AMC GUIDE TO
Mount Washington
AND THE
Presidential Range

Third Edition

Appalachian Mountain Club

Published by

The Appalachian Mountain Club
Boston, Massachusetts 02108

The trail descriptions in this book are taken from the *A.M.C. White Mountain Guide,* 1983 edition, edited by Eugene S. Daniell III and Vera V. Smith.

Due to changes in conditions, use of the information in this book is at the sole risk of the user.

ISBN 0-910146-50-0

Copyright 1983 Appalachian Mountain Club

CONTENTS

LIST OF MAPS v
ACKNOWLEDGMENTS vi
TO THE OWNER
    OF THIS BOOK v

INTRODUCTION
    OVERVIEW — WHY THE PRESIDENTIALS? vii

    NATURAL HISTORY
        THE REGION ix
        THE LANDSCAPE xii
        THE WEATHER xvii
        PLANTS AND ANIMALS xix
        WINTER xxix

    HUMAN HISTORY
        EARLY EXPLORATION AND
            SETTLEMENT xliii
        ERA OF THE GRAND HOTELS xlviii
        THE TWENTIETH CENTURY liv

    BOOKS ABOUT THE PRESIDENTIAL
        RANGE lxi

1. HIKING AND CAMPING
    IN THE PRESIDENTIAL RANGE 1

2. NATIONAL AND STATE AREAS 17

3. MOUNT WASHINGTON 30

4. NORTHERN PEAKS 56

5. GREAT GULF 104

6. SOUTHERN PEAKS 114

7. MONTALBAN RIDGE 128

8. PRESIDENTIAL RANGE IN WINTER	141
9. THE APPALACHIAN MOUNTAIN CLUB AND ITS ACTIVITIES	150
GLOSSARY	158
INDEX	161

LIST OF MAPS

MAP, FOLDED, IN PACKET
    MT. WASHINGTON RANGE

PAGE MAPS
    WILDERNESS AND RESTRICTED
        USE AREAS 22-23
    AMC HUTS 154-155

TO THE OWNER OF THIS BOOK

With the object of keeping pace with the constant changes in mountain trails, the Appalachian Mountain Club publishes a revised edition of this *Guide* at intervals of about four years.

Hiking and climbing in the Presidential Range should provide a combination of outdoor pleasure and healthful exercise. Plan your trip schedule with safety in mind. Determine the overall distance, the altitude to be reached, the steepness of the footway, and, if you are returning to the starting point the same day, allow ample time, as your morning quota of energy will have lost some of its get-up-and-go. Read the caution notes where they appear in this book. They are put there for your guidance and protection.

We request your help in preparing future editions. When you go over a trail, please check the description in the book. If you find errors or can suggest improvements, send a letter or card to the Committee. Even if the description is satisfactory, a note saying, "Description of such-and-such trail is o.k.," will be appreciated. Do not be deterred by the lack of experience. The viewpoint of one unfamiliar with the trail is especially valuable.

Address — White Mountain Guidebook Committee, Appalachian Mountain Club, 5 Joy Street, Boston, MA 02108.

ACKNOWLEDGMENTS

Most of this book is due to the efforts over the years of the White Mountain Guidebook Committee, since its core is the trail descriptions from the first five chapters of the *White Mountain Guide*, 23rd Edition. The current Committee consists of the following members:

Eugene S. Daniell III and Vera V. Smith

Ruth Houghton, *ex-officio*
John E. Auchmoody
D. William and Iris Baird
Lawrence R. Blood
Eugene S. Daniell IV
Benjamin W. English Jr.
John and Margaret Ensor
Joseph J. Hansen
John E. McNamara
Avard Milbury
Kenneth E. Miller
Paul A. Miller
James A. Smith
Stephen and Nina Waite
Edna Welch

Arlyn S. Powell Jr., former director of publications for the AMC, wrote the Introduction, except for the section on winter, which was written by John Coburn.

Introduction

OVERVIEW — WHY THE PRESIDENTIALS?

Why are Mount Washington and its neighboring peaks in the Presidential range of such interest to outdoorspeople?

The peaks are certainly not the highest in the east. A dozen of the Smoky Mountains of Tennessee and North Carolina are higher.

However, Mount Washington *is* the highest peak in the Northeast — a thousand feet higher than Katahdin in Maine and New York's Mount Marcy, highest of the Adirondacks. It is two thousand feet higher than Mount Mansfield in Vermont, highest of the Green Mountains, and three thousand feet higher than anything in Massachusetts.

Mere statistics, however, do not tell the real story. Mount Washington and the other Presidentials provide, some say, the most breathtakingly rugged mountain scenery east of the Rockies. The highest Smokies, although ranging up to 600 feet higher than Mount Washington, are, because of their more southerly location, tree-clad and lack the austere alpine zone that makes the Presidentials seem far higher than they really are. In the northeast perhaps only Katahdin, rising majestically in central Maine, can compare, but it is much more remote from urban vacationers and recreationists.

It is, then, the facts that the Presidential Range is at once accessible to megalopolis and unusual in its natural history that make it of interest today. And, it has always been so. These mountains, only a few hours by car from Boston, form the hub of a recreational area that dates back well over a century.

viii   INTRODUCTION

Mount Washington Summit. Photo Stanley O. Bean

   Thoreau visited here. Hawthorne, Emerson and Whittier wrote about them. Frederick Church, Benjamin Champney, Albert Bierstadt and Winslow Homer all painted here.
   Before describing the hiking trails that crisscross the Presidential Range, let us first look briefly at the natural and human history that can so much enhance our enjoyment of these mountains.

INTRODUCTION

NATURAL HISTORY

The Region

The Presidential Range forms an attenuated *s*-curve in the heart of the White Mountains of northern New Hampshire. Running over fourteen miles from north to south, the range consists of eleven peaks, with Mount Washington, the highest at 6,288 feet, roughly in the center.

To the north of Mount Washington are the Northern peaks — Mounts Clay (5,532 feet), Jefferson (5,715 feet), Adams (5,798 feet) and Madison (5,363 feet). The Southern Peaks consist of Mounts Monroe (5,385 feet), Franklin (5,004 feet), Eisenhower (4,761 feet), Clinton (4,312 feet), Jackson (4,052 feet) and Webster (3,910 feet).

The five highest peaks in the range are the five highest in New Hampshire, and eight are included on the 4,000-Footer list for the state.

Across Pinkham Notch to the east lies the Carter-Moriah Range, and to the west lie the Dartmouth Range, Rosebrook Range and Crawford Notch. To the north is the Pliny Range.

Best access to these mountains is provided by three interstate highways. For those in New York and southern New England, I-91 from New Haven bisects both Connecticut and Massachusetts, and runs up the New Hampshire-Vermont border, passing within fifteen miles of Franconia Notch, at the western boundary of the White Mountains. From Boston I-93 runs up through central New Hampshire directly to Franconia Notch. The Kancamagus Scenic Highway runs from I-93 just south of Franconia Notch (itself a major White Mountain scenic attraction) east to Route 16 in Conway. This is a slow but attractive route to the Presidentials, especially when fall foliage is at its height.

The most direct route from Boston, however, involves leaving I-93 well south of Franconia Notch. From New Hampton Route 104 goes east to Meredith on Lake Winnipesaukee; from there

Route 25 winds through the Lake Country until it intersects Route 16. Take Route 16 north through Conway and North Conway, the "latchkey to the White Mountains," and you will be at the doorstep of the Presidential Range.

Another route from Boston involves taking I-95 north to Portsmouth, New Hampshire. From there take the Spaulding Turnpike north to Rochester, then Route 16 to Conway.

It is also possible to reach the area by public transportation. Concord Trailways runs buses daily between Boston and Conway, and there is air service to nearby Fryeburg, Maine, and Laconia, New Hampshire. There may also be passenger rail service. Check with the AMC's Boston or Pinkham Notch Camp offices for the latest access information.

Just north of Intervale on Route 16 is Glen, nothing more than a few stores and gas stations, really. There begins a circuit of roads, shaped roughly like a French chef's hat, that encompasses the area covered by this book.

If one turns right at Glen and stays on Route 16, the road winds up the Ellis River to Pinkham Notch, where the Appalachian Mountain Club maintains a lodge, dining room, and administrative facilities. Beyond the Notch the Peabody River runs down to Gorham, twenty-four miles north of Glen. This road passes Storyland, Heritage New Hampshire, the Mt. Washington Auto Road, the site of the Glen House, Wildcat Skiway and Dolly Copp Campground.

If one goes straight ahead at Glen, Route 302 runs west along the Saco River for about twelve miles, and then turns north with it toward Crawford Notch. A state park protects the scenic Notch, along with sites of the pioneer Willey and Crawford houses. From its turn northward Route 302 travels eighteen miles, by the old resort hotel at Bretton Woods, to the town of Carroll, embarkation point for the cog railway running to the summit of Mount Washington.

Here the road turns west for five miles to Twin Mountain; then take Route 3 north for two miles, to where Route 115 forks off to the right. This road heads north to Meadows (seven miles), then turns east for four miles to connect with Route 2 a mile above Jefferson Highlands. Turn right on Route 2, and it is eight miles almost due east to Randolph, then another six miles to Gorham. The entire circuit is approximately eighty-eight miles, and encloses more than two hundred square miles of mountain terrain.

Almost all of this territory is part of the White Mountain National Forest, and is undeveloped except along the roadways. (There are, in fact, two wilderness areas on the east and south flanks of Mount Washington — the Great Gulf and Dry River Wilderness. They are currently the only two in the forest and two of the few in the entire East.) There are only two commercial facilities in the area, both dating far back in the history of the Presidential Range. One is the cog railway, running up Mount Washington from the west. The Mount Clinton Road and Base Road form a rough triangle connecting our perimeter road to Marshfield, base station of the railway. The second commercial development is the Mount Washington Auto Road, a toll road leaving Route 16 north of Pinkham Notch Camp and climbing to the summit of Mount Washington.

These three roads are the only paved thoroughfares within the circuit. An unpaved road runs from the Base Road through Jefferson Notch to the vicinity of Bowman, west of Randolph, and another parallels it five miles to the west. Still another goes from Randolph to the Dolly Copp Campground on Route 16. Dolly Copp, Crawford Notch State Park and Pinkham Notch Camp are the three major recreational facilities within the area.

The area covered by this book includes more than just the Presidential Range. There is Pine Mountain (2,404 feet) in the northern corner, and to the south of the Presidentials stretch Montalban and Rocky Branch Ridges. Along the former runs the well-known Davis Path, climbing from Notchland over Mounts Crawford (3,129 feet), Resolution (3,428 feet), Davis (3,840 feet), Isolation (4,005 feet), Stairs Mountain (3,460 feet) and Slide Peak (4,807 feet), before reaching Boott Spur (5,500 feet) on the flank of Mount Washington. From the southeast another roller coaster trail begins near Glen and goes over Mounts Stanton (1,748 feet), Pickering (1,942 feet), Langdon (2,423 feet) and Parker (3,015 feet) before reaching Mount Resolution and the Davis Path.

Despite these long trails in the southern half of the area, most of the hiking trails are concentrated around Mount Washington and in the Northern Peaks near Randolph. In fact, about 150 of 250 miles of hiking trails occupy only about 50 square miles of the 200 in the area.

The longest trails are the Great Gulf Trail (12.8 miles), Dry River Trail (10.5 miles), and Davis Path (14.5 miles). All others are ten miles or less in length. The through Appalachian Trail, running from Maine to Georgia, takes advantage of the trail system to cross all of the Presidentials. Three of the AMC's eight high mountain huts — Madison on Mount Madison, Lakes-of-the-Clouds on Mount Washington, and Mizpah Spring on Mount Clinton — are within this area, and are on the Appalachian Trail as well.

The Landscape

The Presidential Range does not fit into the ridge-and-valley pattern so common to the Appalachians. In fact, the history of these mountains is so complex that most writers content themselves with broad generalities about them.

It seems safe to say, however, that the mountains began on the ocean floor, perhaps 350 to 400 million years ago, when layers of muddy sediment were deposited in a shallow sea. Volcanic ash and lava then filled the sea, until there was a dry land surface. The land sank, and water once again covered the area; another thick layer of sediment was deposited.

Roughly 300 million years ago an upwelling of magma from the earth's interior pushed what was by now miles of layered rock up into a dome. The rock was first compressed and then heated and folded, metamorphosing it into the mica schist and gneiss that form the predominant rocks of the range today. From time to time the area was invaded from below by veins and dikes of igneous rock, but on the surface of the land things were relatively quiet, with erosion playing the major part.

For the last 250 million years wind, frost, and running water have broken down and removed perhaps eight miles of mountain, so that what remains today are the deep roots, once buried far beneath the earth's surface. The last major sculpting, according to some experts, was done 10 to 12 thousand years ago by the last great continental ice sheet.

Evidence of this glaciation is everywhere in the Presidential Range. Where fresh, unweathered bedrock is exposed, scratches and grooves made by rocks embedded in the ice can still be seen. Alignment of the scratches allows geologists to plot the direction of flow of the ice.

Also, *erratics*, or pebbles and boulders carried from other areas and left behind here, tell where the ice went. Rocks from the Pliny Range, eight miles to the north, have been found in the Presidentials. Erratics, identifiable because they are of different composition than local rocks, have been discovered almost on the summit of Mount Washington, along with glacial till, indicating that the ice sheet actually overrode and buried the entire range.

A stream-carved valley is characteristically V-shaped, but the passes, or "notches," of the Presidential Range — Crawford and Pinkham Notches — have the distinctive U-shape of ice-carved valleys. Deep below the surface of the south-flowing ice sheet, rivers of ice were compressed into these passes, gouging out as much as 500 feet of bedrock and leaving them the steep walls that make them so spectacular today.

Another glacial feature of the Presidential Range that is justly renowned is the *cirque*, locally called a "gulf" or "ravine." Formed high on the flank of the northwest to south (shady) or east (downwind) sides of a mountain, a cirque is a U-shaped valley with a steep headwall and gently sloping floor. A glacier gave the valley its distinctive form, the ice sculpting the back and sides to give the walls their steepness and eroding the floor to a gentle slope by its weight and motion.

Tuckerman Ravine, most famous of the Presidential cirques, often has snow in it until July, and scientists agree that it would take very little change in mean annual temperature or winter snowfall to transform the "Snow Arch" into a glacier once more.

Tuckerman, on the eastern flank of Mount Washington, is actually one of the smallest of the principal cirques. Its 800-foot headwall compares to 1,300 in King Ravine (north face of Mount Adams), 1,400 in Huntington Ravine (east face of Mount Washington) and 1,500 in the Great Gulf (north slope of Mount Washington). There are at least eight other cirques in the Presidentials, and other ravines that show signs of some glaciation.

Still another reminder of the passage of the ice sheet is the composition of the soil one finds in the region. Glacial *till* is an unlayered mixture of particles ranging in size from microscopic clay to huge boulders. The boulder-strewn upland field and pasture so common in New England is a sure sign that when the ice melted — and it was 5,000 feet or more thick in some places — it dropped its load of rocks and soil helter skelter, to provide a meager and frustrating living for later farmers.

By contrast, there are also broad valleys in the mountains, called "intervales" by the residents, where agriculture is an easier task. Scientists suggest that that the soil here comes from sediments laid down in lakes created by the ice; these lakes have long since dried up, leaving their flat, fertile beds behind for the farmers.

Geologists have assumed until quite recently that little has happened in the Presidential Range for the last 10,000 years. They have pointed to the absence of *moraines*, the characteristic ridges of debris laid down by glaciers, as evidence that none formed in the mountains following the retreat of the last ice sheet. However, within the last two decades that view has been challenged, and now some scientists see these mountains as being still quite active and interesting geologically.

The first clues came in the odd geometric patterns that pebbles and boulders assumed high in the mountains. In the relatively level alpine meadows, such as the Alpine Garden and Bigelow and Monticello Lawns, these patterns are in the form of nets or polygons. On slopes they are stripes.

It was generally agreed that these patterns were formed by frost action, but it was assumed that only pebble-sized patterns were still being created under modern conditions. Boulder patterns were thought to be 'fossil,' having developed in earlier times when the climate was harsher.

In 1960 and 1961, Will F. Thompson, writing in *Appalachia*, discarded the notion that the Presidential Range was geologically inactive. An AMC member living in the Boston area at the time, Thompson was a physical geographer specializing in mountain terrain. Citing research and observations from mountainous areas all over the world, he argued that these boulder fields, technically called *felsenmeers*, were actually in constant if very slow motion, and were important clues to the topography of the Presidentials.

Earlier theories claimed that the level areas, or alpine meadows, were actually once the surface of a flat plain. The mountains had then been uplifted in two stages, the first exposing the high peaks and the second creating the 'shoulders' at the 5,000-foot level upon which the meadows now exist.

Thompson suggested that there was no uplifted and eroded plain, but rather that these geological features, also found in the Rockies, could be completely explained by a *mass wasting process* — movement of detritus without benefit of a suspending medium such as wind, water or ice.

This process, which was just beginning to be investigated by scientists at the time, is in the same class of phenomena as the familiar frost heaves that make for roller coaster rides on New England roads each winter and spring. It created the boulder rings and stripes familiar to hikers in the Presidentials, and also the above-timberline lawns beloved of mountain wildflower seekers.

Thompson argued that permafrost, long known on the summit of Mount Washington, was actually far more prevalent than was previously suspected. A combination of heavy precipitation, high winds, and low annual temperatures created a climatic condition above timberline in the Presidentials that favored severe frost action and widespread permafrost. This action worked on a silty, stony, frozen soil underlying the boulder fields that covered the 1,500-foot summit cone of Mount Washington and the meadows and cirques below it.

Partial melting and refreezing of this soil layer very slowly churns it and carries it downslope, along with the loose boulders covering it. New soil formed by frost action replaces that which is carried away. On the floors of the cirques, where the soil and boulders would be expected to accumulate from the combination of landslides, avalanches, and soil creep, the debris is carried away by *rock glaciers*, another manifestation of the same process.

These rock glaciers, moving at most a few feet each year, may have obliterated glacial moraines, which is why little evidence remains for post-Ice Age glaciers. Thompson, in fact, believes that there may have been glaciers in the Presidential Range only a few centuries ago, perhaps as late as the "Little Ice Age," a worldwide cool spell in the Middle Ages.

So, glaciation, followed by mass wasting, has shaped the terrain of the Presidential Range as we now know it. The latter force, according to Thompson, was briefly interrupted by the Ice Age, but goes on acting today as vigorously as ever.

So, the questions being asked about the shape of the Presidential Range are still far from having certain answers.

The Weather

Thompson's theory of mass wasting emphasizes the severity of White Mountain weather. There are records to prove it. In April, 1934, the wind gusted to 231 mph on the summit of Mount Washington, the highest wind velocity ever recorded outside a tornado.

The year-round average wind velocity is a brisk 35 mph. In winter, hurricane force winds (75 mph or higher) are common; they blow an average of 104 days a year. Gusts of over 100 mph have been recorded in every month of the year, and gusts of over 150 mph in every month between September and May.

The average annual temperature on the summit of Mount Washington is a chilly 27° F. It has never risen above 71° F., and in January of 1934 the mercury dropped to a record low of −47° F. It is below zero 65 days a year on the average, and in June of 1945 a temperature of −8° F. was recorded — hardly a summer's day by any standard!

On the summit there is usually more than 70 inches of precipitation a year. Much of this falls as snow, which averages 195 inches annually. The winter of 1968-1969 saw the heaviest snowfall on record — over 47 feet. More than four feet fell in one 24-hour period, a record for U.S. weather observatories.

Fog and clouds are also quite common on the summit of Mount Washington, occurring on the average of 305 days a year. Sightseers can expect the summit to be socked-in 55% of the time according to Weather Observatory records. Occasionally a lenticular, or lens-shaped cloud can be seen directly over the summit; it is formed when moisture in the air condenses as it passes over the peak and then evaporates again as the wind descends the other slope.

The combination of low temperature, high winds, and much precipitation creates a unique climate on the Presidential Range summits — an area that has been called an Arctic island in the midst of the temperate zone. The mountains lie at the intersection of two major North American storm tracks, one sweeping up the coast from the Gulf of Mexico and the other a polar track traversing central Canada, the Midwest, and the St. Lawrence River valley. The disturbances created when these two tracks cross are only enhanced in power by their steep rise over the mountains.

It is no wonder, then, that the region has long been of interest to scientists. The Mount Washington Weather Observatory was founded in 1870, the first of its kind in the world. It has been staffed permanently on a year-round basis since the 1930s, which accounts for the detailed knowledge we now have of the climate on the summit. During World War II, all three major military services tested cold-weather equipment and clothing on Mount Washington, and more recently the Air Force has performed icing tests on engines and propellers there.

However, despite the summit buildings, and the road and railroad that lead to them, Mount Washington and the other Presidential peaks are far from civilized. The combination of cold, wind, and rain or snow can create a wind-chill factor that freezes exposed flesh in minutes in winter, and that can kill at any time of the year. These three factors account for what scientists call the *severity* of White Mountain weather, and some claim that it is the equal of any on earth, including Antarctica. More lives have been lost on Mount Washington than on any other peak in North America, mostly due to exposure, or hypothermia.

Despite the danger, though, the Presidentials remain a four-season mecca for Eastern hikers, backpackers, naturalists, rock and ice climbers and skiers. The latter two especially find in Tuckerman and Huntington ravines a challenging and unusual experience. Much of the snow that falls on the summit of Mount Washington is blown into these cirques on the eastern flank of the mountain by northwest winds. One result is the Tuckerman snow bowl, open to skiers far into the late spring and early summer. The skier must hike the two miles from Pinkham Notch Camp to the Ravine, however, and then climb the headwall on foot as well, since there are no lifts or tows.

Plants and Animals

Note: No attempt is made here to provide identification information for the species discussed. A number of field guides are included in the bibliography.

A hike from Pinkham Notch to the summit ridge of the Presidential Range is biologically equivalent to a trip of 1,000 miles due north, to the Canadian Arctic. In terms of climate each 400 feet of the 4,000-foot vertical rise is equivalent to traveling 100 miles north, so it is little wonder that the plants and animals change as one progresses up the mountains.

The hiker begins on the Notch floor in a forest of hardwoods, justly famous for their autumn displays of color. During the ascent, more and more conifers become mixed in with the deciduous trees. Finally the conifers predominate, and the hiker has entered the spruce-fur forest. At timberline (the upper limit of commercial timber, here around 4,200 feet), the conifers stand 50 to 70 feet tall, and the deciduous trees have mostly disappeared. For the next 600 to 1,000 feet of elevation the trees get smaller and smaller, until the hiker reaches treeline, above which there is no continuous forest cover.

Above treeline the combination of frequent fog and cloud cover, cool summer temperatures, heavy precipitation, and high winds creates a climate similar to that in Labrador, north of the continental treeline. Many of the same plants exist in this island of Arctic tundra in the temperate zone, which runs for 8½ miles from Mount Madison to Mount Eisenhower. With an area of approximately 7½ square miles, it is the largest continuous above-treeline alpine zone in the eastern United States.

Given the wide climatic variation between the base and the summit ridge of the Presidential Range, it would be impossible to discuss all the plants and animals that live there. Naturalist L. C. Bliss states that 110 plant species inhabit the alpine zone alone, and another study catalogues 95 insect species that reside in the same area. How vast, then, would be the magnitude of a book of the alpine zone? Still, a general description of the various plant and animal communities of the region will be possible. The Range obviously provides a wide variety of habitats for these communities.

The two notches, Crawford and Pinkham, are at an elevation of about 2,000 feet, and are clothed in New England's ubiquitous northern hardwood forest. They are well watered, with small lakes, beaver ponds, and rivers fed by mountain streams running down the nearby slopes. The climate is also dramatically milder than that of the peaks 3,000 to 4,000 feet above.

On the eastern slope of the Range, at Pinkham Notch Camp (2,032 feet) or at the base of the Mount Washington Auto Road (1,620 feet), the hiker begins ascending in this forest. On the west, beginning at the Marshfield station of the cog railway, the climber is already into the zone of conifers, at 2,700 feet.

The American beech, sugar maple, and yellow birch are the predominant trees here, but "hardwood" is actually a misleading part of the name of this zone, since conifers such as red spruce and eastern hemlock are also quite common. Red maples and paper birches occur as well.

This same type of woodland, with its high, open canopy of trees and its abundance of shrubs growing in the rich humus of the forest floor, covers much of northern New England, including the upper two-thirds of New Hampshire and Maine north of Portland. On the sun-dappled forest floor one may find, besides moss and ferns, Canada violets, foam flowers, red trilliums and Solomon's seals. Flitting among the trees and shrubs will be warblers, thrushes, vireos, rose-breasted grosbeaks and redstarts. Chipmunks and red squirrels, the latter a scolding, brassy lot quite willing to defend their turf from hikers, are the most likely mammals to be encountered. Beavers populate some of the ponds, and in winter the tracks of rabbits and deer abound. Pinkham Notch Camp has been nicknamed "Porky Gulch" because of the porcupines that once made nuisances of themselves in the area. Today raccoons are the major pests. It is even claimed by local residents that bears and moose occasionally appear in the area. Garter snakes, wood toads, and a large number of small rodents are also likely to be encountered from time to time. As to insects, one need hardly mention gnats, mosquitoes, black flies, and midges or 'no-see-ums,' as they are called locally because of their small size; suffice it to say that in the late spring one hardly dares to venture forth without insect repellent.

Between 1,500 and 2,100 feet of elevation, the northern hardwoods begin to give way to the spruce-fir forest. This mixed coniferous-deciduous zone is dominatd by red spruce and balsam fir, but there are also yellow birch, paper birch, mountain-ash and striped maple. Hobblebush, wood sorrel, bluebead lily, false lily of the valley, star flower, bunchberry, goldthread, and creeping snowberry, as well as northern clintonia, painted trillium, and pink lady's slippers, enliven the understory. Birds include juncos and a number of northern warblers — black-throated blues and greens, Canadas and magnolias. In more open areas fireweed, orange hawkweed, wild strawberry, wild sarsaparilla, and yarrow can be found.

Following this transition zone are pure conifers, mostly red spruce and balsam fir. This evergreen forest, which is often associated with New England but which is acutally rare except in its northernmost reaches, is a study in contrast to the hardwood landscape. The trees are densely packed together, and little can grow on the dark, acidic floor beneath. However, in mature woodlands there are openings, and where the light can penetrate, oxalis, goldthread, and bunchberry can grow. In addition to the mixed forest species, a number of birds prefer this habitat, among them the winter wren, Swainson's thrush, hermit thrush, myrtle warbler, kinglet and yellow-bellied sapsucker.

As one progresses still higher, the trees begin to thin out and become stunted. Illustrating the biologist's maxim that fewer species inhabit harsher climates, the number of tree species declines, with only spruce, fir, and paper birch remaining in any numbers. Alpine plants such as Labrador tea, alpine bilberry, mountain cranberry, sedges, and rushes can be found down to treeline, but not much below it. Reaching their upper limit where the alpines reach their lower are such plants as bunchberry, Canada mayflower, oxalis, goldthread, and twinflower. For the first time the birds present are not the ones prevalent throughout the southern Appalachians; now one can see the gray-cheeked thrush, boreal chickadee, gray jay, three-toed woodpecker, pine grosbeak, blackpoll warbler, and, occasionally, spruce grouse.

At treeline only the black spruce and balsam fir remain. This is what ecologists aptly call a zone of tension. It is the place where the last scraggly plants struggle against the increasing rigors of wind and snow. Dwarfed trees and dense, low mats of vegetation called *krummholz*, a German word meaning "crooked wood," are all that survive here. At an elevation of between 4,800 and 5,200 feet, even these plants succumb, and the bare rocks above support only lichens and scattered patches of greenery in sheltered spots.

The location of treeline seems to be influenced by climate primarily. On the north-facing slopes exposed to prevailing winter winds from the northwest, treeline is lower. On the eastern and southern slopes, where snow accumulates in the lee of the peaks, it is higher. (Also, southern exposures enjoy more sunlight during the growing season.) However, why treeline is at half the elevation in the Presidential Range as it is in the Rockies has yet to be adequately explained.

One of the most remarkable phenomena of this tension zone is the *krummholz*. Minute trees, reminiscent of Japanese bonzai, are shaped by wind and snow into grotesque shapes. The tree species are the same as the ones that grow 50 to 70 feet tall only a thousand feet lower on the slope, at timberline, but here they may form mats 4 to 12 inches high — and so dense that in places they will support a person's weight. Though tiny, the plants may be a century or more old.

Scientists are more or less agreed that *krummholz* is shaped by wind and snow. The steady, brisk wind at higher elevations tends to dry plants out very quickly, even given the heavy precipitation of the area. Therefore, it is common to find *krummholz* in the lee of boulders or in natural depressions in the terrain. Also, snow, which inhibits the growing season of these evergreens, provides a beneficial service in return. The plants cannot grow while covered with snow, but in the eight-month winter the snow provides a protective blanket, insulating them from the wind and low temperatures. (Beneath the snow it remains at roughly the temperature at which the snow fell, so beneath the snow cover it may be 40-50° F. warmer than the outside air.) Also, the snow may moisturize the plants at a time when their roots cannot take up water from the frozen ground.

In the alpine zone itself, it is too harsh for full-sized trees, so the plants that predominate are low-lying heaths, grasses, rushes, sedges, lichens, mosses, and the spectacular mountain wildflowers. Scientists speculate that these plants populated the area following the retreat of the continental ice sheet. As the climate became milder, the plants migrated upslope where they became trapped on a climatic "island." Consequently, their closest relatives are found on other alpine islands in New England, the Adirondacks, and in Labrador far to the north.

For two centuries naturalists have investigated this area, and many of its prominent features are named after them — Tuckerman and Huntington Ravines, Cutler River, Oakes Gulf, Bigelow Lawn, Boott Spur. Estimates vary on the number of higher plants that grow above treeline, but the best is probably 110 species, of which 75 are true alpine plants that only grow in this zone. The other 35 are native to the spruce-fir forest, but survive at higher elevations in the *krummholz* mats.

Four of the alpine plants are *endemics* — that is, they only exist in a small geographic area. The dwarf cinquefoil, which only grows in a few spots in the White Mountains, is the most famous of these; alpine avens and bluets occur here and in eastern Canada. The fourth species, bluejoint grass, has not been seen in the area for some years.

L. C. Bliss has identified several plant communities in this zone, each of which is adapted to a particular habitat. The sedge meadow, consisting of Bigelow sedge and some mosses and mountain sandwort, is one of the most common, and grows on the higher slopes. Downslope from these meadows the community may branch out to include large clumps of rushes and low heath shrubs. Lower still is a heath-rush community, which includes three-forked rush, mountain cranberry, alpine bilberry and three-toothed cinquefoil.

In exposed areas where the winds are strong and much of the winter snow cover is blown away, hardy *diapensia* mats thrive. Lapland rosebay, alpine azalea, and alpine bilberry also live in these mats. Near treeline and in protected sites higher up, heath communities exist exclusive of the rushes. Snow falls deep over these communities, but it melts early. Where the snow is deeper still and melts late in the spring, so-called snowbank communities thrive. Hairgrass, goldenrod, dwarf bilberry, and bluets live here, along with the flowers of the spruce-fir community from the slopes below.

There are few actual watercourses or lakes above treeline but near Lakes of the Clouds and the runnels of the Alpine Garden there is a stream/bog community dominated by shrubby willows and birches.

The Alpine Garden and Bigelow Lawn on Mount Washington, Monroe Flats on Mount Monroe, and Monticello Lawn on Mount Jefferson are rightly famous for the mountain wildflowers that bloom among their rocks each spring. In late spring, once the snow has melted, many of the plants listed above as well as dozens of others — rhodora, *Phyllodoce, Cassiope* — blossom. At an elevation of 5,000-5,500 feet, these meadows peak in late June and draw many admirers. The most accessible is the Alpine Garden, which can be reached from the Mount Washington Auto Road and from the summit buildings where the Cog Railway stops, as well as by hikers.

The flowers are protected, as are the other plants in the White

INTRODUCTION

Mountain National Forest, so do not pick them without special permission. Also, be careful to remain on the trails in these areas, since the flora are very delicate — and in some cases quite rare.

There are few animals and birds native to these heights. L. C. Bliss lists nine animals that appear here, mostly small rodents such as mice, shrews, squirrels, woodchuck, porcupine and chipmunks. The snowshoe rabbit may also be seen. Naturalists agree that only two birds nest above treeline, the slate-colored junco and the white-throated sparrow. However, other birds, such as ravens, hawks and an occasional eagle, may be seen in the area.

Insects are the predominant mobile life form here. One study lists 95 native species, including 61 beetles, although it is difficult to distinguish between those insects occurring naturally and the ones blown up on strong winds from the lowlands. There are ten species of black spiders, and anyone who has picked his way among the boulder fields in summer will have been sure to startle a number of them. Of the fourteen species of moths and butterflies that appear here, three are endemic. The White Mountain butterfly lives only above treeline in the White Mountains; its larvae feed on the local grasses. It can be seen fluttering about the sedge meadows most frequently in early July. The White Mountain fritillary and White Mountain locust are also native species localized in this region.

ANIMALS

Mammals

Red squirrel
Eastern chipmunk
Porcupine
Jumping mouse
Vole
Deer mouse
Muskrat
Woodchuck
Beaver
Marten
Fisher
Skunk
Weasel

House mouse
Snowshoe hare
Bat
Mole
Redbacked mouse
White-footed mouse
Masked shrew
Eastern short-tailed shrew
Shrew
White-tailed deer
Moose
Fox
Coyote
Bobcat
Lynx
Black bear
Raccoon
Mink

Reptiles
Painted turtle
Garter snake

Amphibians
Salamander
Bullfrog

Insects
Gnat
Black fly
Deer fly
Mosquito
Bumblebee
Butterfly
Midge
Beetle
Locust
Black spider

BIRDS

Common Loon
Pied-billed Grebe
Great Blue Heron
Green Heron — R
American Bittern
Mallard
Black Duck
Green-winged Teal — R
Blue-winged Teal — R
Wood Duck
Great Horned Owl
Barred Owl
Long-eared Owl

Ring-necked Duck
Common Goldeneye
Barrow's Goldeneye — W
Hooded Merganser
Common Merganser
Goshawk
Sharp-shinned Hawk
Red-tailed Hawk
Red-shouldered Hawk
Broad-winged Hawk
Red-breasted Nuthatch
Bald Eagle — R
Marsh Hawk — R

INTRODUCTION

Saw-whet Owl
Chimney Swift
Ruby-thr. Hummingbird
Belted Kingfisher
Yellow-shafted Flicker
Pileated Woodpecker
Yellow-bellied Sapsucker
Hairy Woodpecker
Downy Woodpecker
Black-backed Three-toed Woodpecker
Northern Three-toed Woodpecker
Eastern Kingbird
Crested Flycatcher — R
Eastern Phoebe
Yellow-bellied Flycatcher
Traill's Flycatcher
Least Flycatcher
Wood Pewee
Olive-sided Flycatcher
Tree Swallow
Bank Swallow — R
Rough-winged Swallow — R
Barn Swallow
Cliff Swallow
Gray Jay
Blue Jay
Raven
Crow
Black-capped Chickadee
Boreal Chickadee
White-breasted Nuthatch — R
Philadelphia Vireo
Osprey
Sparrow Hawk
Spruce Grouse — R
Ruffed Grouse
Virginia Rail
Sora
Killdeer
Woodcock
Common Snipe
Spotted Sandpiper
Herring Gull
Mourning Dove
Black-billed Cuckoo
Brown Creeper
House Wren — R
Winter Wren
Long-billed Marsh Wren — R
Short-billed Marsh Wren — R
Catbird
Brown Thrasher
Robin
Wood Thrush
Hermit Thrush
Swainson's Thrush
Gray-cheeked Thrush
Veery
Bluebird
Golden-crowned Kinglet
Ruby-crowned Kinglet
Cedar Waxwing
Starling
Solitary Vireo
Red-eyed Vireo
Purple Finch
Pine Grosbeak — W

INTRODUCTION

Black and White Warbler
Tennessee Warbler
Nashville Warbler
Parula Warbler
Yellow Warbler
Magnolia Warbler
Cape May Warbler
Black-thr. Blue Warbler
Myrtle Warbler
Black-thr. Green Warbler
Blackburnian Warbler
Chestnut-sided Warbler
Bay-breasted Warbler
Blackpoll Warbler
Palm Warbler
Ovenbird
Northern Water-thrush
Mourning Warbler
Yellowthroat
Wilson's Warbler
Canada Warbler
Redstart
House Sparrow
Bobolink
Meadowlark — R
Redwinged Blackbird
Baltimore Oriole — R
Rusty Blackbird
Common Grackle
Brown-headed Cowbird
Scarlet Tanager
Rose-breasted Grosbeak
Indigo Bunting
Evening Grosbeak
Fox Sparrow
Pine Siskin
Common Redpoll — W
American Goldfinch
Red Crossbill
White-winged Crossbill
Savannah Sparrow
Vesper Sparrow — R
Slate-colored Junco
Tree Sparrow — W
Chipping Sparrow
White-throated Sparrow
Lincoln's Sparrow
Swamp Sparrow
Song Sparrow
Snow Bunting — W

Migrants
Horned Grebe
Double-crested Cormorant
Canada Goose
Brant
Snow Goose
Pintail
Greater Scaup
Bufflehead
Scoter
Golden Plover
Solitary Sandpiper
Greater Yellow-legs
Least Sandpiper
Pectoral Sandpiper
Horned Lark
Water Pipit
White-crowned Sparrow
Lapland Longspur

W = WINTER   R = RARE

Winter

Winter in the White Mountains has special charm. Except for the occasional noise made by the wind rubbing the limbs of trees together there is a great silence in the snow-cloaked woods. This, plus the fact there are fewer hikers about provides an unparalleled opportunity for solitude. The leaves of deciduous trees and shrubs are gone, revealing the lay of the land, its ridges and rolls. Areas which are difficult to reach during warmer weather — swamps, bogs, and ponds — are easily explored when winter's grip is on the land. Travel on snow-carpeted level trails is a relaxing rhythmic glide. Bark and buds reveal themselves, and animal signs are recorded everywhere in the snow. The varied patterns of snow and ice alone are enough to absorb the observant hiker.

Winter has its special perils also. Errors in trip preparation, route finding, and judgment which in summer may cause discomfort can in winter endanger one's life. Wind, cold, wetness, and nutritional requirements must be effectively dealt with to permit enjoyment of the winter woods. Snowshoes or skis must be carefully maintained. Physical stamina and navigational skills are required before venturing too far from one's car. This is not the place to detail the precautions winter naturalists should take to ensure safe enjoyable outings. The reader is urged to obtain either *Don't Die on the Mountain* by Dan Allen or The Adirondack Mountain Club's *Guide to Winter Hiking and Camping*. Both books are available from the AMC.

The White Mountain summer is characterized by variety, color and an abundance of life that is seemingly limitless. During the months from June through August it is possible to observe the full diversity of life in the mountains. However, this season is a short one, and its mood is by no means prevalent throughout the year. From September until mid-May quite a different set of conditions occurs. Lacking are the variety of color and sound and the abundance of species witnessed in the summer months. For those members of the natural community that do not migrate, the months from September to June are a challenge. At stake is their ability to survive through to yet another summer. The obstacles include shortened days, high winds, intense cold, rain, snow and ice. Adaptation to such conditions is the key to survival.

Snow is one aspect of winter that the natural community must not only cope with, but in many cases take advantage of in order to survive. The number of adaptations to winter conditions shown by White Mountain flora and fauna is impressive. In order to better understand these adaptations, it is helpful to know something of the physical properties of snow.

Snow falls in a variety of forms ranging from very dry powder to icy corn snow and wet slush. In the first case, individual crystals or conglomerates are well defined. Relatively low moisture and considerable air space within and between individual flakes keep them from packing too tightly as they accumulate on the ground. It is this loose packing that gives powder snow its light and fluffy characteristics. In the case of very wet snow, flakes may be composed of a very large number of individual crystals. These flakes form under moister cloud conditions. As the large, moisture-laden flakes accumulate on the ground, they tend to compress under their own weight. In the woods while snow is falling, it is interesting to observe the individual flakes with a hand lens and to note the kind of snow cover such flakes produce. Beyond the two examples discussed here, a wide range of snow types is possible.

Whatever form snow may fall in, it can undergo transition due to changing weather conditions following the storm. A warm spell or perhaps even rain will greatly consolidate powder snow lying on the surface. When followed by a cold night, such conditions will produce an icy crust. A cold, dry air mass following a fresh wet snowfall may withdraw enough moisture to make that snow light and fluffy. High wind after a new snowfall will produce drifts and windslab. Varying snow conditions place numerous constraints on the activities of the natural community. Prolonged snowfall without settling or consolidation may completely strand a herd of deer in an area too small to provide sufficient food. Travel becomes more difficult for all species of mammals. For those that feed close to the ground, procuring food is increasingly difficult.

Snow is an effective insulator against extremely cold air temperatures for all that lies beneath. The low-growing botanical world of the forest floor is buffered from the extreme fluctuations of the weather. Above treeline only those areas that accumulate drifted snow or windslab will provide similar protection. Alpine plants that require such protection are therefore isolated into pockets called snowbank communities. Animal residents also take advantage of the insulating properties of snow. Ground-dwelling rodents locate their runways atop the frozen ground surface, beneath the entire thickness of snow cover. Certain species of birds, among them the spruce grouse, hole up beneath the snow-covered branches of spruce trees or other evergreens.

A single winter in the White Mountains will see many snowfalls and a larger number of surface snow transitions. Due to changes in temperature and moisture, the latter may occur daily. The cumulative effect of repeated snowfall and transition may be easily observed. With an ice axe or shovel, dig a hole in undisturbed snow down to ground level and trim one face to a smooth surface, extending from top to base. What you see is a snow profile, a record of the season's climatic events preserved in vertical column. Snows of different textures will be readily distinguishable, as will ice layers indicating rain or thaw conditions. Consecutive snowfalls of the same type may be difficult to distinguish. Often, however, a fine layer of dust will differentiate between storms that occurred several days apart. Look closely at the bottom of the column. Note the increasing similarity of layers there. Distinct crystals no longer appear. Instead the layers are composed of large icy granules made up of many crystals. This metamorphosis is due to increased moisture and pressure from the overlying snow. As snow depth increases during the course of a winter, these lower layers may become almost plastic in consistency, often causing overlying layers to creep downslope. Such creep can occur on quite gentle terrain. When slope angle exceeds 25 degrees and snow accumulation is heavy, such motion may cause an avalanche.

The extensive forest cover on most of our White Mountains makes avalanche danger uncommon. Avalanches are for the most part confined to those slopes at or above treeline which receive unusually high amounts of snow due to drifting or wind-slab formation. Most of these areas are in the large glacial cirques that face south and east, such as Tuckerman Ravine and Huntington Ravine. These areas receive a great deal of snow that has been blown off the adjacent ridges by the prevailing northwest winds that follow a storm. Any area with steep slopes or heavy snow cover may be susceptible to avalanching. The winter traveler should be familiar with potential risks before setting out. Snow rangers are stationed at Tuckerman Ravine throughout the winter to assess regularly hazards in that popular area. One's own knowledge may be further improved by reading a comprehensive treatment of the subject, such as Edward La Chapelle's *The ABC's of Safety*.

Some of the most severe weather in the world occurs above treeline in the Presidential Range, as noted earlier. Winter winds and extreme low temperatures, coupled with a short summer growing season, exclude all but the most suitably adapted plant species from life in the alpine zone. Certain adaptations are shared by a number of species. Low posture is universal among plants of the alpine zone. Close to the ground, the winter gales are buffered by friction from the land surface. The fact that a given species will grow taller in the lee of a large boulder than on nearby open ground attests to the limitations wind places on growth. Smaller leaf area or loss of leaves in the fall helps to protect against wind damage and desiccation. On plants that retain their leaves through the winter, waxy or hairy surfaces also help to prevent loss of moisture and make leaves more resistant to abrasion by wind-blown snow crystals.

Despite these common adaptive strategies, there is no one key to survival. Within the alpine zone, local areas differ greatly in their exposure to wind and sun, snow depth, and soil moisture. It is a combination of these and other factors that determines the requirements for vascular plants growing in a particular location. Such factors combine to form what is called a *microclimate*. Different species that habitually grow under common conditions may be grouped into plant communities. Let us look at four distinct communities and their adaptations to winter.

The hiker who ascends beyond treeline will first encounter the *krummholz* community of dwarf black spruce and balsam fir. These trees are characteristically found in tightly intergrown mats from four inches to eight feet in height. Growing in this manner, each tree can provide a degree of shelter for its neighbor from the wind. In the winter, blowing snow drifts into these wind-sheltered patches. This snow provides the insulation from cold and drying arctic winds that permits the dwarf trees to survive. As a result, the height of a *krummholz* patch is directly controlled by the depth of drifted snow which that patch is able to accumulate. New growth that protrudes above the following winter's snow will be desiccated and killed back. It is for this reason that the growth of individual trees is primarily horizontal rather than vertical, often extending only downwind from the original stalk. The wide variation in height shown by different patches is due to variations in local topography. On the lee side of a boulder or other topographic high, trees will grow flush with the height of that obstacle, gradually tapering off as the area downwind becomes more exposed. In a local depression, the *krummholz* will grow with small plants around the perimeter and taller plants in the center so as to form a roughly level surface with the surrounding topography. If a swath is cut in a patch, the bordering trees will begin to die back where they are not fully covered with snow during the winter. It is for this reason that cutting a campsite in *krummholz* has such a disastrous effect on the surrounding vegetation, sometimes destroying a hundred years of growth.

Spruce and fir, though certainly the most common, are not the only dwarfed lowland species found in the alpine zone. A variety of paper birch, known by its pinkish bark and heartshaped leaves, is also widespread.

A second alpine community that depends upon drifted snow for protection during the winter is known as the snowbank community. This group of species is comprised of both woody and herbaceous plants, most of which are deciduous. These plants establish themselves at the base of cliffs, in depressions or in the lee of rocks and other windbreaks at elevations ranging from 4,800 to 5,800 feet. It is interesting to note that deciduous snowbank communities are often found growing in the lee of a *krummholz* patch. Plants typical of such communities include heaths, sedges, grasses, goldenrods, and an endemic variety of alpine bluet that occurs only in tundra areas in northeastern North America. A number of herbaceous species are also typical of snowbank communities. Among them are Canada mayflower, bluebead lily, Indian poke, and goldthread. These herbaceous members of the snowbank community are among the last to begin growing in the spring, since they must wait until their winter insulation has melted before they can begin the growing season. Some species actually begin to photosynthesize while still snow-covered when enough light is able to filter through.

On moist, gentle slopes about 5,400 feet, a third major community is encountered. This is the sedge meadow. This community is almost completely dominated by the Bigelow sedge, a rather broad-leaved species with a purplish fruit stalk. Both of these features may be recognizable in winter, because the sedges are found in more exposed areas that do not collect a great deal of snow. The plants may become covered by rime or ground-water ice, but often the dry leaves and stalks will protrude. In preparation for winter, sedges withdraw chlorophyll and other organic molecules into their root systems, allowing only skeletal brown leaves to take the full force of the weather. The moist summer conditions of their preferred microclimate and the extensive root systems developed by sedges cause the sedge meadow to produce a more complete soil profile than other alpine plant communities. This in turn provides a suitable anchor for the leafy sedges against high winds.

The fourth group of alpine plants is the rugged *diapensia* community. On rocky and windswept slopes and ridges, these plants are at the limits of habitable terrain. Only the nonvascular lichens, which can withstand almost complete desiccation, exist under harsher conditions. *Diapensia* has thick, waxy leaves and grows in very tight mats one inch or less in height. Completely exposed to winter weather, individual plants have only their neighbors to help them resist damage and uprooting. Matted growth also helps to hold what moisture may reach the thin, rocky soil on which these plants grow during the summer months. Members of this community which make use of a cushion-like growth pattern include mountain cranberry, Lapland rosebay, alpine azalea, and bearberry willow. All have the ability to withstand intense cold without the insulation provided more sheltered communities by snow. *Diapensia* plants have undergone freezing in liquid nitrogen at minus 210°C. and lived to produce seeds.

The lower-slope forest community must also contend with severe winter conditions. Although protected from the extremes found on exposed ridges, plants living below treeline are also subjected to storms, high winds, and cold. Herbaceous or woody, these plants must remain dormant for seven months a year. When spring does arrive and the overlying snow melts, understory plants in the broad leaved birch-beech-maple forest are quick to revive, flower, and reproduce. They must take advantage of the sun that reaches the forest floor between snow melt and the leafing out of the canopy trees above. In the evergreen forest, fewer ground-cover species are found. There, understory plants cannot depend upon annual spring sunlight and must be highly shade-tolerant to survive. The acid soils commonly associated with spruce and fir needle compost also limit understory diversity in the evergreen forest.

Trees in the forest canopy cannot wait winter out beneath a blanket of snow. Large trees almost invariably show scars from the high winds that send limbs crashing into one another and from storms that overload branches with ice and snow. The loss of a limb opens the door to attack by fungus or insects and can permanently weaken the tree. The winter hiker who ventures into the woods after a major storm will witness these and other signs of winter damage firsthand. Smaller trees, particularly birches, may be bowed or snapped off by ice loading. Trees growing in exposed areas have their top branches trained by the prevailing winds. The tops of these 'flagged' trees show branches pointing downwind in the shape of a pennant. Violent gusts can make the entire tree a victim of windthrow.

Evergreens commonly occur in the White Mountains in both mixed and pure stands. Since these trees maintain their foliage during the winter, loss of water through the needles presents a real threat. The cold winter winds contain very little moisture and have a strong drying effect. Surface and ground water is generally frozen and inaccessible. To protect against moisture loss, the surfaces of evergreen leaves and stems are covered with a thick waxy or resinous coating as the tree prepares for winter. The needle-like leaf form also offers less surface area from which water can evaporate.

While evergreen needles are small, they do keep quite a bit of snow from reaching the ground. Trees grow closely together and prevent drifting. As a result, the snow cover beneath evergreen stands tends to be less than in hardwood stands or open country. Less snow means increased mobility for wildlife. Deer will take advantage of this and yard among evergreens. These yards are most often along the borders of an evergreen forest, close to the more palatable food supplies of an adjacent broadleaved stand. Animals such as the red squirrel, which have a food source of cones and tassels within the spruce-fir forest, are very active. Where snow buries the lower limbs of evergreens, air pockets are formed. They provide warmth and protection for snowshoe hares and other ground dwellers. Young evergreens and dwarfed *krummholz* will often become completely buried during the winter, forming many air pockets beneath a seemingly even surface of snow. Snowshoers must avoid these "spruce traps" lest they find themselves waist deep in snow, entangled in a mass of twisted branches. Nonetheless, the winter naturalist seeking animal signs will do well to begin the search among the spruce and fir.

Somewhere along the line, deciduous trees found it more energy-efficient to put out new leaves each spring then to maintain them through the winter. In the fall, they withdraw what nutrients and organic molecules they can from the leaves before letting them go. Most notably chlorophyll, the photosynthetic pigment that gives leaves their green color, is broken down and sent to the branches and ultimately the roots. Our spectacular autumn colors result from the predominance of anthocyanin pigments left in the leaves after the chlorophyll is gone.

By November the deciduous forest stands naked of its summer foliage. Only an occasional brown leaf still clings to the branches of the American beech. In the valleys and south of the mountains, oaks retain their dried leaves well into the winter. However, they are not ordinarily found above 1,000 feet of elevation in the White Mountains. The loss of leaves deprives the naturalist of the easiest means of distinguishing one tree from another. Identifying species in the winter requires attention to bark, twigs, buds, and overall growth form.

Using these observations, the various types of birch are among the easiest to pick out. There are two white-barked species, paper birch and gray birch. Both are early colonizers of open areas such as old fields and clearcuts, where they may grow in almost pure stands. The famous Shelburne birches are one such stand that developed after a disturbance.

The gray birch is the smaller of the two trees, reaching 30 feet high at maturity in 30 to 40 years. The bark of young trees and limbs is brown with white breathing pores called *lenticels*. The angle between limb and trunk is small. Trunks of older trees become white and show prominent black horizontal lenticels. Gray birches often grow in clumps of three to five trees. The trees are very susceptible to loading by ice during a freezing rain. After such a storm, the winter hiker will find them, with glazed trunk and branches, bent over and touching the ground. It is this gray birch that Robert Frost wrote of in his poem entitled *Birches*.

The paper birch has a life span of a hundred years or more and may reach a height of 80 feet. Young trees and limbs are bronze in color. The bark of mature trunk and limbs is a shiny white with only occasional lenticels. It tends to peel off in narrow strips that run around the tree. Branches leave the trunk at greater angles than those of the gray birch.

A third common species of birch in the White Mountains is the yellow birch. Like the paper birch, the yellow birch is a larger forest tree, reaching 100 feet. Yellow birch is easily recognized by its lustrous yellow or silver bark that peels off in narrow translucent strips. Young twigs have a slight taste of wintergreen.

All birches produce male and female flowers on the same tree. The cone-shaped male catkins are produced in late summer and are conspicuous on the bare branches throughout the winter. Female flowers remain protected as buds until early spring. Flowering occurs in April and May.

Two trees that often grow in association with the yellow birch on moist upland soils are the American beech and the sugar maple. The former is recognized by the smooth light-gray bark on younger trees or upper limbs. Beech twigs display narrow, pointed winter buds with scaled outer surfaces, looking something like cigars. A single large beech is often surrounded by numerous pole-size trees that have sprouted from the older tree's roots. It is almost possible to map the root system by the location of these sprouts.

Sugar maples are another gray-barked tree, though slightly darker than the beech. The bark of young maples will show irregular cracks, and older trees are often deeply furrowed. If you examine a twig carefully you can see that the flat scars left when the leaves peel off are opposite one another. This is not the case with beech or birch. Forest sugar maples have tall straight trunks, 60 to 70 feet high, with few branches on their lower portions.

Three other maples are commonly found in the White Mountains. The red maple grows very well in sunless and swampy soil that would be too moist for many other trees. It is recognized by its gray bark (smooth when young and scaled when older) and conspicuous red twigs. This tree grows to a slender 60 feet, generally with a narrow crown. The striped maple is a small, shrubby tree which grows well beneath a canopy of other hardwoods. Its furrowed dark-brown or green bark sports vertical white stripes, giving the tree its name. When the tree reaches about three inches in diameter, these stripes turn gradually browner and are less easily distinguished. Finally, the mountain maple has a bushy growth form and often forms thickets up to 20 feet high. Its thin, slightly fissured bark is a light reddish-brown. The tree is most easily identified by its hairy green to red-brown twigs, which reveal a brown pith when broken.

The white ash is a common tree in fertile, moderately well-drained soils up to about 2,000 feet of elevation. This tree's gray bark has deep, even furrows. Opposite branching gives white ash limbs an angular appearance. Above 2,000 feet another ash is rather common. The American mountain-ash is not an ash at all, but a relative of the apple tree. This tree rarely grows over 25 feet. Its light-brown bark may be slightly scaly. Clusters of bright-red fruits about the size of blueberries often remain on the tree until mid-winter. If present, these are a dead giveaway.

However, they are prized by many birds and may not last. If not, look for their large, round, sticky buds.

In open, burned-over areas and on the borders of marshes and beaver ponds, the quaking aspen is common resident. This tree tends to grow in even-aged stands with paper and gray birch. The three species require a great deal of sunlight to germinate and tend to be the first invaders of open areas in the White Mountains. Beneath their protective shade, an understory of shade-tolerant spruce and fir is often established. The quaking aspen is best identified by its generally smooth gray-green bark. Compared with the bark of other trees, the green tint is most notable. Black wounds and aberrations of the bark are not uncommon in older trees. Smooth, slightly sticky winter buds are also apparent.

The hobblebush grows in cool, moist woods up to about 3,000 feet. It is a straggling shrub 3 to 8 feet tall whose branches are said to "hobble" horses which try to move through them. Hobblebush buds are favorite deer food and make the shrub simple to identify in winter. They are brown, furry, and always in twos. Each bud is protected by two small leaves giving the twig the appearance of tiny hands pressed together in prayer.

Perhaps the most interesting tree in the winter woods is the tamarack. Tamaracks are slender, have reddish, scaly bark, and may grow to 70 feet or more. They bear small spherical cones that stand upright on the branch. The leaves are needle-shaped and generally grow in clusters. The tamarack strongly resembles our most common evergreens. However, the tamarack sheds its needles each fall. It is the only deciduous conifer in the White Mountains. The winter hiker coming upon a mixed stand of tamarack and black spruce is likely to think that the tamaracks are dead. Many a wintering tamarack has been felled by an axeman who supposed it good for firewood only. Tamarack and black spruce commonly grow together in swamps and peat bogs at elevations up to 4,000 feet. Although both trees will grow well on drier sites, they seem to have a competitive edge over other species in very moist soils. With or without needles, the well-spaced branches of the tamarack have a frail, Oriental quality that is singularly beautiful.

The most gregarious of winter creatures must certainly be the black-capped chickadee. This tiny gray-and-white bird has a metabolic rate so high that it must be in almost constant search of food. Chickadees will nonetheless abandon this pursuit in a moment to investigate any mimicked or unfamiliar sound made by the winter traveler. They are particularly quick to congregate when a tree is being felled. The birds will inspect chips and sawed ends for insect eggs and pupae, which form the bulk of their winter diet. Lacking such a reward, the winter hiker may still gather quite a flock of these curious onlookers by repeating a shrill descending whistle or a loud kiss on the back of the hand. Keep your eye out for an occasional brown-capped cousin, the boreal chickadee.

The white-breasted nuthatch is another common winter insectivore. Though similar in color to the black-capped chickadee, the nuthatch is easily distinguished by its stubby tail, squat appearance and the absence of a black throat patch. The two birds often flock together in the winter. The white-breasted and the rarer red-breasted nuthatch are equally at home walking right side up or upside down along the trunk of a tree as they search the bark for insects. Like the chickadee, they diversify their diets to include dry fruits and seeds. In the hunt for insects, they are joined by downy and hairy woodpeckers. Although very similar in coloration, these two may be distinguished by the size of the beak. Both birds are found in mixed, open woods, close to civilization. They seem to like humans and can be almost as gregarious as nuthatches and chickadees. Is the outgoing nature displayed by winter insectivores due to true friendship, or to a pragmatic recognition of the human ability to attract insects? Whatever the case, they are a happy sight in the winter woods.

The other major group of winter birds is the seed eaters. Their primary diet consists of dried fruits and seeds from various weeds and forest trees. Seed from evergreens, aspen, alder, and birch are favorites. The larger birds will take acorns and beechnuts when they can be found. Winter buds also provide a tender meal. Many of these birds will vary their diet with insects, especially in the summer.

One seed eater worthy of special mention is the slate-colored junco. This dark-gray white-breasted bird is about the size of a chickadee and is nearly as common in the winter woods. When the junco spreads it tail in flight, two white tail feathers flash out on either side and unmistakably reveal its identity. The other winter seed eaters of the White Mountain area are too numerous to describe in detail here. They include:

Pine Siskin	White-winged Crossbill
Common Redpoll	Blue Jay
Goldfinch	Canada Jay
Purple Finch	Ruffed Grouse
Evening Grosbeak	Spruce Grouse
Pine Grosbeak	Tree Sparrow
Red Crossbill	Song Sparrow

The common raven, so visible on the high ridges in the summer, remains in the mountains through the winter. Ravens have a widely varied diet that includes carrion.

Four owls may be found in the White Mountains during the winter. Boreal and snowy owls are migratory birds that occasionally come far south. Barred and great horned owls inhabit the region year-round. These birds feed on small mammals and perching birds. Sighting one is a rare treat.

With ground cover obliterated by snow and a majority of lower elevation forest trees leafless, winter becomes an ideal time to examine the basic landforms that underlie the forest. Long views are possible even below timberline. Landslide and avalanche scars may be seen on steep slopes. The effects of the continental ice sheet are apparent. These range from the large U-shaped north-south trending notches and polished, striated bedrock surfaces to boulder trains and hillside gravel terraces. "Erratic" boulders transported by glacial ice and set down atop bedrock of a different composition are easily recognizable. Features from alpine glaciation of the White Mountains prior to the ice sheet, the bowl-shaped cirques of the Presidential Range, Tuckerman and Huntington Ravines, stand out.

In the woods, smaller and more recent landforms may be discovered by the winter naturalist. Snow cover, as it conforms to the local topography, may make drainage patterns more apparent even when streams are invisible. Of course, it is hard to be certain about features that are only reflected by the snow cover. However, intelligent guessing is half the fun for the winter naturalist. One favorite is the two- to three-foot narrow rise that runs along one end of a large, open field of snow. On the other side of this rise a stream flows out of the open space. What's this? If you guess beaver dam, you're right. Often a mound of snow in the middle of the pond will reveal the location of the beavers' lodge. These and other "snow stumpers" provide endless entertainment. And, examining the winter landscape helps us better understand the foundations of the natural community through which we travel.

HUMAN HISTORY

Early Exploration and Settlement

The first name applied to the Presidential Range in the literature of the West appeared in 1628, according to White Mountain historian Frederick W. Kilbourne. "The Christall hill," as the citation went, must have been viewed from afar, for Europeans did not visit the mountains until 1642. The name White Mountains was first applied by John Josselyn in his *New England's Rarities Discovered* (1672). There is no clear consensus among scholars on the origin of this name, but it is the one that has stuck.

The original Algonquin name for Mount Washington was *Agiocochook* or *Agiochook*, according to a narrative published in

1736. This has been translated as meaning "at the mountains on that side." This is one name among several put foward, none of which can be ascribed with certainty to the peak. Nevertheless, the name was adopted by nineteenth century poets, and "Old Agiochook" was a common epithet applied to the mountain.

The same mist of uncertainty clouds the early history of the region, primarily, according to Kilbourne, because resident tribes had already been decimated by disease and warfare before the first British settlers moved into the area. The Abenakis, one of the ten major Algonquin nations, occupied most of New Hampshire, including the region around the Presidential Range. Vestiges of their wigwam villages, surrounded by wooden palisades, have been found in the river valleys and intervales in this century. These hunting and fishing people also grew some corn; corn hills and other hints of their agriculture survive, along with earthenware, pipes, and burial mounds.

At the time of first contact with Europeans, Passaconaway was chief of the nation. He welcomed the settlers and their missionaries, selling them land, converting to Christianity and abiding by their laws. In 1660 his son Wonalancet assumed the chieftancy and tried to keep the peace, but hostilities broke out and many of the Abenakis retreated to Canada.

Wonalancet's nephew Kancamagus was the last chief of the Abenakis in New Hampshire. Although he, like his forebears, tried to maintain good relations with the colonists, he was finally provoked in 1689 into an attack on Dover, New Hampshire. Armed expeditions were sent out and overcame Kancamagus and the other tribes of the region; the survivors fled to Canada. By the time of Chocorua, a famous chief after which a prominent peak of the White Mountains was named, even friendly Abenakis were hunted for their scalps. Chocorua's fetched a bounty of 100 pounds sterling in Boston. The names of a number of famous Abenakis remain associated in some way with the region. A waterfall in the Great Gulf, for instance, is named for Weetamoo, a princess who is said to have had six husbands, a story which the Six Husbands Trail commemorates.

The Italian expolorer Verrazano is credited with being the first European to see the White Mountains. He spied them on a coastal cruise in 1524 and recorded them in his log. In 1605 Champlain may have seen them from afar, after which they appeared on several antique maps, but it was not until 1642 that Darby Field visited them. From his account it is evident that he climbed Mount Washington, perhaps being the first person to do so. He was accompanied at least part of the way by two Abenakis; but it is uncertain whether or not they attained the summit with him. Tradition has it that the tribe thought that superior beings lived there because of the violent storms and landslides, and therefore tribesmen were reluctant to ascend the peaks.

Field's glowing account of the mineral riches to be had there — crystals he thought were diamonds — led to several later expeditions. There were no riches, though, and the region was left until the turn of the nineteenth century to other explorers, scientists and naturalists. They found riches indeed — the plants, animals, insects, weather, and geological phenomena discussed earlier.

"It was not until the latter part of the eighteenth century," Kilbourne states, "that the New England colonies were sufficiently established, and the country secure enough from Indian depredations, for the settlement of the remoter regions to be thought of and attempted." The first town in the region, Fryeburg, Maine, was chartered in 1762 and settled a year later. At the time the town was 60-70 miles into the wilderness. Conway, New Hampshire, was founded in 1765, and North Conway in 1766. Most of the other towns in the region were first settled in the following decade.

The real frontier drama of the Presidential Range, however, lies not in the incorporation of towns but in the settlement of the mountain country. One of the first pioneers in Crawford Notch, west of the Presidentials, was Abel Crawford, who unsuccessfully tried to colonize a spot at the north end of the Notch, in the valley of the Ammonoosuc River, near present-day Fabyan. He sold out to his father-in-law, Eleazar Rosebrook, who came to the region in 1792 with his wife and two children.

Crawford, "rather than be crowded by neighbors," moved twelve miles farther into the wilderness, where he built what was to become the first Crawford House inn. In the meantime the Tenth New Hampshire Turnpike was built twenty miles through the Notch at a cost of $40,000, raised by lottery.

The Notch had been discovered in 1771 by hunter Timothy Nash, who was in pursuit of a moose when he found it. Governor Wentworth, when told about the pass, immediately recognized its importance as a route from the upper Connecticut River valley to the seacoast. He offered Nash a land grant if he could bring a horse through the Notch, which he soon did with fellow hunter Benjamin Sawyer. A rough road was later built, and then the Turnpike.

Rosebrook built the first inn in the White Mountains, in 1803. At his death in 1817 his property went to his grandson, Ethan Allen Crawford, a man of great height and strength whose name more than any other is connected with the early settlement of the region. This is certainly because his wife, Lucy Howe Crawford, very ably chronicled their life together in her *History of the White Mountains,* a book so simply and powerfully written that it is still enjoyed by modern readers.

Besides farming, Crawford made his living as a guide and hotelier. He cut the first path up Mount Washington in 1819. It is now the oldest continuously maintained mountain footpath in the country. By 1820, newspaper advertisements were bringing intrepid men and women to the area to see the sights.

In 1825, following a fire, Crawford rebuilt his house as a hotel. In 1832, such was the traffic through the Notch that he built a still larger establishment. However, his health declined and, debt-ridden, he left his beloved White Mountains after twenty years of toil. Years later he returned and died near the site of his long-time home in the Notch.

It would be easy to assume from such a brief account that there was no hardship or heroism involved in the settlement of this region. These pioneers, after all, became guides and hotel proprietors only a few years after they arrived. There were no vast prairies to navigate, no deserts to cross, no hostile tribes to fend off — nothing, in short, of the superhuman effort Americans have come to expect of their pioneers through a steady diet of Western literature and cinema. However, as the journals of the era show, the challenges of this frontier were sufficient.

Perhaps the best indication of this was the Willey House disaster, an event which still colors the folklore of the region. Narrated by both Lucy Crawford and Samuel Willey's brother Benjamin, the tale is also the foundation for Nathaniel Hawthorne's short story, "The Ambitious Guest."

Midway between the Rosebrook and Crawford farms, in the very heart of Crawford Notch, the Willey House was, like the others, a lonely inn in the wilderness. In late August of 1826, following a long drought, a tremendous rainstorm swept through the mountains, flooding farms and inundating the turnpike. The following day a traveler found the Willey House deserted, as if the family had left in great haste. When the news reached the settlement in the valley, a search was mounted. Over the next several days the bodies of husband, wife, two children, and two hired hands were discovered among the debris of a huge landslide. The bodies of the three other children were never found. By a freak of fate, a ledge between the house and the mountain slope protected the dwelling from the slide, which split into two parts that cascaded down on either side. The residents, or so it is speculated, heard the landslide amid the storm and ran for safety. Ironically, if they had remained where they were, all would have been saved. Instead they were caught and crushed by the rocks and mud washed down from the mountain that now bears their name. Now in the heart of Crawford Notch State Park, the Willey House site is marked with a monument. It is a spot of profound beauty. Landslide scars still mar the face of Mount Willey.

The Era of the Grand Hotels

A history teacher, looking for a simple way to describe the human habitation of the Presidential Range, might devise the following scheme —

Seventeenth Century — Exploration
Eighteenth Century — Settlement
Nineteenth Century — Exploitation
Twentieth Century — Preservation

As noted in the previous section, even the first settlers in Crawford Notch, farmers and woodsmen though they were, saw the potential for exploiting the scenic grandeur of the Presidentials, and became hoteliers and guides as well. By late in the nineteenth century, this early vision of the mountains had been fully realized. Resort hotels dotted the landscape, catered to by a rail network bringing vacationers from all over the East. Both a railway and a carriage road climbed Mount Washington, and there was a thriving seasonal community on the summit to serve the whims of the visiting travelers. Attracting artists and writers as well as other distinguished visitors, the region was as much a chic watering place in its heyday as the French Riviera is now.

Late in this era, the timber barons came, stripping the mountain slopes and starting forest fires with their steam locomotives. It was this despoliation, and the outrage it caused among the White Mountain visitors and residents, that more than anything else led to the theme of the twentieth century: Preservation.

Early access to the Presidential Range depended, naturally, on the available transportation. The first in the region, as mentioned earlier, was the turnpike from the seacoast at Portland, Maine, through Crawford Notch to the upper Connecticut River valley. The earliest settlers, most notably the Crawfords, did much to keep this road open in spite of floods, landslides, and blizzards, for their livelihoods depended on it. The earliest traffic was commercial, farm produce from the hinterland exchanged for finished goods coming in through the seaport. Noncommercial visitors tended to be scientists and explorers, not tourists.

INTRODUCTION

Catering to this trade were half a dozen inns in Crawford Notch. The first, as noted previously, was built by Eleazar Rosebrook on the site of his decade-old homestead at the north end of the Notch in 1803. In 1816 Ethan Allen Crawford and his wife Lucy came to take care of Rosebrook, and after his death the following year ran an inn on the spot until forced out of the region by debt in 1837.

At about the same time that Rosebrook opened his inn, a second waystation was opened by Henry Hill at the Willey House site, halfway through the Notch, and a third was begun by Able Crawford, Rosebrook's son-in-law, at the south end of the Notch.

Life was precarious for these early settlers in the first quarter of the nineteenth century. In 1818, Ethan Allen Crawford's house burned; he immediately moved a smaller building to the site, but it was inadequate to house guests, so he had to send them on to his father Abel's, which was converted into an inn at the time for this reason. And, of course, the slide that killed the Willey family in 1826 was part of a storm and flood that also did extensive damage to both Crawford establishments.

Despite the hazards of life in the Presidentials at that time, however, much progress was made. In 1819 the first path to Mount Washington was built by the Crawfords, father and son; it is now called the Crawford Path. A year later Ethan guided a party of scientists and naturalists who named the peaks of the Presidentials with the names that most of them bear today. The following year a path was built to the summit near wehre the cog railway runs today. In 1823 Ethan Allen Crawford built the first buildings on the summit of Mount Washington, two stone huts that were soon abandoned because they accumulated moisture.

By 1825 tourists had begun to come to North Conway, which opened its first hotel in 1812. The town was the terminus of a stagecoach line from Center Harbor on Lake Winnipesaukee, which brought travelers from southern New Hampshire — and the outside world. By the quarter-century mark North Conway

INTRODUCTION

was a full-fledged resort town with five hotels.

At the same time the Conway region was developing, business was booming in Crawford Notch. Ethan Allen Crawford built a new hotel in 1824-1825, which he enlarged in 1832. With his father he built the Notch House, between the present Crawford House site and the Gate of the Notch, in 1828. It was managed by his brother T. J. Crawford for almost a quarter of a century.

Nathanial Hawthorne first visited the area in 1832. He was to write several stories with White Mountain settings in his lifetime, and was only one of many famous writers to vacation here. Among others to come were Henry Wadsworth Longfellow, Henry David Thoreau, Ralph Waldo Emerson, Francis Parkman, John Greenleaf Whittier, and William Cullen Bryant. By the end of the decade the region was established as a true resort. Until the end of the nineteenth century people came to the White Mountains summer after summer, staying several weeks at a stretch in their favorite hotels, visiting with summertime friends and amusing themselves with the grand mountain scenery.

It was a great era for the region, an era that brought with it a new generation of entrepreneurs. In 1837 Horace Fabyan relieved the debt-ridden Ethan Allen Crawford of his property at the north end of Crawford Notch. He renamed the place the Mount Washington House, and ran it for fifteen years. In 1845 he built another hotel at the Willey House site, and in 1851 took over management of the Conway House. Dr. Bemis, a long-time summer visitor to the region, assumed the reins at the Crawford House at the south end of the Notch in 1840. Even though Ethan Allen Crawford returned to the region in 1843 to live out his few remaining years, an age had ended, and a new one had begun.

By mid-century painters were coming to North Conway. They were to include Thomas Cole, Asher B. Durand, Benjamin Champney, Albert Bierstadt, and John Kensett, a group later to be called the Hudson River School. Because of their interest in the region, these Eastern landscape painters have been collectively labeled the White Mountain School locally. Their work is much studied and prized today.

INTRODUCTION

Around mid-century the spotlight shifted somewhat; hotels continued to be built and refurbished in Crawford Notch, and periodically burned down so the whole cycle would repeat itself. However, in 1852 the railway was completed from Portland, Maine to Gorham, New Hampshire, at the head of Pinkham Notch, on the eastern side of the Presidentials. With the railway came a hotel, Alpine House, and Gorham rapidly became one of the chief resort towns of the region. In the same year, 1852, the first hotel was constructed in Pinkham Notch — the Glen House — near where the present Auto Road begins its ascent of Mount Washington.

Commercial interest was also growing in the summit of Mount Washington. Until 1852 no permanent building was successfully constructed in that weather-whipped and rocky place, but in that year the first Summit House hotel was put up. The following year a rival hotel, the Tip-Top House, opened. Timothy Estus built an 'observatory' tower on the summit in 1854, but it was quickly abandoned as impractical and was torn down two years later.

Accompanying the opening of new areas to commerical activity were changes in the transportation network in the region. Until mid-century, although railways came to the main resort towns, transportation in the mountains was confined to stage coach, horseback riding, or foot travel. (In 1840 the Crawfords' path to the summit of Mount Washington was improved into a bridle path; at the ripe age of 75, Abel Crawford made the first horseback ascent of the mountain.) At this time the Presidential Range was not nearly so accessible as all the hotel-building might suggest, and, indeed, the summit of Mount Washington could be reached in a single day from only five inns in the entire region.

It is no wonder, then, that the Mount Washington Road Company was chartered in 1853, with General David O. Macomber as president. The idea was to build a carriage road to the summit of Mount Washington so that stagecoaches might carry visitors up and down in comfort. The idea was more easily envisioned than it was carried out, for the company failed in 1855-1856 due to the high cost of construction, after four miles had been completed. It remained for the Mount Washington Summit Road Company to finish the job in 1861, completing the world's first mountain toll road, which rises 4,700 feet in eight miles. The road is substantially the same one that is the Mount Washington Auto Road today, a testament to the engineering skill and daring of an earlier era. (For a good description of what can be seen from the Auto Road, which leaves Route 16 opposite the Glen House site, see Peter Randall's *Mount Washington*.)

On the other side of the mountains an even more daring engineering project was under way. In 1852 Sylvester Marsh, a founder of the city of Chicago and the man who began the meat packing industry there, was looking for a new avenue for his genius and fortune. He conceived of building the world's first mountain cog railway to the summit of Mount Washington. When he went to the New Hampshire legislature in 1858 for a charter to that effect, his idea was considered so preposterous that he was offered a charter to build a "railroad to the moon" if he desired it.

However, in 1866 he began construction, and two years later his railway was open to Jacob's Ladder. The following year it was completed to the summit, and a turnpike had been built from Fabyan to the Base Station. "Old Peppersass," Marsh's first experimental locomotive, is still on display at the Base Station. (For a good description of what can be seen from the cog railway, see, again, Randall's *Mount Washington*.)

The year 1870 saw the advent of the last great era of hotel-building in the White Mountains. It resulted from increasing numbers of visitors brought to the area by an improved transportation system, and lasted until the turn of the century, when the motor car ushered in a new age. (It is interesting to note that until 1874, when the railway was opened to Fabyan, Crawford Notch was still accessible only by a long and uncomfortable stagecoach ride.)

Again, the transition saw a change in fortunes of the resort towns in the region. Gorham, at the north end of Pinkham Notch, went into decline after the Alpine House burned in 1872. During the same period Jackson, at the south end of the Notch, underwent a period of growth and development.

'Growth and development' is also the best way to describe the activity on the summit of Mount Washington at the time. In 1862 Colonel John R. Hitchcock leased both summit hotels. When his Alpine House burned a decade later, he connected the two summit hotels, while at the same time beginning construction of a new Summit House. In 1870 a train shed was built on the summit, and in 1874 the world's first mountain weather station went into operation there. When the new Summit House was completed in 1873, the old Tip-Top House was turned into a dormitory and later became the first office of "Among the Clouds," the first newspaper printed on top of a mountain. A stage office was constructed in 1878, so that by 1880 there were six buildings — a veritable small town — on the summit of Mount Washington.

There was activity in Crawford Notch during this period, too. In 1876 the railway was extended from Fabyan to the cog railway Base Station, and two new hotels were built in the vicinity.

The harbinger of the end of this era came in 1899, when the first automobile ascended the carriage road. By 1904 an annual road race, "The Climb to the Clouds," was being run. The huge and sumptuous Mount Washington Hotel, built on virgin ground a mile from Fabyan, was completed in 1901-1902, but it has been something of an afterthought to the history of the region. Today it is the only hotel in this region from this era not to have been torn down or burned to the ground. In 1908, the Summit House and all other buildings on the summit of Mount Washington except the old Tip-Top House burned. In 1915, a new Summit House opened, after five years in the building, but by then the twentieth century — and a new era in the Presidentials — was well under way.

The Twentieth Century

The history of the Presidential Range in the twentieth century begins in 1867, when the New Hampshire legislature passed a law permitting the governor to sell all of the state's public lands to pay for school maintenance. The governor quickly did so, at very low prices, to half a dozen lumber barons who systematically clearcut large forested areas in the White Mountains between 1875 and 1915.

By 1907, 650 million board-feet a year were being cut in the region to fuel the building boom accompanying the Industrial Revolution in New England. Also, it was learned at about this time how to make paper from pulpwood, so for the first time softwoods as well as hardwoods were in demand. A forestry study of the period indicates that New Hampshire was "the most intensively lumbered state, per acre of wooded area, of any of the states . . . ."

River driving was initially tried as a method of getting logs to the mill, but New Hampshire's rivers and streams were too small; the railway, then, became the principal mode of transportation for the lumber companies. Each laid its own tracks into the wilderness it had purchased, until the whole region was a network of rail lines. When the trains were not hauling out logs, they took excursion parties in on their flat-cars. When an area was logged out, the tracks were taken up and moved to the next area to be stripped. The ruins of old lumber camps dot the region today, and a number of the abandoned rail beds have been used for hiking trails.

Compared to other areas of the White Mountains, the Presidential Range was relatively unscathed by timber harvesting, perhaps because of its remoteness and steep slopes. One rail line ran up the south branch of the Israel River to accommodate logging near the Northern Peaks. The wood was hauled out to Berlin for milling. From the south, lines ran up the Rocky Branch from Jackson and the Dry River through Crawford Notch to provide access to the southern Presidentials.

However, the damage caused by lumbering was sufficient to raise a cry throughout the region. An area just west of Crawford Notch was described as follows in an editorial entitled "The Trail of the Sawmill" in the *Boston Transcript* of July 20, 1892:

> The beautiful Zealand Valley is one vast scene of waste and desolation; immense heaps of sawdust roll down the slopes to choke the stream and, by the destructive acids distilled from their decaying substance, to poison the fish; smoke rises night and day from fires which are maintained to destroy the still accumulating piles of slabs and other mill debris.

Other criticisms of the timber industry in New Hampshire at the time were even more histrionic, one account comparing the devastation to that of the Holy Land around Jerusalem. Adding destruction to devastation were forest fires, many of them blamed on the timber harvesters and their spark-belching locomotives, which ignited dry slash left after lumbering. In 1903 such fires destroyed more than 10% of the White Mountain forests. Altogether 554 serious fires were reported to the authorities during the first eight months of that year.

Such events were obviously a grave threat to the White Mountains as a summer resort area, since its appeal to visitors depended on its scenic beauty. In 1888 the historian Francis Parkman made an early plea for their importance in attracting visitors. Writing in the February, 1893 *Atlantic Monthly,* Julius H. Ward proclaimed the White Mountains as being "worth infinitely more for the purpose of a great national park than for the temporary supply of lumber which they furnish to the market."

By the turn of the century there was a strong public sentiment in favor of a forest preserve maintained by the U.S. government where conservation — or at the very least selective timber harvesting — would be practiced. The Society for the Protection of New Hampshire Forests was founded in 1901 to pursue this aim, and in 1903 the New Hampshire legislature passed a bill favoring such a preserve.

The New Hampshire resolution was introduced into the U.S. Congress that same year as a bill, but it met with intense political opposition. Much legislative maneuvering during several Congressional sessions was needed to get what came to be known as the Weeks Act finally passed in 1911. What had started as a specific bill to protect the White Mountains, introduced by and named after a native of Lancaster, New Hampshire, ended up, because of the legislative compromises needed to get it enacted, as a general doctrine in which the government asserted its right to protect the headwaters of navigable rivers and to acquire watersheds for that purpose. In 1912 the commission empowered to apply the new law purchased more than 30,000 acres on the northern slopes of the Presidentials. By 1914 the total acreage exceeded 224,000, approximately one-third of the area within the purchase boundary; acquisitions included the all-important Mount Washington, except for the summit area.

In 1912 the state of New Hampshire purchased a 6,000-acre tract in the heart of Crawford Notch and made it into a state park.

A strong force behind passage of the Weeks Act was the Appalachian Mountain Club, an organization founded by Massachusetts Institute of Technology professor and later director of the Harvard Observatory E. C. Pickering in 1876 "for the advancement of the interests of those who visit the mountains of New England and adjacent regions, whether for the purpose of scientific research or summer recreation."

The Club early focused on the White Mountains, so much so that historian F. W. Kilbourne calls the region "an A.M.C. preserve." Its first efforts were devoted to taking over maintenance of some of the system of footpaths cut in the Presidentials and nearby ranges for half a century by guides and explorers.

In the 1920s the AMC hired a professional trail crew, the first of its kind in the country. Today the crew numbers thirty seasonal employees and two full-time staff members. It maintains three hundred and fifty miles of trail in the White Mountains, as well as twenty backcountry shelters and campsites. Today the Club is a nationally recognized authority on the subject of trail building and maintenance.

An important part of the trail system in New Hampshire is the Appalachian Trail (AT), a long-distance hiking trail from Maine to Georgia first conceived in the 1920s. When the Appalachian Trail Conference was founded to clothe this conception in reality, it discovered that the AMC had already formed some links in its trail network, so that most of the AT in New Hampshire could be routed along existing trails, Today the AMC is a strong force in the Conference at a time when the AT is being brought under the aegis of the National Park Service. The Club and it various New England chapters are responsible for more than 275 miles of the AT in the northeast.

Along the AT in New Hampshire are eight high mountain huts, the only alpine-style hut system in this country. The system began with a shelter constructed on Mount Madison by the AMC in 1888 to provide protection for hikers caught in inclement weather. This hut was later enlarged, and a second was built on the flank of Mount Washington in 1915 at Lakes of the Clouds. Today a string of eight, each a day's hike from the next, traverses the White Mountains, running from Carter Notch to Lonesome Lake, west of Franconia Notch. There is also a base camp at Pinkham Notch, at the foot of Mount Washington. The original intent of the hut sytem was that "trampers," in a time when camping was a major expedition involving hundreds of pounds of equipment, could walk this entire scenic area with only a knapsack on their backs, thus making it accessible to many who could not otherwise enjoy its beauty. At first only shelters from the weather, the huts are now equipped with bunks and serve meals, the makings for which are packed in on the backs of young hut crewmembers. The huts also dispense information, provide educational programs, and serve as a base for search and rescue operations.

Shortly after the turn of the century it was evident to the perceptive eye that another great change was coming to the

White Mountains. The era of the grand hotels was ending, never to return. The historian Kilbourne wrote about this in 1916:

> The advent of the automobile, with its almost immediate leap into general use for touring, greatly to the regret of many, including some landlords, has largely transformed in character the summer hotel and tourist business in the White Mountains, as well as elsewhere. While the volume of travel has increased, the majority of the visitors to the region are now of the transient variety, making in most cases but a fleeting stay at any one place and consisting largely of those who are "doing" the Mountains in their "motor-car."

Now motorists stopped at the resort hotels for a meal, or perhaps to stay overnight; at most they stayed a few days, using the hotel as a jumping off point for touring nearby sights. The summer-long sojourn, where people returned year after year to spend weeks or even months at the same hotel, was a thing of the past. Needless to say, establishments suffered, especially those off the major scenic highway routes. The volume of railway traffic also dropped noticeably. Shortly after World War II the trains were more or less dead as a means of passenger transportation; the one or two that remain are now scenic attractions in their own right, to be ridden like a carnival ride.

Gone too are the most of the old resort hotels. One knowledgable inhabitant of the region estimates that no more than half a dozen remain open in the entire area. Now the tourists stay in motels or own condominiums or vacation homes in the mountains, if they are not roughing it.

With the new modes of transporting and sheltering visitors have come new attractions. There are now 'theme' parks such as

Storyland and Heritage New Hampshire near Jackson. Ski areas now try to stay open all year with gondola rides or alpine slides.

Speaking of skiing, it was not until the 1920s that this sport came to the mountains, the harbinger of another important twentieth-century trend in the region — its use by visitors throughout the year. Kilbourne notes that in the nineteenth century only intrepid inhabitants and a few foolhardy mountaineering enthusiasts could be found anywhere near the Presidential Range in winter. However, the phenomenal growth of downhill skiing in New England, and more recently of ski touring, has made the region a four-season resort area today. For this reason the AMC keeps several of its huts open through the winter now, and Pinkham Notch Camp is a starting point for winter ice climbers, snowshoers, and ski tourers, as well as summer hikers and campers.

The set piece of winter sports in the Presidentials, though, has always been spring skiing in Tuckerman Ravine. There the snow often lasts into May, and once winter avalanche danger has subsided, wilderness skiers hike up the two miles from Pinkham, then climb the precipitous headwall for each run, since there is no lift. This tradition began in the 1930s and produced some exploits not matched in recent times. Among them were the three Inferno Races sponsored by the Dartmouth Outing Club. They ran from the summit of Mount Washington to Pinkham.

The coming of snowshoeing, ski touring and other sports to the Presidential Range area has not necessarily been all to the good. The growth of backcountry recreation and tourism has created problems and controversies. Pressure to develop the backcountry has been fairly constant down through the years.

For instance, in the 1950s skiers were pushing for a lift on Mount Washington in the Great Gulf area. To combat this threat and others, preservationists got it designated as a primitive area in 1961. When Congress passed the Wilderness Act in 1964, the Great Gulf was included in the new Wilderness system automatically. The shelters in it have been torn down by the Forest

Service, and a permit system was instituted to control use and access. In 1974 the Presidential Dry River Wilderness was added.

As early as 1915 there was a plan on the books for a scenic railway to the summit of Mount Washington (in addition to the cog railway), but the plan was abandoned. In the 1930s the Works Progress Administration drew up plans for a scenic highway crossing all the Presidential peaks, and got as far as sending surveying crews into the field. However, this plan too never came to fruition, some say because of high-level AMC members in the Roosevelt administration. Within the last few decades planning for Interstate-93 has included some alternate routes through the more scenic reaches of the White Mountains. A recent compromise route calls for a scenic parkway through Franconia Notch, west of the Presidentials.

The story of the Presidentials since World War II has been the story of the White Mountain National Forest. The Forest has grown over the years as hotel properties and other inholdings have been acquired, until it now totals 741,444 acres. Approximately 85% of the land within the designated purchase boundary is now part of the forest, a very high percentage as national forests go. Because it is situated so close to the East Coast megalopolis the Forest is one of the ten most heavily used national forests in the country. This great popularity has led to much concern among users about overcrowding and the degradation of the backcountry. With 200,000 people a year visiting the summit of Mount Washington by one means or another, the Presidentials are among the most populous mountains in the world. The development of lightweight backpacking equipment in the 1960s and 1970s as well as the growth of a 'clean camping' ethic, has helped to minimize the impact of those visitors who have the most direct effects on the backcountry, but it has still been necessary to impose some controls. Tent platforms are provided at several backcountry sites now so that pitching tents will not damage the environment. In the Great Gulf Wilderness area, a quota system is in effect to insure that its use will not exceed its ability to recuperate from human intrusion. Several other areas of the Forest have been proposed as Wilderness areas, engendering much debate between those who support as much Wilderness as possible and those who would like to see the areas available for a wider variety of uses. This debate is not likely to end for some time to come.

Nor is the future of the Presidential Range likely to be any less eventful than its past or present. What does seem likely is that the theme will continue to be "conservation" for the remainder of the century, and that the mountains will continue to come under pressure as the numbers of users and types of use increase.

BOOKS ABOUT THE PRESIDENTIAL RANGE

General Books

Burt, F. Allen, *The Story of Mount Washington,* University Press of New England (Dartmouth Publications), 1960

Crawford, Lucy, *History of the White Mountains,* edited by Stearns Morse, Appalachian Mountain Club, 1978 (reprint)

Ford, Daniel, *The Country Northward,* New Hampshire Publishing Company, 1976

Hill, Evan, *A Greener Earth,* photographs by David MacEachran, Society for the Protection of New Hampshire Forests, 1977

Kidder, Glen M., *Railway to the Moon,* privately published, 1969

Kilbourne, Frederick W., *Chronicles of the White Mountains,* Heritage Books, 1978 (reprint)

Oakes, William, *Scenery of the White Mountains,* New Hampshire Publishing Company, 1960 (reprint)

Olson, W. Kent and Brooks Atkinson, *New England's White Mountains,* photographs by Philip Evans, Amory Lovins and George DeWolfe, Appalachian Mountain Club,

Friends of the Earth, and New York Graphic Society, 1978

Randall, Peter, *Mount Washington: A Guide and Short History,* University Press of New England, 1974

Tanner, Ogden *et al., New England Wilds,* Time-Life Books, 1974

Tree, Christina, *How New England Happened: The Modern Traveler's Guide to New England's Historical Past,* Little, Brown and Company, 1976

Getting Along in the Presidential Range

Allen, Dan, *Don't Die on the Mountain,* New Hampshire Chapter of Appalachian Mountain Club, 1972

U. S. Forest Service (White Mountain National Forest), *Your Hike in the White Mountains,* Government Printing Office, 1976

Various pamphlets and leaflets are also available from the White Mountain offices of the Forest Service and Appalachian Mountain Club.

Hiking Guides

AMC White Mountain Guidebook Committtee, *AMC White Mountain Guide,* Appalachian Mountain Club, 1983

Appalachian Trail Conference, *Appalachian Trail Guide — New Hampshire-Vermont,* ATC, 1983

Doan, Daniel, *Fifty Hikes in New Hampshire's White Mountains,* New Hampshire Publishing Company, 1977 (revised)

Doan, Daniel, *Fifty More Hikes in New Hampshire,* New Hampshire Publishing Company, 1983 (revised)

Randolph Mountain Club, *Randolph Paths,* RMC, 1977

Reifsnyder, William, *High Huts of the White Mountains,* Appalachian Mountain Club, 1979

There are also a number of hiking and backpacking guides to the East Coast and the U.S. as a whole that include chapters on the Presidential Range and its environs.

Maps

Appalachian Mountain Club, *Mount Washington Range*, AMC 1983

Appalachian Trail Conference, *Appalachian Trail Map No. 10*, ATC, 1968

Preston, Philip, *Washington and Lafayette Trail Maps*, Waumbek Books, 1982

Randolph Mountain Club, *Randolph Valley and the Northern Peaks*, RMC, 1979

White Mountain National Forest, *White Mountain National Forest*, U.S. Forest Service, 1979

The Presidential Range in Winter

Cole, Peter and Rick Wilcox, *Shades of Blue: A Guide to Ice Climbing in New England*, Eastern Mountain Sports, 1976

Ford, Sally and Daniel, *25 Ski Tours in the White Mountains*, New Hampshire Publishing Company, 1977

Ski Touring Council, *Ski Touring Guide*, 15th edition, STC, 1978

Tapley, Lance, *Ski Touring in New England and New York*, Stone Wall Press, 1977

Ziegler, Katey (editor), *Ski Touring Guide to New England*, 4th edition, Eastern Mountain Sports, 1979

Nature Guides to the Presidential Range

Appalachian Mountain Club, *AMC Field Guide to Mountain Flowers of New England*, AMC, 1977 (reprint)

Bliss, L. C., *Alpine Zone of the Presidential Range*, privately published, 1963

Burke, C. John and Marjorie Holland, *Stone Walls and Sugar Maples: An Ecology for Northeasterners*, Appalachian Mountain Club, 1979

Jorgensen, Neil, *A Guide to New England's Landscape*, Pequot Press, 1977

Steele, Frederic, *At Timberline: A Nature Guide to the Mountains of the Northeast,* Appalachian Mountain Club, 1982

Steele, Frederic L. and Hodgdon, Albion R., *Trees and Shrubs of Northern New England,* Society for the Protection of New Hampshire Forests, 1975

Thompson, Betty Flanders, *The Changing Face of New England,* Houghton Mifflin Company, 1977 (reprint)

Thompson, Will F., "The Shape of New England Mountains," *Appalachia* (12/60; 6/61; 12/61), Appalachian Mountain Club

Additionally, within the next few years the Sierra Club is expected to publish a comprehensive naturalist's guide to northern New England by Neil Jorgensen. The first volume in a two-volume set, on southern New England, came out in 1978. There are also a number of bird and flower identification guides available that cover species found in the Presidential Range, but that are not specifically directed at the area.

Periodicals

Appalachia, Appalachian Mountain Club
New Hampshire Profiles
Mount Washington Observatory Bulletin

Bibliography

Bent, Allen H., *Bibliography of the White Mountains,* New Hampshire Publishing Company and Heritage Books, 1972 (reprints)

Wright, Walter W., "The White Mountains: An Annotated Bibliography, 1918-1947," *Appalachia* (12/48), Appalachian Mountain Club

SECTION 1

Hiking and Camping in the Presidential Range

This book describes hiking trails in the Presidential Range of New Hampshire.

THE WEATHER

The climate gets much cooler, windier, and wetter at higher elevations. Since 1932, there has been a permanent US weather station on top of Mt. Washington, which is under cloud cover about 55 per cent of the time. On an average summer afternoon, the high temperature on the summit is only about 52° F (11° C); in the winter, about 15° F (−9° C). Average winds throughout the day and night are 26 mph in summer and 44 mph in winter. Winds have gusted over 100 mph in every month of the year, over 120 mph at least once in every year 1952 through 1977, and set the world record of 231 mph in April 1934. Over 300 inches of snow fell on the summit in each winter 1969 through 1977, with almost twice as much in 1969. Other mountains also have severe conditions, in proportion to their height and exposure. Mt. Washington averages about 25° F (14° C) cooler than Boston in all seasons, and gets about twice as much precipitation.

Before going above timberline in winter, hikers should build up experience gradually. Section 8, *The Presidentials in Winter*, discusses winter hiking. **Caution.** Except for Section 8, trail descriptions in this *Guide* are meant to apply in summer conditions (mid-June through September). A reliable source of water in summer at high elevation may be frozen from November through May. Many rescues take place in late winter and early spring, because hikers are unprepared for continuing severe mountain winter conditions. In early May, long after snow is gone from the lowlands, snowshoes or skis may be needed in the mountains. Even at the end of May, snow can remain several feet deep in such places as Mahoosuc Notch or some of the ravines in the Presidential Range.

In the spring, dirt roads may be impassable due to washouts and deep mud until yearly maintenance is done. Trails may not be cleared of fallen trees and brush until late summer, and not all trails are cleared every year. Mosquitoes and black flies are at their worst on windless days in late May and June. Even in midsummer, hikers above treeline should be prepared for cold weather with a wool sweater, hat, mittens, and a wind parka, which will give comfort on sunny but cool days and protection against sudden storms. By early November, snow tires may be needed on roads above 1000 feet elevation.

STREAM CROSSINGS

Rivers and brooks are often crossed without bridges on White Mountain trails. In normal low water, it is usually possible to jump from rock to rock, perhaps using a stick from the bank for balance. If you need to wade across, wearing boots, but not necessarily socks, is recommended. Higher waters come in the spring as snow melts, in the fall when trees drop their leaves and take up less water, or after heavy rainstorms. Do not plan hikes with potentially hazardous stream crossings during these high-water periods. Rushing current can make swimming extremely hazardous, and several deaths have resulted. If you are cut off from roads by swollen streams, it is better to make a long detour, even if you need to wait and spend a night in the woods. For such unplanned bivouacs, wool sweaters and coats can be supplemented by very lightweight, insulating metallized "space blankets" sold in outdoor stores. Flood waters may subside within a few hours, especially in small brooks. It is particularly important not to camp on the far side of a brook from your exit point if the crossing is difficult and heavy rain is predicted.

HIKING AND CAMPING

PROTECTING THE ENVIRONMENT

Carry In — Carry Out

Trash receptacles are not available in trail areas (except at some trailheads), and visitors are asked to bring trash bags and carry out everything — food, paper, glass, cans — they carry in. Cooperation with the "carry in — carry out" program so far has been outstanding, and the concept has grown to "carry out *more* than you carried in." We hope you will join in the effort. Your fellow backcountry users will appreciate it.

Use Special Care Above Timberline

Extreme weather and a short growing season make these areas especially fragile. Just footsteps can destroy the toughest natural cover, so please try to stay on the trail or walk on rocks. And, of course, don't camp above timberline.

Limit the Size of Your Group

The larger the group the greater the impact on the environment and on others. Please limit the size of your groups to a dozen or less.

Guidelines for Backpacking Campers

Those who camp overnight in the backcountry tend to have more of an impact on the land than day hikers do. Repeated camping on one site compacts the soil and makes it difficult for vegetation to survive. Trash may accumulate and trees may be attacked for firewood, and popular campsites begin to resemble disaster areas. How to preserve the mountains for all to enjoy? Two possible methods are: first, to camp in well-prepared, designated sites, supervised by caretakers, or second, to disperse camping over a wide area, out of sight of trails and roads, and to camp with full respect for wilderness values.

Restricted Use Areas (RUAs) and Wilderness Areas

To limit or prevent some of the adverse impacts of concentrated, uncontrolled camping, the US Forest Service (USFS) has adopted regulations for a number of areas in the National Forest.

Those areas as of 1982 are listed and shown on a map in Section 2 of this *Guide*. Camping is never allowed above timberline. In RUAs, camping and wood or charcoal fires are not allowed within 200 feet of trails or within ¼ mile of roads, except on designated campsites. For further information, see Section 2 and consult any of the USFS, AMC, or other offices listed there, such as the Forest Supervisor in Laconia (603-524-6450) or Pinkham Notch Camp (603-466-2727).

Bring Your Own Tent or Shelter

Shelter buildings are often full, so each group should carry all needed shelter, including whatever poles, stakes, ground insulation, and cord are required. Do not cut boughs or branches for bedding.

Help Preserve Nature's Ground Cover

If a shelter is full, or if you camp away from shelters, try to choose a clear, level site on which to pitch your tent. Site-clearing and ditching around tents are too damaging to soils and vegetation.

Find a Site Out of Sight

As opposed to "concentrated" use at huts or shelters, the object of "dispersed" use is that campers remain unseen. Look for a spot more than ¼ mile off roads, and more than 200 feet off the trail, following any local RUA rules (but dispersed camping has advantages and rewards even where not required by such rules). Use a compass, and check landmarks carefully to find your way to and from your campsite.

Streams — Not Too Close

You will want to find water near your site, but try to put your tent on the same side of the trail as the water, so your path back and forth to the water won't wear a visible track across the main trail. To avoid polluting water supplies, camp at least 200 feet away. Other reasons not to camp too close to a stream or pond are

HIKING AND CAMPING

to avoid soil compaction at vulnerable shorelines and to stay above sudden floods.

Don't Be Cut Off

A heavy storm can quickly swell a quiet stream into a rushing torrent. This is especially true during spring runoff, but it can also occur during the summer or fall. In the White Mountains people have been killed trying to cross swollen streams. So, sometimes, it may be important to camp on the side of a river more accessible to civilization.

Use a Portable Stove

In some camping areas, a "human browse line" is quite evident, because people have gathered firewood over the years: limbs are gone from trees, the ground is devoid of dead wood, and vegetation has been trampled as people scoured the area. A stove puts the least pressure on the land. But be careful; stoves can be dangerous.

If You Do Build a Wood Fire . . .

You'll need a campfire permit. In the national forest follow USFS rules (see Section 2). On private land you must have the owner's permission to build a fire, and on state land, you need a state fire permit. Look for wood well away from the site. If you don't disturb the natural vegetation around the site, you will help provide a more enjoyable experience for the next camper. Of course you will put out your fire completely before you leave, but think about dismantling your fireplace so that your fire site is not obvious to others. Make sure, too, that there are no bits of aluminum foil or other unsightly debris left in the ashes.

Water for Drinking and Washing

Wash your dishes and yourself well away from streams, ponds and springs. It's handy to carry a small screen or cloth to filter the dishwater, so you don't leave food remnants strewn about the woods.

Most hikers drink from the streams without ill effect, and indeed, the pleasure of quaffing a cup of water fresh from a (presumably) pure mountain spring is one of the traditional attractions of the mountains. Unfortunately, in many mountain regions, including the White Mountains, the cysts of the intestinal parasite *giardia* are present in some of the water. A conservative practice is to boil water for 20 minutes or to use an iodine-based disinfectant. Chlorine-based products, such as Halazone, are ineffective in water that contains organic impurities and they deteriorate quickly in the pack. Remember to allow extra contact time (and use twice as many tablets) if the water is very cold.

Think About Human Waste

Keep it at least 200 feet away from water sources. If there are no toilets nearby, dig a trench 6 to 8 inches deep for a latrine and cover it completely when you break camp. The bacteria in the organic layer of the soil will then decompose the waste naturally. (Don't dig the trench too deep, or you will be below the organic layer.)

Hammock Camping

Some campers use hammocks rather than tents. Hanging between trees eliminates even that crushing of groundcover caused by tents. (Hammocks, however, have certain limitations during bug season!) We can all practice low-impact camping by making conscious efforts to preserve the natural forest.

FOLLOWING TRAILS

Most hiking trails are marked with paint on trees or rocks, or (on older trails), with blazes cut into trees. The Appalachian Trail, which crosses most of the higher White Mountains, has vertical rectangular white paint blazes throughout. Side trails off the Appalachian Trail are marked in other colors, such as blue. Above timberline, cairns (piles of rocks) mark the trails. Because hikers have trodden out the vegetation, the footway is usually visible except when it is covered by snow or by fallen leaves. In winter, signs at trailheads and intersections and blazes also are often covered by snow.

There has been logging at one time or another in most of the White Mountains. Trails following or crossing the logging roads require special care at intersections in order to distinguish the trail from diverging roads.

Around shelters or campsites, trodden paths may lead in all directions, so look for signs and paint blazes. If a trail is lost and is not visible to either side, it is usually best to backtrack right away to the last mark seen and look again from there: regularly maintained trails, such as those described in this book, should not just "peter out." Piles of wood or brush are sometimes used to block false trails. Such paths have eroded to the point of becoming rocky stream beds — if a trail seems to disappear at a small brook, it may follow the stream bed.

Caution. Hikers should always carry a compass, and should bear in mind their approximate location on the map. Before entering the woods, make certain which is the north end of the compass needle. Also, remember that the sun, after rising in the east, swings through the south in the middle of the day and sets in the west.

Compass Directions

Directions of the compass given in the trail descriptions are based on *true north,* instead of magnetic north, unless otherwise specified. This is important. At the present time there is a deviation of approximately 17 degrees between true north and magnetic north in the general area of the Presidential Range. The compass needle points *west* of true north in the northeastern United States. On the map included with this book, the black longitudinal lines, from bottom to top, point to true north. The diagonal light-brown lines point to magnetic north. In a few places, iron or other mineral deposits may affect compass functioning.

If You Become Lost...

If you become lost from a trail in the White Mountains, it is not necessarily a serious matter. In many instances, retracing your steps will lead you back to the point of departure from the trail. Distances are, as a rule, so short that it is possible to reach a highway in half a day, or at most in a whole day, simply by going downhill, skirting the tops of any dangerous cliffs, until you come upon a river or brook. The stream should then be followed downward. Special cautions for dangerous sections of trails appear within the text.

FOR SAFETY AND COMFORT

Let someone else know where you will be hiking. Have the latest guidebook and maps. A good group size is three to four people. Do not let inexperienced people get separated from the group.

Plan to finish your hike with daylight to spare. Hiking after dark, even with flashlights, makes finding trails and crossing streams distinctly harder, and if your flashlight fails, you have a real problem. Remember the shorter days in fall and winter.

Wear comfortable hiking boots. Get the latest weather report and any necessary wilderness entry or campfire permits. If you are going above timberline, carry extra warm and windproof clothing.

Good things to have in your pack for a summer day hike in the White Mountains include: maps, guidebook, water bottle, compass, knife, rain gear, windbreaker, wool sweater(s), hat, waterproof matches, enough food plus extra high-energy foods in reserve (such as chocolate or candy), first aid supplies (including personal medicines, aspirin, bandaids, gauze, and antiseptic), needle and thread, safety pins, parachute cord, trash bag, "mountain money" (toilet paper), and a (small) flashlight with extra batteries.

Bluejeans dry out too slowly in our wet conditions. Most fabrics dry faster than cotton, and wool keeps much of its value even when wet.

For an overnight backpack, you will also need, unless you've made a reservation in an AMC hut, a sleeping bag, pad, tent (shelters are often full), enough lightweight nutritious food, some extra clothes, and probably a stove and fuel. Of course, too much gear can become a burden. At a campsite, you may need to hang up your food to protect it from raccoons or bears.

For emergencies there is a toll-free New Hampshire State Police number 1-800-852-3411. You might want to jot this number down in a handy place, such as the inside front or back cover of this book, along with the AMC Pinkham Notch Camp number (603-466-2727).

THE TREES AND BUSHWHACKING

You can judge your elevation, to an extent, by the vegetation around you. Especially if you want or need to travel off trails, or "bushwhack," a closer acquaintance with the trees can help you to plan your route.

The rich variety of species on the lower slopes diminishes to only a few higher up. In the valleys of the southern White Mountains, at around 1000 feet elevation, some of the most striking trees are the tall white pines, with their needles in 5's. (Smaller ones occasionally occur to about 3000 feet.) A little higher than most white pines, often in ledgy areas, may be some red pines, with thicker twigs and longer needles in 2's. The red maples, with *v*-shaped divisions between leaf lobes, provide autumn glory, as do red oak leaves with their many, irregular, sharp-pointed lobes (white oaks' are rounded).

On some plots in the Hubbard Brook Experimental Forest, between 2000 and 3000 feet above sea level, foresters have found that 90 percent of the trees are either yellow birch (with thin, peeling bark layers), beech (with smooth gray bark on younger trees or limbs), or sugar maple (with *u*-shaped spaces between its leaf lobes). Sugar maple seedlings apparently prefer to grow under yellow birches, and beech saplings like to grow under sugar maples, while none of the three particularly favors growing under its own kind.

Above about 3000 feet elevation, most of the trees are small evergreens: balsam firs and spruces. If you want to tell them apart, spruce needles have a square cross section and can be rolled between finger and thumb. Balsam needles are flat and do not roll. Hemlocks grow at lower elevations; their needles are flat, like the firs', but shorter.

Near timberline, the small "scrub" or "krummholz" trees grow thickly together and are hard to walk through without a trail, especially uphill, or on ridge crests where they are tangled by the wind. The woods below 3000 feet are more open in all seasons, especially when the leaves are off the trees. So, when bushwhacking, you'll usually go faster if you minimize the distance you travel above 3000 feet. You can often find an old logging road, close to your objective, leading down from about the 2700-foot level to regular trails or roads. There are so many of these old logging roads that only a few of them appear on the maps included with this *Guide*. The first trees to grow into abandoned roads are often white birches, so sometimes an old road will pick up again on the far side of a birch grove.

When bushwhacking on a compass course without other good clues, look at the compass very frequently. Otherwise, for example, while you are trying to slab east along the south side of a descending ridge, you might circle around and end up slabbing west along the north side.

Above timberline, small, delicate alpine flowers can be seen, especially in June in the Alpine Garden on Mt. Washington. Plants, from lichens through trees that grow above about 4000 feet elevation are described in the AMC's *Field Guide to Mountain Flowers of New England*.

SKIING

Some alpine ski trails are described briefly in the text. To locate them, refer to the index under *Skiing*. Except for alpine skiing on Mt. Washington, discussed at the end of Section 3, this

Guide does not try to cover any kind of skiing (alpine, downhill, or cross-country). Several cross-country (ski-touring) trails are mentioned where they happen to cross hiking trails. They are not indexed.

Abandoned ski trails, owing to their width and their usual zigzag course on steeper slopes, may provide better views than regular summer trails do. On the other hand, they are less shady, the footing may be poor and rough, and some of them cross swampy places that are difficult when not frozen.

On ski trails currently used in winter, summer hiking may promote erosion, a serious concern. Accordingly, the USFS requests that summer hikers not make a practice of using ski trails.

ROCK CLIMBING

Because of extreme hazards to inexperienced or insufficiently equipped climbers or groups, rock climbs are not described in this book. Detailed information concerning a particular route may be obtained from the AMC Mountain Leadership Committee.

Rock climbing is not recommended for hikers in general: it requires special techniques and equipment, and there is greater risk for the unskilled than on trails. Even a slight slip may entail serious consequences. Rock climbing in the White Mountains should not be undertaken except by roped parties under qualified leaders.

OTHER HAZARDS

There are no poisonous snakes or other dangerous animals (except possibly humans) in these mountains. Deer-hunting season is in November, when you'll see many more hunters than deer. The few bears tend to keep well out of sight, except at some popular campsites. Actually, the main risks to look out for on any hiking trip are probably not in the woods at all, but on the highway, going to or from your trailhead.

DISTANCES AND TIMES

The distances and times that appear in the tables at the end of trail descriptions are cumulative from the starting point at the head of each table. Estimated distances are preceded by *est.*

Times are based on a speed of 2 mph, plus an additional half-hour for every 1000 feet gained in elevation. Times are included only to provide a consistent measure for comparison among trails and routes. When no time is given, the route described may be considered a leisurely walk or stroll. With experience, hikers will learn how to correct these standard times for their own normal paces. Bear in mind, however, that if your average pace is faster than the standard time, it will not necessarily be so on trails with steep grades, in wet weather, if you are carrying a heavy pack, or if you are hiking with a group. And in winter, you should roughly double the time it would normally take for you to complete a hike.

The final entry in the distance-time summaries at the end of trail descriptions usually gives the metric equivalent of the total distance, although neither the USGS maps nor the USFS yet use metric measures.

ABBREVIATIONS

The following abbreviations are used in trail descriptions.

hr.	hour(s)
min.	minute(s)
mph	miles per hour
in.	inch(es)
ft.	foot, feet
km.	kilometer(s)
yd.	yard(s)

N.	North (proper name only)
S.	South (proper name only)
E.	East (proper name only)
W.	West (proper name only)
Mt.	Mount (proper name only)
AMC	Appalachian Mountain Club
US	United States
USFS	United States Forest Service
USGS	United States Geological Survey
WMNF	White Mountain National Forest

The following abbreviations are used for organizations that maintain trails, shelters, and other facilities for the public.

AMC	Appalachian Mountain Club
AT	Appalachian Trail
HA	Hutmen's Association
JCC	Jackson Conservation Commission
NHDP	New Hampshire Division of Parks
RMC	Randolph Mountain Club
SPNHF	Society for the Protection of New Hampshire Forests
SSOC	Sub Sig Outing Club
WMNF	White Mountain National Forest

FIRES AND FIRE CLOSURES

Permits to build fires within the WMNF are required except at improved roadside campgrounds, where adequate facilities are provided. Permits can be obtained free of charge from the Supervisor, USFS, Laconia, NH, or from the District Rangers located at Plymouth, Bethlehem, Conway, and Gorham, NH, and Bethel, ME, and from AMC facilities. Campfire permits will be issued for the entire season, except for the Great Gulf and Presidential-Dry River Wilderness Areas. Further information is in Section 2.

During periods when there is a high risk of forest fires, the Forest Supervisor may temporarily close the entire WMNF against public entry. Such general closures apply only as long as the dangerous conditions prevail. Other forest lands throughout New Hampshire or Maine may be closed during similar periods through proclamation by the respective governors. These special closures are given wide publicity so that local residents and visitors alike may realize the dangerous condition of the woods.

MAPS, GUIDES, AND LITERATURE

Extra copies of the maps with the *Guide* may be purchased separately at the AMC Boston and Pinkham Notch offices and at some book and outdoor equipment stores. Elevations of mountain summits not given in the text of this *Guide* may be determined from the maps.

The published topographic quadrangles of the US Geological Survey cover all of New Hampshire. The new USGS 7.5 min. quadrangles are gradually becoming available. Pamphlets published by the WMNF are available free of charge at the Forest Supervisor's Office in Laconia, NH 03246.

A detailed map of the Randolph Valley and the Northern Peaks is available (1979 edition) on plastic-coated paper from the Randolph Mountain Club, Randolph, NH 03570. Cost $1.50.

The following may be purchased at the AMC offices at 5 Joy Street, Boston, MA 02108, and the Pinkham Notch Camp: *Guide to the AT in New Hampshire and Vermont,* published by the Appalachian Trail Conference; *Randolph Paths,* a detailed guide to paths and places around Randolph, published in 1977 by Randolph Mountain Club, Randolph, NH 03570.

COOPERATION

The AMC earnestly requests that those who use the trails, shelters, and campsites heed the rules of the WMNF, NHDP, and SPNHF (see Section 2), especially those that have to do with camping. The same consideration should be shown to private owners.

Trails must not be cut in the WMNF without the approval of the Forest Supervisor at Laconia, NH. The New England Trail Conference advises that trails should not be blazed or cut elsewhere without consent of the owners and without definite provision for maintenance.

The AMC guidebook Committee appreciates the comments and suggestions sent in by members of the Club and others, in preparation of this edition. Since the purpose of this book is to furnish accurate details in the text and on maps, information from any source will be welcome. If you find inaccuracies, signs missing, obscure places on the trails, or a map that needs correcting, please send report to White Mountain Guide Committee, AMC, 5 Joy Street, Boston, MA 02108.

SECTION 2

National and State Areas

WHITE MOUNTAIN NATIONAL FOREST (WMNF)

Most of the higher White Mountains are within or adjoin the White Mountain National Forest (WMNF). In the Presidential Range, the Great Gulf and Dry River-Davis Path areas within the WMNF have been set aside for preservation as Wilderness Areas. A free wilderness permit is required for overnight camping in the Great Gulf Wilderness from June 15 to September 15. Also, camping and fires are restricted to designated sites in a number of Restricted Use Areas (RUAs) in the Forest, described below and shown on the map, pp. 22 and 23. By protecting the plants, water, soil, and wildlife of the White Mountains, these areas should help to provide a higher quality experience for the visitor.

CAMPFIRE PERMITS

The laws of the states of Maine and New Hampshire and regulations of the Secretary of Agriculture require that permits be obtained to build campfires anywhere in the WMNF, except at improved roadside campgrounds maintained by the USFS, where no campfire permits are required. Permits are not required to use portable stoves. Campfire permits are not required when snow is on the ground. Permits may be obtained from the District Forest Rangers or other WMNF offices, or from AMC huts or offices listed below. Applications may be made personally, by letter, or by telephone, any time before the planned trip.

WMNF OFFICES AND RANGER DISTRICTS (R.D.'s)

Androscoggin R.D., 80 Glen Rd., Gorham, NH 03581 (at south end of town along NH Rte. 16). Tel. 603-466-2713.

Saco R.D., Kancamagus Highway (RFD 1, Box 94), Conway, NH 03818 (near east end of highway). Tel. 603-447-5448.

Forest Supervisor, P.O. Box 638, Laconia, NH 03246. Tel. 603-524-6450.

The Androscoggin Ranger District has been open seven days a week in the summer from about 8:00 A.M. to 5:00 P.M. or later. The Saco Ranger District Visitors' Center is open in the summer seven days a week, as follows: 8:00 A.M. to 5:30 P.M. Monday through Thursday; 8:00 A.M. to 10:00 P.M. Friday and Saturday; and 9:00 A.M. to 5:30 P.M. on Sunday. Otherwise, the offices are open during normal business hours.

The WMNF also has information centers on the Kancamagus Highway in Passaconaway and at the west end in Lincoln, and in Campton. Campfire and wilderness entry permits as well as other information are available there as well as at Ranger District offices. The Lincoln Center has been open seven days a week for most of the year from about 9:00 A.M. to 7:00 P.M.

AMC OFFICES

Fire permits and further information are also available from the AMC at Pinkham Notch Camp, Gorham, NH (603-466-2727), 7:30 A.M. to 10:00 P.M. seven days a week, and on summer days, at the Old Bridle Path trailhead in Franconia Notch. Fire permits are also available from the USFS and from fire wardens. Information can also be obtained at AMC huts during their operating season and from the caretakers of shelter sites.

NATIONAL AND STATE AREAS

FIRE AND CAMPING REGULATIONS

The use of portable stoves is encouraged and does not require a permit. Operate stoves with reasonable caution. Wood or charcoal campfires require permits and must be made in safe, sheltered places and not in leaves or rotten wood, or against logs, trees, or stumps. Before you build a fire, clear a space at least 5 ft. in radius of all flammable material down to the mineral soil. Under no circumstances should a fire be left unattended. All fires must be completely extinguished with earth or water before you leave a campsite, even temporarily. Firewood may be obtained only from dead trees. Green trees may be cut only with a permit from the District Rangers.

All camp refuse should be carried out *(Carry in/Carry out)*, and when you break camp the site must be made tidy and attractive. No rubbish or refuse should be thrown into any stream, spring, pond, or into or beside any road or path. Bathing and washing clothes or dishes is absolutely prohibited in certain streams that are used for domestic water supply by neighboring towns. Hunting and fishing must conform to the laws of the state in which the lands are situated. The policy of the USFS is to make all campsites available for the general public instead of leasing them to individuals for private use. Sites are available on a first-come, first-served basis.

For more detailed camping guidelines, see Section 1.

WILDERNESS AREAS

The national Wilderness Preservation system, which included the Great Gulf, was established in 1964 with passage of the Wilderness Act. The Presidential Range-Dry River Wilderness was created in 1974, and in 1979 numerous additional areas within the WMNF were also proposed for Wilderness Act protection.

20　　　　　　　　　　　SECTION 2

Permits are now required only for overnight camping in the Great Gulf Wilderness Area. They may be obtained from the Androscoggin Ranger District office in Gorham, NH 03581 (603-466-2281) from May 1 to October 31, or at Dolly Copp Campground from July 1 to Labor Day. No permits are required for day use in either the Great Gulf or the Presidential-Dry River Wilderness Areas. Permits for overnight camping are not required in the Presidential-Dry River Wilderness Area.

Shelter buildings are contrary to Wilderness Act policy, so eventual dismantling of all shelters in Wilderness Areas is planned.

Great Gulf Wilderness

This area includes some 5552 acres of WMNF land; see map, pp. 22 and 23.

Beginning on the north side of the Mt. Washington Auto Rd. at a point about 0.8 mi. up from NH Rte. 16, the boundary generally follows the road to about 0.5 mi. below the summit of Mt. Washington, turns right along the Gulfside Trail, then goes over Mt. Adams to Madison Hut, along the Osgood Trail over Mt. Madison and down to the Great Gulf Trail, turns east for a short distance and then right (south) to the Auto Rd.

The Gulfside and Osgood trails (except for a short segment) are just *outside* the Great Gulf Wilderness.

Presidential-Dry River Wilderness

This area includes the Dry River valley and parts of the Montalban Ridge, see map, pp. 22 and 23. Its general boundary is as follows: beginning at the New Hampshire Division of Parks-WMNF boundary on the Webster Cliff Trail, it follows that trail, then the Crawford Path to where the line turns south at the base of Mt. Washington summit cone, and goes just southwest of the Glen Boulder Trail, follows the Rocky Branch Ridge down to where the line turns west across Mt. Crawford, and then north along the WMNF boundary to the Webster Cliff Trail. The

Webster Cliff Trail and Crawford Path are entirely in the Presidential RUA, but just outside the Presidential-Dry River Wilderness Area.

RESTRICTED USE AREAS (RUAs)

Overnight camping is permitted in almost all of the WMNF. The object of the RUA program is not to hinder backpackers and campers, but to disperse their use of the land so that people can enjoy themselves in a clean and healthy environment without causing deterioration of natural resources. Overnight camping and fires are therefore regulated to limit damage in some areas of the WMNF that are threatened by overuse and misuse. Following are the current RUA regulations in 1982. Contact the USFS in Laconia, NH (603-524-6450), or any Ranger District office for up-to-date information. Ask for a current *Restricted Use Area Map*.

In summary, the 1982 RUA rules call for **no camping and no wood or charcoal fires:**
 1. **above timberline** (where trees are less than 8 ft. in height);
 2. **within 200 ft. of certain trails,** except at designated sites;
 3. **within a quarter mile of certain roads, rivers, and sites,** except in or on campgrounds, shelters, and designated sites.

Stoves are permitted for day use, even in RUAs. RUAs as of 1982 are listed below, but the list may change from year to year, since new areas may need this protection and old ones may not. Because hikers and backpackers have cooperated with RUA rules, many trails once designated as RUAs are no longer under formal restrictions. However, common sense and self-imposed restrictions are still necessary to prevent trailside damage.

The RUAs, Wilderness Areas, and other regulated areas as of 1982 are numbered as on the map, pp. 22-23. RUA boundaries and approved overnight sites within RUAs are indicated by prominent signs. Specific rules are posted at each site.

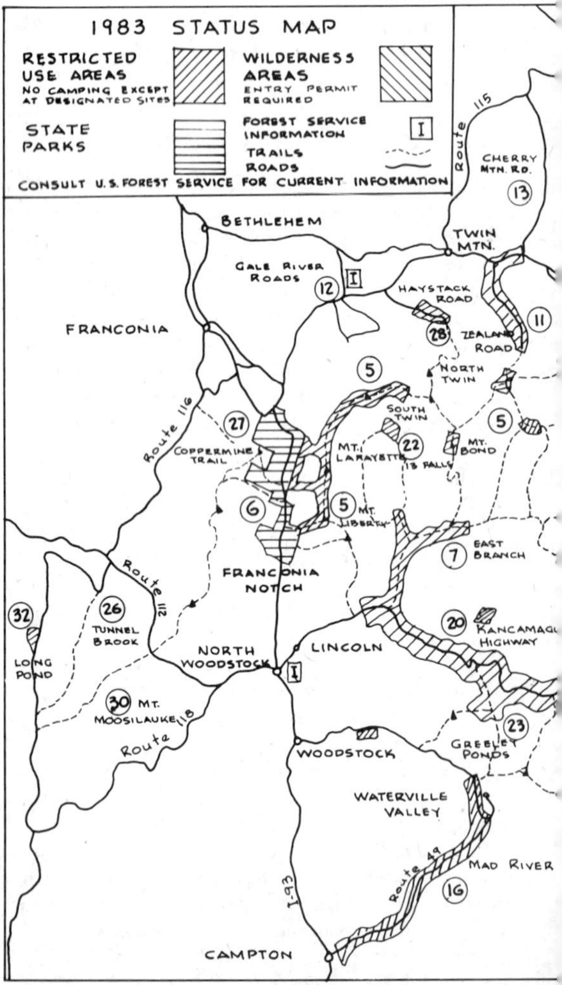
1983 STATUS MAP
RESTRICTED USE AREAS
NO CAMPING EXCEPT AT DESIGNATED SITES
WILDERNESS AREAS
ENTRY PERMIT REQUIRED
STATE PARKS
FOREST SERVICE INFORMATION
TRAILS
ROADS
CONSULT U.S. FOREST SERVICE FOR CURRENT INFORMATION
Route 115
CHERRY MTN. RD.
13
BETHLEHEM
TWIN MTN.
GALE RIVER ROADS
12
HAYSTACK ROAD
11
FRANCONIA
28
ZEALAND ROAD
5
NORTH TWIN
Route 116
SOUTH TWIN
27
5
COPPERMINE TRAIL
MT. LAFAYETTE
22
MT. BOND
13 FALLS
6
5
MT. LIBERTY
EAST BRANCH
7
FRANCONIA NOTCH
Route 112
32
26
TUNNEL BROOK
20
KANCAMAGU
HIGHWAY
LONG POND
NORTH WOODSTOCK
LINCOLN
30
MT. MOOSILAUKE
Route 118
23
WOODSTOCK
GREELEY PONDS
WATERVILLE VALLEY
MAD RIVER
Route 49
I-93
16
CAMPTON

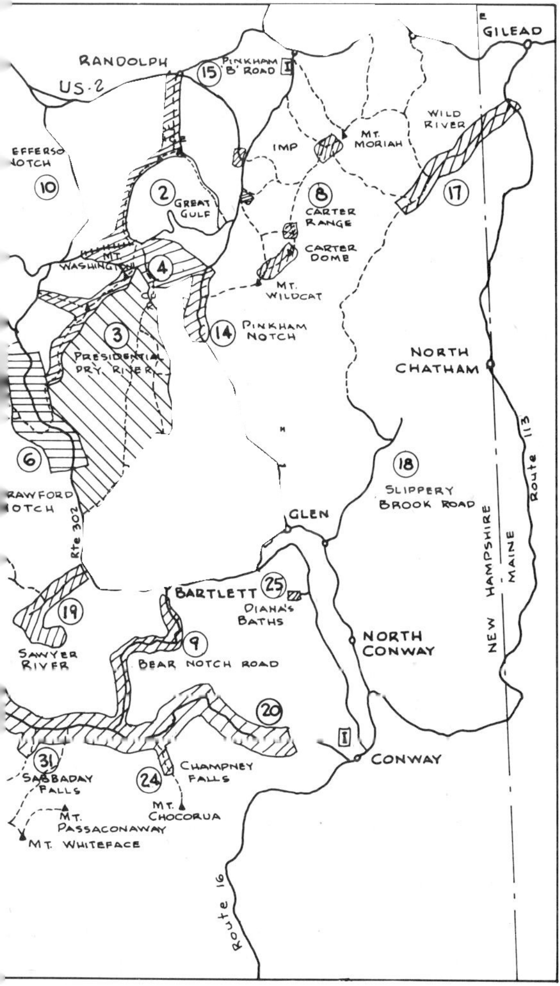

NATIONAL AND STATE AREAS 23

Use Regulations for Specific RUAs

1. **Presidential Range RUA.** *No camping, no wood or charcoal fires above timberline* (where trees are less than 8 ft. high). *No camping, no wood or charcoal fires within 200 ft. of trails,* except at shelters, in huts, and at Mizpah-Nauman campsite. *Removal, without permission, of any tree, plant, or shrub is prohibited.*
2. **Great Gulf Wilderness.** See Section 5.
3. **Presidential-Dry River Wilderness.** *No camping, no wood or charcoal fires above timberline* (where trees are less than 8 ft. high). *No camping, no wood or charcoal fires within 200 ft. of trails,* except at designated sites.
4. **Cutler River Drainage RUA** (Tuckerman and Huntington Ravines). *No camping allowed year-round* except at Harvard Mountain Club Cabin in Huntington Ravine and at Hermit Lake Shelters in Tuckerman Ravine. *No campfires.* Stoves only. Tickets for shelters in Tuckerman Ravine are sold on first-come, first-served basis at Pinkham Notch Camp. *Inquire* before hiking in to the ravine. There is a caretaker at Hermit Lake.
6. **Crawford Notch** (NH state park). Crawford Notch State Park 603-374-2272. *No camping, no wood or charcoal fires* are allowed in the state parks except at Lafayette Campground in Franconia Notch and the Dry River Campground in Crawford Notch. Fees. AMC Lonesome Lake Hut: *no camping around hut.*

No camping, no wood or charcoal fires within a quarter-mile of the following roads except at campgrounds that are designated sites (fees charged).

ROAD	CAMPGROUNDS
14. Zealand Rd. — Ammonoosuc River	Zealand, Sugarloaf

NATIONAL AND STATE AREAS

15. NH Rte. 16 — Pinkham Notch   Dolly Copp, Barnes Field

This completes the list of RUAs as of 1982. Again, contact the USFS (603-524-6450) for current status, or consult up-to-date RUA map.

SCENIC AREAS

The USFS has established the Pinkham Notch scenic area of 5600 acres to preserve the area's outstanding and unique beauty. Information may be obtained by writing to the Forest Supervisor, WMNF, Laconia, NH 03246.

NATIONAL FOREST — BACKGROUND

Under the Weeks Act, and subsequent legislation passed by the states of Maine and New Hampshire, the USFS was authorized to purchase approximately 850,000 acres in the White Mountains and adjoining regions. The total area of the WMNF, including lands acquired and approved for purchase, is currently about 752,000 acres, of which about 47,000 acres are in the state of Maine.

As lands are acquired they are placed under the care of the USFS, and their immediate supervision is delegated to the Forest Supervisor, whose office is at Laconia, New Hampshire. Anyone who plans to camp in the WMNF, to buy timber, or to use the resources of the Forest in other ways, should communicate with a District Ranger in person, by mail, or by telephone.

It is important to remember that this is not a National Park, but a National Forest. Parks are established primarily for preservation and recreation. National Forests are managed for multiple use. In the administration of National Forests the following objectives are considered: recreation development, timber production, watershed protection, and wildlife propagation. It is the policy of the USFS to manage logging operations so that trails, streams, camping-places, and other spots of public interest are protected. Mountain recreation has been identified as the most important resource in the WMNF.

To preserve the rare alpine flora of the Mt. Washington Range and to assure that the natural conditions on the upper slopes of the WMNF are maintained, removal of any tree, shrub, or plant without permission is prohibited. See the AMC's *Field Guide to Mountain Flowers of New England*.

The boundaries of the WMNF are usually marked wherever they cross roads or trails. The printed notice faces outward from the Forest. Throughout the mountains red-painted corner posts and blazes indicate either WMNF boundaries or the boundaries of various tracts acquired.

PUBLIC CAMPS AND SHELTERS

There are no public campgrounds for motor camping in the Presidential Range except for the Dolly Copp campground in the Northern Peaks area.

Trailside Shelters and Tent Sites

Shelters are overnight accommodations for persons carrying their own bedding and cooking supplies. The more popular shelters are often full, so bring tents or tarps. Dishwashing should be done at a location away from any surface water. Please heed the rules of neatness, sanitation, and fire prevention, and carry out everything — food, paper, glass, cans, etc. — that you carry in. Do your part to keep the backcountry clean. (See Section 1 for more detailed guidelines.)

Around many shelters or sites are tent platforms or tent pads, providing camping areas for numbers of people given in paren-

NATIONAL AND STATE AREAS

theses in the table below. Less formalized tent sites are also often available, but they may be scarce.

Please note that the facilities listed below are described as follows:
- C — Cabin and capacity
- S — Shelter and capacity
- T — Tent site and capacity

Guide Section	Facility	Capacity	Maintaining Organization	Trail
3	Hermit Lake Shelters***	86	AMC	Tuckerman Ravine
4	The Log Cabin	C-10	RMC	Lowe's Path
4	Crag Camp	C-14	RMC	Near Spur Trail
4	Gray Knob	C-12	Town of Randolph	Near Lowe's Path
4	The Perch	S-8	RMC	Perch Path
6	Nauman	T-16	AMC	At Mizpah Hut
7	Resolution	S-8	AMC	Davis Path
7	Mt. Langdon	S-8	WMNF	Mt. Langdon
7	Rocky Branch No. 1	S-8 S-10	WMNF	Rocky Branch
7	Rocky Branch No. 2	S-10	WMNF	Rocky Branch

Contact Pinkham Notch Camp, Gorham, NH 03581 (1-603-466-2727), for up-to-date information on shelters, tent sites, huts, and trails.

THE APPALACHIAN TRAIL (AT)

This 2,035-mile footpath, running from Springer Mountain, Georgia to Katahdin in Maine, traverses the backbone of the White Mountains in a southwest to northeast direction from

---

***No tents at Hermit Lake. Shelters only. Charge. Tickets only at Pinkham Notch Camp.

Hanover, NH to Grafton Notch, ME, approximately 154 miles within New Hampshire. Its route traverses most of the major peaks and ranges of the White Mountains, following many historic, heavily used local and circuit hiking routes. Persons interested in following this section as a continuous path should consult the Appalachian Trail Conference's guidebook, *Guide to the Appalachian Trail in New Hamsphire and Vermont*. In 1978, new USFS signs were posted at trail junctions on the AT, giving distances (some of which, unfortunately, were incorrect). Information on the Appalachian Trail and the several guidebooks which cover its entire length can be secured from the Appalachian Trial Conference, P.O. Box 236, Harper's Ferry, WV 25425.

With the passage of Public Law 90-543 "The National Trails System Act," by Congress on October 2, 1968, the Appalachian Trail became the first federally protected footpath in this country and was officially designated the Appalachian National Scenic Trail. Under this act the Appalachian Trail is administered primarily as a footpath by the Secretary of Interior in consultation with the Secretary of Agriculture and representatives of the several states through which it passes. In addition, an Advisory Council for the Appalachian National Scenic Trail was appointed by the Secretary of Interior. It includes representatives of each of the states and the several hiking clubs recommended by the Appalachian Trail Conference.

STATE PARKS

As of 1982, the state of New Hampshire had 181 distinct and separate areas comprising over 110,000 acres under the jurisdiction of the State Department of Resources and Economic Development. State parks are supervised by the Director of Parks in the New Hampshire Parks Division; forest properties by the Director of Forests and Lands. Offices are in the State House Annex, Concord, NH 03301.

NATIONAL AND STATE AREAS

In Crawford Notch on US Rte. 302, camping is available from mid-May to mid-October at Dry River Campground, with 30 tent sites, 3 miles south of the park buildings. There is a charge. Natural attractions (see Section 6) include Mts. Webster, Willard, and Willey, Arethusa Falls — reached by a side road 3 miles south of the Willey House site, and by a trail (about a mile to the falls) — Silver and Flume cascades, and Frankenstein Cliff.

Other State Campgrounds

The following New Hampshire state park also offers a campground near hiking trails.

Moose Brook State Park, Gorham. Excellent campground and bathing in park, 42 tent sites. Open mid-June to Labor Day. Trails in the park connect to Randolph trails. There is a charge.

In state campgrounds, tent sites cannot be reserved. Campers must appear at the park office to register. The camping period is limited to TWO WEEKS from mid-June to Labor Day. Extensions may be obtained before and after that period at the discretion of park managers. Anyone camping in a state park must have a tent or a camping unit. Camping with only a sleeping bag is not permitted. Write NH Division of Parks and Recreation, Concord, NH 03301 for information on camping in state parks.

SECTION 3

Mount Washington

Mt. Washington (6288 ft.) is the highest peak east of the Mississippi and north of the Carolinas. It was seen from the ocean as early as 1605, and its first recorded ascent was in 1642 by Darby Field and two Indians. It is a huge mountain mass with great ravines cut deep into its sides. Above the ravines are comparatively level stretches called "lawns," which vary in elevation from 5000 to 5500 ft. From these lawns rises the bare, rock-strewn cone or summit, the climate of which is similar to that of northern Labrador. The mountain is on the watershed of three rivers, the Androscoggin, the Connecticut, and the Saco.

This section covers trails on the east slopes of Mt. Washington itself and local trails around the summit. For other approaches see Section 4 *Northern Peaks*, 5 *Great Gulf*, 6 *Southern Peaks*, and 7 *Montalban Ridge*, which together cover the Presidential Range. For a day hike up Mt. Washington in the summer, popular trails are: from the west, at the Marshfield Station of the cog railway (2700 ft.) via the Ammonoosuc Ravine Trail and Crawford Path (Section 6); or, from the east at Pinkham Notch Camp (2000 ft.) via the Tuckerman Ravine Trail, all the way or via Lion Head.

Most of the Presidential Range is in Restricted Use Areas (camping restricted) and Wilderness Areas (see Section 2). On the east, in Cutler River drainage (Tuckerman and Huntington Ravines), overnight camping is permitted only at existing shelters, except in winter; see "Hermit Lake Shelters" below.

For those interested in the geological history of Mt. Washington and the Presidential Range, *The Geology of the Mt. Washington Quadrangle* is published by the New Hampshire Department of Resources and Economic Development (603-271-2343).

The visitor who ascends the mountain on foot should carry a compass and should bear in mind that the cog railway on one slope and the Mt. Washington Auto Rd. on another make a line, although a very crooked one, from west to east. If you become lost in a cloud, remember which side of the mountain you are on. Once you have climbed to the upper reaches of the mountain, go north or south, as the case may be, skirting the heads of ravines, and sooner or later you will approach the road or the railroad, landmarks that cannot be missed in the darkest night or the thickest fog, except in winter, when they may be obliterated by snow.

Caution. The appalling and needless loss of life on this mountain has been due largely to the failure of robust hikers to realize that wintry storms of incredible violence occur at times, even during the summer months. Rocks become ice-coated, freezing fog blinds and suffocates, winds of hurricane force exhaust the strongest hikers, and, when they stop to rest, a temperature below freezing completes the tragedy.

If you experience difficult weather, abandon your climb. Storms increase in violence with great rapidity toward the summit. The highest wind velocities ever recorded were attained on Mt. Washington (see Section 8). Since *the worst is yet to come,* turn back without shame, before it is too late. Don't attempt Mt. Washington if you have coronary problems or are below par physically in any way.

See *The Presidential Range in Winter,* Section 8, for detailed information and advice regarding winter climbing.

THE COG RAILWAY

The original Mt. Washington Railroad, known as the cog railway and now extending from the Marshfield station to the summit, was completed in 1869. Its maximum grade, 13½ in. to the yd., is equaled by only one other railroad (excluding funicular roads), that on Pilatus in the Alps. When the cog railway is in operation, walking on the track is not permitted; use the Jewell (Section 4) or the Ammonoosuc Ravine (Section 6) Trail.

There is a parking area below the Marshfield station, owned and operated by the cog railway — fee charged.

The cog railway ascends a minor westerly ridge in a nearly straight line to the treeline near Jacob's Ladder (4834 ft.). This trestle, at its highest point about 30 ft. above the mountainside, is the steepest place on the road. Traces of the old Fabyan Bridle Path may be seen from time to time. After crossing the shoulder toward Mt. Clay, the line curves right and crosses the Westside Trail close to the edge of the Great Gulf. Between the Great Gulf and the cog railway lies the Gulfside Trail (Section 4), which, if you are ascending the summit, soon turns right and crosses the tracks. From the Gulf Tank (5638 ft.) there is a fine view across the Gulf toward the Northern Peaks. Just below the summit, the Bourne monument may be seen on the right.

Cog Railway (map 6)

Distance from the Marshfield station
  to Mt. Washington summit: 3 mi., 1 hr. 10 min. via railway

SUMMIT BUILDINGS

No hotel or overnight lodging for the public is available on the summit of Mt. Washington. The new summit building, named in honor of former NH Governor Sherman Adams and operated by the NH Division of Parks and Recreation during the summer season (mid-May to mid-October) has food service, pack room, souvenir shop, public rest rooms, telephone, and a post office. It houses the Mt. Washington Observatory, the Mt. Washington Museum, and facilities for park personnel. There has been a year-round weather observatory on Mt. Washington from 1870 to 1886 and from 1932 to the present.

The Yankee Building was built in 1941 to house transmitter facilities for the first FM station in northern New England. It is now leased by WMTW-TV and houses two-way radio equipment for various state, federal, and local organizations. This building is closed to the public.

The transmitter building and powerhouse for WMTW-TV and WHOM-FM, built in 1954, provides living quarters for station personnel and houses television and microwave equipment. The structure, built to withstand winds of 300 mph, is not open to the public.

The Stage Office, built in 1975 to replace a similar building constructed in 1908, is owned by the Mt. Washington Auto Road Company and used only in connection with their operation.

The first Summit House on Mt. Washington was built in 1852. The first Tip Top House hotel, built in 1853, suffered a fire in 1915. It is now owned by the State of New Hampshire and is part of the Mt. Washington State Park. Plans call for restoring this ancient stone building at a future date. Its use is yet to be decided. At present it is closed to all but park use. The second Summit House, 1873-1908, was destroyed by fire.

THE MOUNT WASHINGTON AUTO ROAD

This road, constructed in 1855-61 and long known as the "Carriage Road," extends from the Glen House site on NH Rte. 16 (Pinkham Notch Highway) to the summit. With long zigzags and an easy grade, it climbs the prominent northeast ridge named for Benjamin Chandler, who died of exposure on the upper part in 1856. Since the upper half is above treeline, it is an interesting way to ascend on foot. The Old Jackson Rd., a hiking trail, is the best approach to the Auto Rd. from Pinkham Notch Camp. Automobiles are charged a toll paid at the foot of the mountain.

The road leaves Rte. 16 opposite the Glen House site (1632 ft.), crosses the Peabody River, and passes the beginning of the Osgood Trail, which diverges right just where the road enters the woods. (There are plans to relocate Rte. 16 about 1.5 mi. north of the Glen House site.) After sharp curves right and then left, just above the 2-mi. mark, the Appalachian Trail crosses. To the right it follows the Madison Gulf Trail (Section 5), "Lowe's Bald Spot," a fine viewpoint about 0.3 mi. from the road, is reached by this trail and a side trail. To the left, the Old Jackson Rd. (trail), after junctions with the Nelson Crag Trail and then the Raymond Path, leads south to Rte. 16 at Pinkham Notch Camp. The Halfway House (3840 ft.) is on the right at treeline. Just above, where there is a fine view to the north, the road skirts a prominent shoulder, known as the Ledge. A short distance above this point the Chandler Brook Trail to the Great Gulf leaves right. Just above the 5-mi. mark, on the right and exactly at the sharp turn, there are some remarkable folds in the rocks beside the Auto Rd. At this point, near Cragway *Spring*, the lower section of the Nelson Crag Trail enters left, and a few yards above, the upper section diverges left. At about 5.5 mi. the road passes through the patch of high scrub in which Dr. B.L. Ball spent two nights in a winter storm in October 1855. A short distance above the 6-mi. mark, the Wamsutta Trail descends right to the Great Gulf, and the Alpine Garden Trail diverges left. The trench-like structures near the road are the remains of the old Glen House Bridle Path, built in 1853. At the loop of the road at about 6.5 mi. the Nelson Crag Trail enters left, and just below the 7-mi. mark the Huntington Ravine Trail also enters left. Just above, in the middle of a lawn known as the "Cow Pasture," the remains of an old corral are visible. A little beyond on the right are the cog railway and the Lizzie Bourne monument at the spot where she perished in September 1855 (the second recorded fatality on the mountain).

Because of continued theft and destruction of trail signs, they are now placed on the trails about 100 ft. from the Auto Rd. The names of some trails that leave the road are painted on a rock at that point.

There are plans to remove the emergency shelters along the Auto Rd.

Mt. Washington Auto Rd. (map 6)
Distance from Glen House site (on NH Rte. 16)
to Mt. Washington Summit: 8 mi. (12.9 km.), 5 hr.

MOUNT WASHINGTON

AMC PINKHAM NOTCH CAMP and VICINITY

This camp, originally built in 1920 and greatly enlarged since then, is located on NH Rte. 16 (Pinkham Notch Highway) practically at the height-of-land in the Notch, about 0.8 mi. north of the public parking area near Glen Ellis Falls, about 10 mi. north of Jackson and 11 mi. south of Gorham. It offers food and lodging to the public throughout the year and is managed similarly to the AMC huts (see Section 9). The telephone number is 603-466-2727. Automobiles may be parked at Pinkham Notch Camp.

Concord Trailways offers daily bus service to and from South Station in Boston.

The Tuckerman Ravine Trail, the Lost Pond Trail and the Old Jackson Rd. all start at the camp. The base of the Wildcat Mountain gondola lift, which operates winter and summer, is about 1 mi. north on Rte. 16.

A number of walking trails have been constructed for shorter, easier trips in the Pinkham vicinity. Among these are the Direttissima and the Crew-Cut Trail (see below). There are also several ski-touring trails. For information on local ski touring consult personnel at the Camp Trading Post.

Glen Ellis Falls and Crystal Cascade

Glen Ellis Falls are on the Ellis River about 0.8 mi. south of Pinkham Notch Camp. The path leaves the west side of NH Rte. 16 (Pinkham Notch Highway) at the public parking area, passes through a tunnel under the highway to the east side, and leads in about 0.3 mi. to the foot of the main fall, which is about 70 ft. high. Below it are several pools and smaller falls.

Crystal Cascade is easily reached by the Tuckerman Ravine Trail (see below).

SECTION 3

The Direttissima (MMVSP)

This trail, which runs between the Glen Boulder Trail and Pinkham Notch Camp, was cut in 1969-71 to avoid hiking on NH Rte. 16 (Pinkham Notch Highway), as well as the sometimes difficult crossing of the Ellis River via Lost Pond Trail. It runs through the woods on the west side of Rte. 16, more or less parallel to the road.

Its start at Pinkham Notch Camp just south of the highway bridge over the Cutler River is indicated by a sign at the edge of the woods. Marked by red paint blazes, the trail turns sharp left about 10 yd. into the woods and follows a cleared area south. It turns slightly west at the end of this clearing and winds generally south, crossing a small brook, skirts through the upper (west) end of a gorge, and then crosses the New River.

The trail continues past an excellent viewpoint looking down the Notch, climbs alongside a cliff, crosses another runoff brook, and ends at the Glen Boulder Trail near the junction of the Chimney Bypass and the Chimney branch of that trail, above the Chimney.

Direttisima Trail (map 6)

Distance from Pinkham Notch Camp

to Glen Boulder Trail: *est.* 0.6 mi., 35 min.

Crew-Cut Trail, George's Gorge, Liebeskind's Loop (MMVSP)

This trail system, in the woods north of Pinkham Notch Camp and between the Old Jackson Rd. and NH Rte. 16 (Crawford Notch Highway), offers some easy, low-level woods walking through interesting terrain with two good lookout points.

Crew-Cut Trail

The Crew-Cut starts at the Old Jackson Rd., leaving right after a stream crossing near where the abandoned section of the road proper enters on the right from Rte. 16, and where the Old Jackson Rd. starts to climb steeply. After crossing a stony, dry brook it runs generally east-northeast, crossing two runoff brooks, in one of which there is usually *water*. On the east bank of this brook the George's Gorge Trail leaves left, leading up beside the brook, steeply in some places, for example when it passes Chudacoff Falls, until it reaches a knob, from where it descends west to the Old Jackson Rd. in its upper, flat section.

The Crew-Cut continues its same general line, rising gradually through open woods in a long slabbing of the slope and crossing several gullies. It skirts southeast of the steeper rocky outcroppings until it reaches the base of a cliff. At this point the main trail turns sharply right (south) while a very short side trail leads straight ahead and directly up to a lookout, "Lila's Ledge." From this ledge you can look straight in at the Wildcat ski-trail complex, down the Notch over the AMC buildings, and up at Mt. Washington over Huntington Ravine.

The main trail makes a sharp turn around the nose of the cliff and then resumes its generally east-northeast direction. In about 50 ft. Liebeskind's Loop enters left, coming down from the knob at the high point on the George's Gorge Trail. The Crew-Cut continues its descent over a few small ledges and through open woods until it passes east of a small high-level bog formed by an old beaver dam. Shortly thereafter, it goes through open woods again, emerging at the top of the grassy slope on Rte. 16 almost opposite the south end of the Wildcat parking lot.

Crew-Cut Trail
Distance from Old Jackson Rd.
  to NH Rte. 16: *est.* 1 mi., 45 min to 1 hr.
  (with time allowed for lookout)

Liebeskind's Loop

Liebeskind's Loop, cut in 1974, makes a loop hike possible (using the Crew-Cut, George's Gorge, Loop, and Crew-Cut trails) without resorting to return either by Rte. 16 or by the steep section of the Old Jackson Rd. The Loop leaves right (east) near the top of the George's Gorge Trail just before the latter makes the final short ascent to the knob, where a short spur to the left (south) leads to an excellent view of Wildcat Mountain and

Huntington and Tuckerman ravines. It descends to a swampy flat, then rises through a spruce thicket to the top of a cliff, where there is a fine lookout with a good view down Pinkham Notch. Here the trail turns left and runs along the edge of the cliff, finally descending by an easy zigzag in a gully to a beautiful open grove of birches. The cliff above this grove offers interesting possibilities for rock climbers. The trail continues east, descending through two gorges and skirting the east end of rises until it finally climbs a ridge and descends 50 yd. on the other side to join the Crew-Cut Trail just east of Lila's Ledge. The Crew-Cut can then be followed back to the starting point.

This loop hike is best made in the direction described, since the Gorge is most interesting on the ascent and the Loop is more interesting on the descent.

Liebeskind's Loop Trail

Distance from Crew-Cut start

to Crew-Cut start (loop): *est*. 2 mi., 1½ to 2 hr.
(with time allowed for lookouts)

Old Jackson Road (AMC)

This trail runs north from Pinkham Notch Camp to the Mt. Washington Auto Rd. It is part of the Appalachian Trail and is blazed in white. It diverges right from the Tuckerman Ravine Trail about 50 yd. from the camp. After about 0.3 mi. it begins to ascend steeply and steadily and the Crew-Cut Trail leaves right (east). Upon reaching the height-of-land, where the George's Gorge Trail leaves right (east), the Old Jackson Rd. descends slightly, crosses several brooks, and at a large one takes a sharp left uphill (1977 relocation). After a short, steep climb it slabs along, the Raymond Path enters left, several small brooks are crossed, and then the Nelson Crag Trail enters left. Continuing north the trail climbs slightly, continues through an old gravel pit and meets the Auto Rd. just above the 2-mi. mark, opposite the Madison Gulf Trail.

Old Jackson Rd. (map 6)
Distance from Pinkham Notch Camp
   to Mt. Washington Auto Rd.: 1.8 mi. (2.9 km.), 1¼ hr.

NELSON CRAG TRAIL (AMC)

This trail leaves the Auto Rd. left with the Old Jackson Rd. and Raymond Path, just above the 2-mi. mark and opposite the Madison Gulf Trail. It soon diverges right and bears southwest, then almost due west, climbing steadily with some sharp ascents. After about 1 mi. it rises steeply out of the scrub, emerging on a watershed ridge from which there is an unusual view of Pinkham Notch in both directions. It then bears slightly north, climbs moderately over open ledges, and joins the Auto Rd. near Cragway *Spring,* at the sharp turn about 0.3 mi. above the 5-mi. mark. A few yards above, the trail again diverges left from the Auto Rd. and climbs steeply to the crest of the ridge. It travels over Nelson Crag, crosses the Alpine Garden Trail, passes between two humps and again joins the road at the east corner of the big loop, about 0.5 mi. below the 7-mi. mark.

Nelson Crag Trail (map 6)
Distances from two-mile mark on Auto Rd.
   to about 0.3 mi. above five-mile mark: 1.6 mi., 1 hr. 40 min.
   to about 0.5 mi. below seven-mile mark: 2.6 mi. (4.2 km.), 2½ hr.

TUCKERMAN RAVINE TRAIL (WMNF)

Tuckerman Ravine is a remarkable glacial cirque in the southeast side of the mountain, named for the botanist Professor Edward Tuckerman.

Below Hermit Lake the tractor road, or Fire Trail, has superseded the original trail, which had become badly eroded after many years of heavy usage.

Information on Hermit Lake camping shelters appears below.

The path leaves the west side of Rte. 16 (Pinkham Notch Highway) at Pinkham Notch Camp 10 mi. north of Jackson. In about 0.3 mi. it crosses a bridge to the south bank of Cutler River. A few yards beyond it turns sharply right and climbs to the best viewpoint of the Crystal Cascade, a few steps off the path, right.

From this point the path bears left, ascends gradually for a short distance and then turns right. At this point Boott Spur Trail leaves left. The Tuckerman Trail continues ahead with two long switchbacks. Above these, the path continues west, ascending by steady grades. At about 1.3 mi. the Huntington Ravine Trail diverges right. A short distance above, the trail crosses two branches of the Cutler River, and then the Huntington Fire Rd., which is the best route to Huntington Ravine in winter, leaves right. Above here, at 2.1 mi., the Raymond Path enters right, at a point where the Tuckerman Trail turns sharply left. About 250 yd. farther, the Boott Spur Link diverges left, and directly opposite the Lion Head Trail diverges right.

Just beyond the buildings, the trail joins the old trail near Hermit Lake. By following the old trail east a few yards to the top of a short rise, a remarkable view is obtained, especially in winter. The cliff on the right is Lion Head, so called because of its appearance from the Glen House site. The more distant crags on the left are the Hanging Cliffs of Boott Spur.

The main trail keeps to the right (north) of the stream. It ascends a well-constructed footway into the floor of the ravine, and finally, at the foot of the headwall, bears right and ascends a steep slope of debris, where the Snow Arch can be found on the left in the spring, when the snowfield above the Snow Arch usually extends across the trail. The arch is formed by a stream of snow meltwater which flows under the snowfield. The snow in the ravine may persist until late summer, although the arch does not always form. ***Caution.*** Do not approach too near the arch and *under no circumstances* cross or venture beneath it: one death and some narrow escapes have already resulted. Sections weighing tons may break off at any moment. If the snow extends across the trail, it is better to use the Lion Head Trail. In the spring and fall the WMNF often closes the section of trail up over the headwall because of snow and ice. In the winter this section is impassable except for experienced and well-equipped snow and ice climbers. When ascending the headwall, be careful not to start rocks rolling, since such carelessness may put others in serious danger.

Turning sharp left at the top of the debris slope and traversing under a cliff, the trail emerges from the ravine and climbs almost straight west up a grassy, ledgy slope. About 200 yd. below Tuckerman Junction, the Alpine Garden Trail, which leads to the Lion Head Trail, the Alpine Garden and Mt. Washington Auto Rd., diverges right. At Tuckerman Junction, at the top of the plateau, the Tuckerman Crossover leads almost straight ahead (southwest) to the Crawford Path near the Lakes of the Clouds Hut; the Southside Trail leads west and northwest, skirting the cone to the Davis Path; and the Lawn Cutoff leads left (south) to the Davis Path. The Tuckerman Ravine Trail turns sharp right and, marked by cairns and painted rocks, ascends the rocks to the Auto Rd. near the summit. About a third of the way up the cone, at Cloudwater *Spring,* the Lion Head Trail enters right.

In descending, the trail leaves the right side of the Auto Rd. a few yards below the lower parking area.

Tuckerman Ravine Trail (map 6)
Distances from Pinkham Notch Camp
  to Crystal Cascade: *est.* 0.4 mi.
  to Huntington Ravine Trail: *est.* 1.3 mi., 1 hr.
  to Raymond Path: 2.1 mi., 1¾ hr.
  to Lion Head Trail and Boott Spur Link: 2.3 mi.
  to Hermit Lake shelters: 2.4 mi., 2 hr.
  to Snow Arch: 3.1 mi., 2¾ hr.
  to Tuckerman Junction: 3.6 mi., 3½ hr.
  to Mt. Washington summit: 4.1 mi. (6.6 km.), 4½ hr.

Hermit Lake Shelters

The Hermit Lake Shelters are lean-tos open to the public. Tickets for shelter space must be purchased at Pinkham Notch Camp in person (first come, first served) for a nominal fee. The tickets are nontransferable and nonrefundable. They may be purchased for a maximum of seven consecutive nights. Overnight use is limited to the 86 spaces in the shelters. Ten tent sites for 40 people are available between December 1 and April 1. Fee $1.75 per person per night. Users may no longer kindle charcoal or wood fires; people intending to cook must bring their own small stoves. Day visitors and shelter users alike are *required to carry out all their own trash and garbage*. No receptacles are provided. This operating policy is under continual review, so it can change from time to time. Information is available at the caretaker's residence. There is no warming room open to the public, and refreshments are not sold.

RAYMOND PATH (AMC)

This old trail extends from the Mt. Washington Auto Rd. to the Tuckerman Ravine Trail.

It leaves the Auto Rd. along with the Old Jackson Rd. and the Nelson Crag Trail just above the 2-mi. mark, opposite the Madison Gulf Trail. Soon, the Nelson Crag Trail diverges right. A little farther, so does the Raymond Path. It crosses several streams, first a branch of the Peabody and then branches of the Cutler River. It crosses the Huntington Ravine Trail near the largest stream and ends about 0.5 mi. beyond, at the Tuckerman Ravine Trail.

Raymond Path (map 6)
Distances from Glen House site on NH Rte. 16
to north terminus of Raymond Path: 2 mi., 1 hr. 10 min.
to Tuckerman Ravine Trail: 4.4 mi., 2¾ hr.
to Hermit Lake (via Tuckerman Ravine Trail): 4.7 mi., 3 hr.

MOUNT WASHINGTON

to Mt. Washington summit (via Tuckerman Ravine Trail): 6.4 mi. (10.3 km.), 5½ hr.

HUNTINGTON RAVINE TRAIL (AMC)

This ravine was named in honor of Professor J. H. Huntington in 1871.

Caution. This is the most difficult trail in the White Mountains. Although experienced hikers who are comfortable on steep rock probably will encounter little difficulty when conditions are good, the exposure on several of the ledges is likely to prove extremely unnerving to novices and to those who are uncomfortable in steep places. The trail is very dangerous when wet or icy. Extreme caution must be exercised at all times. Descent by this trail is strongly discouraged. Since retreat under unfavorable conditions can be extremely difficult and hazardous, one should never venture beyond the "Fan" in deteriorating conditions or when weather on the Alpine Garden is likely to be severe. During late fall, winter, and early spring, this trail (and any part of the ravine headwall) should be attempted only by those with full technical ice-climbing gear and training. In particular, the ravine must not be regarded as a viable "escape route" from the Alpine Garden in severe winter conditions.

Between Raymond Path and the boulders, care must be taken to differentiate the trail from a service road that crosses the trail.

The trail diverges right from the Tuckerman Ravine Trail about 1.3 mi. from Pinkham Notch Camp. In about 0.3 mi. it crosses the Cutler River and, in another 150 yd., the brook that drains Huntington Ravine. At about 0.5 mi. from the Tuckerman Ravine Trail, it crosses the Raymond Path. Above this junction it crosses the brook and the Huntington Ravine Fire Rd. several times. In the floor of the ravine there are some interesting boulders near the path; their tops afford good views of the ravine. Beyond the scrubby trees is a steep slope, covered with broken rock, known as the "Fan," whose tip lies at the foot of the deepest gully. To the left of this gully are precipices, the lower is known as the "Pinnacle." After passing through the boulders the path ascends the left side of the Fan for about 60 ft., then turns right, and, marked by yellow blazes on the rocks, crosses a stream and ascends the north (right) side of the Fan to its tip. The trail then climbs the rocks to the right of the main gully. The route follows the line of least difficulty and should be followed carefully over the ledges, which are dangerous, especially when wet. Above the first ledges the trail climbs steeply through scrub and over short sections of rock, with some fairly difficult scrambles, to the top of the headwall where it crosses the Alpine Garden Trail. From this point it ascends gradually to the Mt. Washington Auto Rd. just below the 7-mi. mark.

Huntington Ravine Trail (map 6)

Distances from Pinkham Notch Camp

to Huntington Ravine Trail: 1.3 mi., 1 hr.

to Raymond Path: 1.8 mi., 1 hr. 20 min.

to top of Fan: 3 hr.

to Alpine Garden Trail crossing: 3.3 mi., 4 hr.

to seven-mile mark on Auto Rd.: 3.5 mi., 4 hr. 25 min.

to Mt. Washington Summit (via Auto Rd.): 4.5 mi. (7.2 km.), 5 hr.

RAVINE OF RAYMOND CATARACT

There is no trail up the ravine, just north of Lion Head. Underbrush has completely covered most of a former footway. Water in the ravine may be unfit to drink (summit drainage).

LION HEAD TRAIL (AMC)

This trail diverges right from the Tuckerman Ravine Trail just below Hermit Lake, opposite the foot of the Boott Spur Link. Running north, it diverges from the original trail (used as a winter route) in about 150 yd. and climbs the steep slope by switchbacks, reaching treeline in about 0.5 mi. The trail then bears left, ascends the open slope to the left, and rejoins the original trail about 0.2 mi. farther along, just below the lower Lion Head. The trail continues over the lower and upper Heads, with impressive views and with little grade over the open spur to the Alpine Garden Trail, which it crosses. After passing through a belt of scrub, it ascends to the Tuckerman Ravine Trail, which it enters at Cloudwater *Spring* about a third of the way up the cone of Mt. Washington.

Lion Head Trail (map 6)
Distance from leaving to rejoining Tuckerman Ravine Trail:
1.1 mi. (1.8 km.), 1¾ hr.

Note. The old Lion Head route is closed for summer use due to its steepness and severe erosion. It may be used as a direct winter route when conditions permit.

BOOTT SPUR TRAIL (AMC)

Boott Spur (5500 ft.) is the prominent ridge running south from Mt. Washington, connected by Bigelow Lawn. This was the route for many early ascents of Mt. Washington.

The trail diverges left from the Tuckerman Ravine Trail 350 ft. above the side path to Crystal Cascade, at a sharp right turn. It crosses the John Sherburne Ski Trail, bears right, soon crosses a small brook (*water unreliable*), bears sharp left at the base of a rocky ledge, and, a short distance beyond, makes a sharp right turn and ascends a former logging road, which it leaves in about 0.3 mi. to emerge on a restricted outlook across Pinkham Notch. Descending slightly, the trail shortly makes a sharp right turn, where a side trail (left) leads in 120 ft. to a view east. The trail then passes through some interesting woods, ascends the south side of a small wooded ridge, crosses a south outlook and turns right. It soon reaches a short moist area and ascends (northwest) a steep slope. Halfway up the slope a side trail leads left 300 ft. to a brook *(last water)*. At the top of this slope a side trail leads right (east) to an interesting outlook (30 ft.) with the first view of Split Rock on the treeless ridge.

At this junction the trail turns left, continues upward at moderate grades, heads more north, shortly makes a sharp left turn, and comes out on a scrub point with a view of the summit of Mt. Washington and north toward Gorham. Turning more to the west, the trail enters thicker woods and ascends steadily for 0.3 mi. where a short trail right leads to Ravine Outlook, with Lion Head directly in front of the summit. A few steps farther on this side trail, Tuckerman Ravine comes into full view. The main trail continues ahead for 0.1 mi., then emerges from the trees, soon bears left (south) and slabs the ridge to Split Rock, which you can pass through or go around. The trail then turns right, rises steeply over two minor humps to a broad, flat ridge, where Boott Spur Link (right) descends to the Tuckerman Ravine Trail near Hermit Lake. Above this point the trail follows the ridge, which consists of a series of steplike levels and steep slopes. The views of the ravine are excellent, particularly where the path skirts the dangerous Hanging Cliff, 1500 ft. above Hermit Lake. After passing the summit of the Spur, the trail ends at the Davis Path.

Boott Spur Trail (map 6)

Distances from divergence with Tuckerman Ravine Trail
to first view of Pinkham Notch: 5 mi., 25 min.

to path to brook: 9 mi., 1 hr.

to ravine outlook: 1.6 mi., 1 hr. 50 min.

to Split Rock: 1.9 mi., 2 hr. 10 min.

to Boott Spur Link: 2.1 mi., 2 hr. 25 min.

to Davis Path junction: 2.8 mi., 3 hr.

Distances from Pinkham Notch Camp
to Davis Path junction: 3.3 mi., 3¼ hr.

to Mt. Washington summit (via Davis and Crawford paths) 5.4 mi. (8.6 km.), 4¾ hr.

Boott Spur Link (AMC)

This trail diverges left from the Tuckerman Ravine Trail just below Hermit Lake, opposite the foot of the Lion Head Trail. It immediately crosses two branches of Cutler River and the John Sherburne Ski Trail, then runs straight up the side of the ridge very steeply through scrub until it tops the ridge, and ends in a few yards at Boott Spur Trail.

Boott Spur Link (map 6)
Distance from Tuckerman Ravine Trail
to Boott Spur Trail: .6 mi. (1 km.), ¾ hr.

GLEN BOULDER TRAIL (AMC)

This trail from NH Rte. 16 (Pinkham Notch Highway) to the Davis Path reaches treeline at a low altitude, and in conjunction with the Wildcat Ridge Trail forms the most direct route between Carter Notch and Lakes of the Clouds huts.

The trail, blazed in orange, leaves the west side of Rte. 16 at the parking area near Glen Ellis Falls. It ascends gradually for about 0.3 mi. to the base of a small cliff. You can go up the cliff via the "Chimney Route" or, preferably, take the Chimney Bypass, which goes around to the right of the cliff. After a short, steep climb on the Bypass, the Direttissima from Pinkham Notch Camp enters from the right (north). The Glen Boulder Trail swings south, the Chimney Route enters left, and then a short branch trail leads left to an outlook on the brink of a cliff, which commands a fine view of Wildcat Mountain and Pinkham Notch. The main trail turns west, rises gradually, then steepens, reaching the north bank of a brook draining the minor ravine south of the Gulf of Slides in about another 0.5 mi. Near here, the Avalanche Brook Ski Touring Trail crosses (with blue plastic markers); it is not suitable for hiking. Following the brook, which soon divides, the trail turns southwest, crosses both branches *(water)* about 0.9 mi. from the road. It is level for 200 yd., then climbs rapidly the northeast side of the spur through evergreens, giving views of the minor ravine and spur south of the Gulf of Slides. Leaving the trees, it climbs about 0.3 mi. over open rocks to the Glen Boulder, an immense stone perched on the end of the spur, a familiar landmark for all who travel Rte. 16. The view is wide, from Chocorua around to Mt. Washington, and is particularly fine of Wildcat Mountain.

From the boulder the trail climbs steeply up the open spur, about 0.5 mi., then ascends moderately through high scrub. About 0.8 mi. above the boulder a side trail descends right about 40 yd. to a *spring*. The main trail continues to Slide Peak, the low peak heading the Gulf of Slides, then turns north, descends slightly, soon leaves the scrub, and about 0.3 mi. below the summit of Boott Spur, enters the Davis Path.

Descending, diverge left from the Davis Path at a sign about 0.3 mi. below the summit of the Spur.

Glen Boulder Trail (map 6)

Distances from Glen Ellis parking area on NH Rte. 16

to to outlook: 0.4 mi., 25 min.

to brook crossing: 0.9 mi., 40 min.

to Glen Boulder: 1.5 mi., 1¾ hr.

to spring: 2.2 mi., 2 hr. 25 min.

to Slide Peak: 2.5 mi., 2 hr. 40 min.

to Davis Path junction: 3.1 mi. (5 km.), 3 hr. 10 min.

to Boott Spur summit (via Davis Path): 3.5 mi., 3½ hr.

to Crawford Path junction (via Davis Path): 4.9 mi., 4¼ hr.

to Mt. Washington summit (via Davis and Crawford paths): 5.6 mi., 5 hr.

to to Mt. Washington summit (via Davis Path, Bigelow Lawn Cutoff, and Tuckerman Ravine Trail): 5.1 mi., 4¾ hr.

to Lakes of the Clouds Hut (via Davis Path, Camel Trail and Crawford Path): 5.1 mi., 4 hr. 5 min.

MOUNT WASHINGTON

THE GULF OF SLIDES

The broad ravine southeast of Boott Spur is known as the Gulf of Slides from the many landslides and winter avalanches that have scarred its upper slopes. Enclosing the ravine on the south is the spur on which the Glen Boulder is located. The ravine can be reached by the Gulf of Slides Ski Trail (see below).

ALPINE GARDEN TRAIL (AMC)

This trail leads from the Tuckerman Ravine Trail through a series of grassy lawns called the Alpine Garden to the Mt. Washington Auto Rd. It forms a convenient connecting link between the trails on the east side of the mountain. Aside from its beauty, it allows various combinations of routes for those who do not wish to visit the summit.

The tiny alpine flowers, best seen in June, include the five-petaled white Diapensia, the bell-shaped pink-magenta Lapland Rosebay, and rarer blooms. (See the AMC's *Field Guide to Mountain Flowers of New England* and *At Timberline: A Nature Guide to the Mountains of the Northeast.*) No plants should be picked without written USFS permission. Hikers are urged to stay on trails or walk on rocks so as not to kill fragile alpine vegetation.

The trail diverges right from the Tuckerman Ravine Trail a short distance above the ravine headwall, about 200 yd. below Tuckerman Junction. It leads northeast, bearing toward Lion Head, and crosses the Lion Head Trail. About 50 yd. before the crossing is a WMNF sign "Right Gully" with a right arrow, to guide winter hikers and skiers. Beyond the crossing the trail leads north, its general direction, until it ends at the road. It traverses the Alpine Garden and crosses a tiny stream, which is the headwater of Raymond Cataract. (*This water is unfit to drink: it consists largely of drainage from the summit buildings.*) The cataract itself is not visible from the trail, which soon approaches the head of Huntington Ravine and crosses the Huntington Ravine Trail. Here, a little off the trail, there is a fine view of this impressive ravine. Rising to the top of the ridge, the trail crosses the Nelson Crag Tail, then descends and soon enters the old Glen House Bridle Path, constructed in 1853, whose course is still plain although it was abandoned about a century ago. In a short distance the Alpine Garden Trail leads left and in a few yards enters the Auto Rd. a short distance above the 6-mi. mark, and opposite the upper terminus of the Wamsutta Trail.

Alpine Garden Trail (map 6)
Distances from Tuckerman Ravine Trail
   to Lion Head Trail crossing: *est.* 0.3 mi.
   to Huntington Ravine Trail crossing: *est.* 1.3 mi.
   to Auto Rd. junction: 1.8 mi. (2.9 km.), 1 hr.

SOUTHSIDE TRAIL (AMC)

This trail diverges right (west) from Tuckerman Crossover about 10 yd. southwest of Tuckerman Junction and, skirting the southwest side of the cone of Mt. Washington, enters the Davis Path near its junction with the Crawford Path. It forms a link between Tuckerman Ravine and the Westside Trail.

Southside Trail (map 6)
Distance from Tuckerman Crossover
   to Davis Path junction: about 0.3 mi., 10 min.

TUCKERMAN CROSSOVER (AMC)

This trail leaves the Tuckerman Ravine Trail left (southwest) at Tuckerman Junction (where the latter trail turns sharply right to ascend the cone). It rises again gradually across Bigelow Lawn, crosses the Davis Path, then descends somewhat steeply to the Crawford Path, which it meets along with the Camel Trail a short distance above the upper Lake of the Clouds. Turning left on the Crawford Path, the Lakes of the Clouds Hut is reached in a few hundred feet.

Tuckerman Crossover (map 6)
Distances from Tuckerman Junction
  to Crawford Path junction: 0.8 mi.
  to Lakes of the Clouds Hut (via Crawford Path): 0.9 mi. (1.4 km.), ½ hr.

LAWN CUTOFF (AMC)

This trail diverges right from the Davis Path about 0.5 mi. north of Boott Spur and leads north across Bigelow Lawn to the Tuckerman Ravine Trail at Tuckerman Junction. With the Tuckerman Ravine Trail it forms the shortest route from Boott Spur to the summit of Mt. Washington.

Lawn Cutoff (map 6)
Distance from Davis Path
  to Tuckerman Ravine Trail junction: 0.4 mi. (0.7 km.), ¼ hr.

CAMEL TRAIL (AMC)

This trail, connecting Boott Spur with the Lakes of the Clouds Hut, takes its name from certain ledges on Boott Spur, which, seen against the skyline, resemble a kneeling camel.

The trail is the right of the two that diverge right (east) from the Crawford Path a short distance above the upper Lake of the Clouds (the Tuckerman Crossover is the left of the diverging trails). It ascends easy grassy slopes, crosses the old location of the Crawford Path, and continues in a practically straight line across the level stretch of Bigelow Lawn. It aims directly toward the ledges forming the "camel," passes under the camel's nose, and joins the Davis Path about 100 yd. northwest of the Lawn Cutoff.

SECTION 3

Camel Trail (map 6)
Distance from Crawford Path
  to Davis Path junction: 0.7 mi. (1.1 km.), 25 min.

WESTSIDE TRAIL (WMNF)

This trail, partially constructed by pioneer AMC trailmaker J. Rayner Edmands, is wholly above timberline. By avoiding the summit of Mt. Washington, it saves nearly 1 mi. in distance and 700 ft. in elevation between points on the Northern Peaks and on the Crawford Path. The trail diverges left from the Crawford Path, at about 5500 ft., just where the path begins to climb the cone of Mt. Washington, and skirts the cone. It crosses under the Mt. Washington cog railway just before entering the Gulfside Trail.

Westside Trail (map 6)
Distance from Crawford Path
  to Gulfside Trail junction: 0.9 mi. (1.4 km.), 35 min.

TRINITY HEIGHTS CONNECTOR

This newly constructed trail allows the Appalachian Trail to make a loop over the summit of Mt. Washington. From the true summit (marked by a large sign) it runs approximately northwest for 0.3 mi. to the Gulfside Trail, not far from its junction with the Crawford Path.

SKIING

For skiers on Mt. Washington, "winter" means December to June. Tuckerman Ravine or the Mt. Washington Auto Rd. offer skiing opportunities throughout this season. The Auto Rd. can be packed, icy, and rough at times, especially after a vehicle has traveled to or from the summit, as when the staff changes shifts at the Mt. Washington Observatory. The areas between the top of the Tuckerman headwall and the summit cone, and Chandler Ridge near the 6-mi. mark on the Auto Rd., afford good spring skiing at all levels, but are hard to reach because of their elevation. Usually, the cog railway resumes operations on May 30, and there is frequently good skiing on the cone for a few weeks after that. Skiing areas in the ravine, in the Gulf of Slides, or on any other part of the mountain above timberline, are subject to wide temperature variations within short periods of time. The difference between corn snow and ice or bathing suits and parkas may be an hour, or even less, when clouds roll in or the afternoon sun drops behind a shoulder of the mountain. Skiers should prepare accordingly.

Tuckerman Ravine

By late February or early March sufficient snow has accumulated in this ravine to provide open-slope skiing at all levels. Because of the nature of the ravine, the snow is pocketed as it falls and blows over the headwall. As it drifts in, slopes of all degrees form. High on the headwall they are very steep; on the floor they are gradual. By the middle of March, when the snow is deepest, the drop from the top of the headwall to the floor is about 800 ft., and climbing on the headwall is hazardous because snowslides are likely.

In the first half of April the snow is well packed and conditions are usually ideal. Descents over the headwall and down the various gullies are only for expert skiers. For intermediate skiers, there are the lower slopes on the headwall and in the gullies for open running under ideal conditions.

During the last half of April the snow settles and melts, crevasses form along the upper stretches of the headwall, and large cracks appear in the floor. Masses of snow and ice that continually break off from the upper gullies and the headwall and roll into the ravine are a hazard. Extreme care should be exercised, and the more dangerous parts of the upper slopes should be avoided. Those who run the headwall should take care to avoid the crevasses.

The skiing season in the ravine continues through to May, and often enough snow is available for persistent skiers until June.

The ravine area and the John Sherburne Ski Trail (see below) are patrolled by the USFS and the Mt. Washington Volunteer Ski Patrol. Sections that are unsafe because of ice or possible avalanches are posted at the shelter area.

John Sherburne Ski Trail (WMNF). This ski trail connects Tuckerman Ravine to Pinkham Notch Camp. It is named for the late John H. Sherburne, Jr., through whose efforts this trail in large part came about. It leaves NH Rte. 16 (Pinkham Notch Highway) about 200 ft. south of the camp and ascends to the little headwall of the ravine by a zigzag course, keeping at all times left (south) of the Tuckerman Ravine Trail and the Cutler River. Just below Hermit Lake a short side trail leads right to the Hermit Lake Shelters. From the top of the little headwall to the floor of the ravine the trail lies on the north of the stream. It is 10 to 50 ft. wide, and the slope is suitable for expert and intermediate skiers at some points, but less expert skiers can negotiate this trail because of its width. There should be 15 in. of packed snow for good skiing.

Tuckerman Ravine Trail, a graded path 6 to 12 ft. wide, extends from the camp to the Hermit Lake Shelters area. It usually can be climbed on foot by skiers without sealskins or other climbing aids, since the trail is generally well packed by USFS vehicles and heavy hiking traffic. Downhill skiing is not permitted because of the risk it creates for those ascending or descending on foot.

Skiing on the Mount Washington Auto Road

The Auto Rd. offers easy access to the summit and such places as Chandler Ridge. Many portions of the upper half of the road are often blown bare, but the 4 miles from the Halfway House to NH Rte. 16 (Pinkham Notch Highway), a drop of 2200 ft., make a good run from late December to the middle of April for novice and intermediate skiers. Good skiing requires 5 in. of packed snow. However, because of winter truck traffic, the road may be badly rutted and cut up, and consequently poor for skiing. There are plans to remove the emergency shelters along the road.

Old Jackson Rd. With 8 in. of snow, this is a good run for all levels. It may be used as the ski route between Pinkham Notch Camp and the Auto Rd. It drops 650 ft. and can be run in 30 min. The ascent takes 1 hr. Skiers should use the old trail instead of the relocation; enter the Old Jackson Rd. below the 2-mi. mark, about 0.2 mi. below where the relocation and the Madison Gulf Trail meet at the Auto Rd.

Raymond Path. This is not a ski run, but it affords a route between Tuckerman Ravine Trail and the Auto Rd. It is wide on the level sections, but narrow and difficult on the steep pitches. In deep snow, the trail is often obscure. It drops, not uniformly, about 700 ft. toward the north and east.

Gulf of Slides

This area, which is situated somewhat similarly to Tuckerman Ravine, receives a large volume of snow that remains in the ravine, so open-slope skiing is possible well into the spring (April and May). Its slopes, though less severe than those in Tuckerman, are more uniform and avalanche frequently.

Gulf of Slides Ski Trail (WMNF) leaves Rte. 16 about 100 yd. south of Pinkham Notch Camp and ascends west 2200 ft. in about 2.5 mi. to the bowl of the Gulf of Slides.

SECTION 4

The Northern Peaks

This name is given to the northern part of the Presidential Range, which extends north and then northeast from Mt. Washington with peaks in the following order: Mt. Clay (5532 ft.), Mt. Jefferson (5715 ft.), Mt. Adams (5798 ft.), Mt. Madison (5363 ft.). Pine Mountain (2404 ft.) stands at the end of the range across the Dolly Copp (Pinkham B) Rd. The four main peaks constitute a great ridge 5 mi. long that averages over 5000 ft. above sea-level, and each of these four peaks rises several hundred feet above the ridge. Two prominent minor summits of Mt. Adams form a part of the crest of the main ridge, Sam Adams (5585 ft.) and John Quincy Adams (about 5470 ft.).

The AMC Mt. Washington Range map (map 6) shows all of the Northern Peaks. The 1979 RMC map of the Randolph Valley and Northern Peaks is available for $2; its larger scale is useful for the dense trail network on the north slopes. The guidebook *Randolph Paths,* 1977 ed., is $1.50 (Randolph Mountain Club, Randolph, NH 03570).

This entire section is a Restricted Use Area, with no camping, wood, or charcoal fires permitted above timberline or within 200 ft. of trails (see Section 2). Hikers are urged to stay on trails when above timberline, to preserve thin soils and fragile alpine plants.

The upper part of the mass of the Northern Peaks is covered with fragments of rock. Above 5000 ft. there are no trees and little scrub. Radiating from this high region are ridges, most important being the Osgood, Howker, and Gordon Ridges of Mt. Madison; Durand and Nowell Ridges and the Israel Ridge, or Emerald Tongue, of Mt. Adams; the Castellated Ridge extending northwest from Mt. Jefferson to Mt. Bowman, the Ridge of the Caps extending westerly and the two Jefferson Knees easterly from Mt. Jefferson; and an unnamed but very salient ridge extending westerly from Mt. Clay. The most important valleys or ravines are the Great Gulf and its offshoots Jefferson Ravine

THE NORTHERN PEAKS 57

and Madison Gulf, Bumpus Basin, the valley of Snyder Brook, King Ravine, Cascade Ravine, Castle Ravine, and Burt Ravine. All except the Snyder Brook valley, Cascade and Burt ravines are marked examples of the glacial cirque.

In 1860 or 1861, Gordon, the guide, made a partial trail over the peaks to Mt. Washington, and some sections still exist. In 1875-76 Lowe's Path was cut, the branch path through King Ravine was made in 1876, and the Osgood Path was opened in 1878. From 1878 until the beginning of the lumbering in about 1902, Watson, Nowell, Peek, Cook, Sargent, and Hunt led trail-making on the Northern Peaks, and in 1892, J. Rayner Edmands began a system of graded paths. The network of trails they created was greatly damaged by lumbering (1901-06), and some trails were obliterated. The more important ones have since been restored. On the Northern Peaks the USFS now maintains about twenty miles of trails, the AMC about thirty, and the RMC about sixty.

On the Northern Peaks, the Appalachian Trail follows the Gulfside Trail, Osgood Trail, Osgood Cutoff, and Madison Gulf Trail for a total (Clay-Washington col to west Branch of Peabody River) of 8.5 mi.

The Northern Peaks can be reached from the summit of Mt. Washington, from the AMC hut at the Lakes of the Clouds (see Section 6), or, best of all, from the AMC hut at Madison Spring. There are motels at Randolph and Gorham, and overnight cabins at Lowe's (100 yd. east of Lowe's Path), and farther west on US Rte. 2. There is public camping at Dolly Copp Campground and Moose Brook State Park in Gorham.

There is free parking at Pinkham Notch Camp, the Glen House site, Dolly Copp Campground, the Appalachia and Randolph East parking areas, and at Bowman. A nominal parking fee is charged at Lowe's store.

The highest points from which to climb the Northern Peaks, except the summit of Mt. Washington, are the junction of Pine Link and Dolly Copp, also called Pinkham B Rd. (1650 ft); the

2-mi. mark (about 2650 ft.) on the Mt. Washington Auto Rd. where the Madison Gulf Trail begins (see Section 5); Jefferson Notch at the foot of the Caps Ridge Trail (3000 ft.), the easiest point on a road from which to obtain a high summit; and the Marshfield Station of the cog railway, about 2700 ft.

From the Marshfield station, reached by automobile, the foot of the Caps Ridge Trail may be reached via Boundary Line Trail in about an hour.

The Memorial Bridge

This is a memorial to J. Rayner Edmands, Eugene B. Cook, and other pioneer pathmakers — King, Gordon, Lowe, Watson, Peek, Hunt, Nowell, and Sargent. It crosses Cold Brook a little below Cold Brook Fall, which is visible from the bridge. The Link and the Amphibrach Trail use this bridge to cross the stream.

Madison Hut (AMC)

In 1888, at Madison Spring (4825 ft.) a little north of the Adams-Madison col the AMC built a stone hut that was later demolished. The present hut, rebuilt and improved since the fire of 1940, accommodates fifty guests on a coed basis and is open to the public from mid-June to mid-September. For current information contact Reservation Secretary, Pinkham Notch Camp, Box 298, Gorham, NH 03581 (603-466-2727).

Madison Hut (map 6)

Distances from Madison Hut
  to Mt. Madison summit: 0.5 mi., ½ hr.
  to Mt. Adams summit (via Star Lake Trail): 0.9 mi., 55 min.
  to Mt. Jefferson summit: *est.* 2.8 mi., 2 hr. 10 min.
  to Mt. Washington summit: *est.* 6.3 mi., 4¼ hrs., (3 hr. 10 min. returning)

Distances to Madison Hut
  from AMC Pinkham Notch Camp (via Old Jackson Rd. and Madison Gulf Trail): 6.1 mi., 4 hr. 50 min.

THE NORTHERN PEAKS

from Lakes of the Clouds Hut (via Crawford Path, Westside, and Gulfside trails): 6.8 mi., 4 hr. 40 min.

from Appalachia parking lot (via Valley Way): 3.5 mi., 3½ hr.

from Glen House site on NH Rte. 16 (via Osgood Trail, Madison Gulf Cutoff, and Madison Gulf Trail): *est.* 5.1 mi., 4½ hr.

from Jefferson Notch Road (via Caps Ridge Trail and Mt. Jefferson): 5.1 mi., 4¼ hr.

The Parapet and Star Lake

One-quarter mile south of the hut, and beyond Star Lake "The Parapet," a 4925-ft. rocky ridge at the head of Adams-Madison col overlooking Madison Gulf, affords fine views of Mt. Washington, the Carter Range, the Great Gulf, and the country around Conway. It is reached by the Parapet Trail.

Star Lake, reached by the Star Lake Trail 0.1 mi. from Madison Hut, is a small, shallow body of water among jagged rocks, from which there are good views. The mossy areas around the lake are usually muddy and wet underfoot; visitors should use great care not to damage the vegetation.

Shelters

The Log Cabin (RMC). About 1890 Dr. W. G. Nowell built this cabin on a former campsite at a spring at 3300 ft. altitude, beside Lowe's Path. It is maintained by the RMC and is open to the public. The cabin is closed but it has no stove, cooking utensils, or blankets. There is room for about ten. No wood fires are permitted in the area, and guests are requested to leave the cabin clean and carry out all trash.

The Perch (RMC). This is an open log shelter built on the site of J. Rayner Edmands's shelter of the same name — at about 4200 ft. on the Perch Path, which runs from the Randolph Path to the Israel Ridge Path. It is open to the public and accommodates eight. There are also four tent platforms at the site; the caretaker at Gray Knob often visits to collect the $1 overnight fee for use of either the shelter or tent platforms.

Crag Camp (RMC). At the edge of King Ravine near the Spur Trail (about 4200 ft.), this former private camp of Nelson Smith is now open to the public at a charge of $2.50 per person per night. It is a closed cabin, supplied with cooking utensils and a gas stove in the summer, with room for about fourteen. During July and August it is maintained by a caretaker. At other times fees may be sent to the Randolph Mountain Club, Randolph, NH 03570. Wood fires are *not* allowed in the area. Hikers are required to limit groups to ten and stays to two nights. All trash is to be carried out. Any infraction of these rules or acts of vandalism should be reported to the above address.

Gray Knob (Town of Randolph and RMC). This winterized cabin is on Gray Knob Trail at its junction with Hincks Trail, near Lowe's Path (about 4400 ft.). It is open to the public at a charge of $2.50 per person per night. Gray Knob has room for about twelve and is supplied with a gas stove and cooking utensils in the summer. There is a caretaker year round. Rules are the same as for Crag Camp. Reports of infractions may be sent to the Randolph Mountain Club.

GULFSIDE TRAIL (WMNF)

This trail leads from Madison Hut to the summit of Mt. Washington. It threads the principal cols, but avoids summits of the Northern Peaks. Its altitudes range from about 4815 ft. close to the hut, to 6288 ft., and it affords extensive and varying views. Barring the slope of Mt. Washington, the highest altitude is 5520 ft. in the Adams-Sam Adams col. The trail is marked by large cairns, each topped with a yellow-painted stone, is well defined, and, though care must be used, can be followed even in dense fog or when obscured by snow. On these heights dangerous winds and low temperatures are likely to occur with little warning at any season of the year. If such storms cause serious trouble on the

THE NORTHERN PEAKS 61

Gulfside Trail, do not attempt to ascend the cone of Mt. Washington, where conditions are usually worse. If impossible to go to the hut at Madison Spring or at Lakes of the Clouds, retreat into one of the ravines, using the Jewell Trail to reach the Marshfield station of the cog railway; the Randolph Path for the Perch; Spur Trail for Crag Camp; or Castle Ravine Trail about 0.9 mi. to the protection of Roof Rock. The steel emergency refuge at Edmands Col was removed in 1982. If it is impossible to reach any of the shelters, descend without trail into one of the ravines. A night of discomfort in the woods is better than exposure on the heights, which may prove fatal.

The name Gulfside was given about 1892 by J. Rayner Edmands, who, in that and subsequent years, located and made the greater part of the trail, sometimes following trails that had existed before. All but about 0.8 mi. of the trail was a graded path, some parts paved with carefully placed stones, a work cut short by Edmands's death in 1910. The whole length is part of the Appalachian Trail.

Part I. Madison Hut-Edmands Col

The trail begins at Snyder Brook between Mts. Madison and Adams not more than 30 yd. from the hut. After leading southwest through a patch of scrub, it aims to the right (north) of Mt. John Quincy Adams, ascends a steep, open slope, and near the top of this slope is joined from the right by the Air Line Trail, which coincides with it for a few yards. From here there is a striking view of Mt. Madison.

The path is now on the high plateau between the head of King Ravine and the peak of John Quincy. On the right is a view into the ravine. The Air Line Trail branches left, toward Mt. Adams. Much of the Gulfside Trail for about the next 0.5 mi. is paved with carefully placed stones. It rises gently southwest, curving a little more south, then steepens, and at 0.9 mi. from the hut reaches a grassy lawn in the saddle (5520 ft.) between Mt. Adams and Sam Adams.

Here, where several trails intersect at a spot nicknamed

"Thunderstorm Junction," there is a massive cairn about 10 ft. high. Entering the junction right is the Great Gully Trail, coming up across the slope from the southwest corner of King Ravine. Here also, the Gulfside is crossed by Lowe's Path, ascending from Bowman to the summit of Mt. Adams. A few yards down Lowe's Path, the Spur Trail branches right for Crag Camp. The summit of Mt. Adams is about 0.3 mi. from the junction (left), via Lowe's Path. There is no trail to Sam Adams (5585 ft.), but this peak, marked by a conspicuous cairn, may be reached easily in 0.2 mi. over the rocks from the junction; it affords a good view.

(A cairned trail, known as the "White Trail," runs from Thunderstorm Junction along the ridge south from Sam Adams to a terminus at the Israel Ridge Path where it rejoins the Gulfside about 100 yd. south of Peabody Spring. This is merely to explain the line of cairns that runs roughly parallel to the Gulfside on the ridge to the north: in bad weather stay on the Gulfside.)

Continuing southwest from Thunderstorm Junction and beginning to descend, the Gulfside Trail is joined on the left by the Israel Ridge Path coming down from Lowe's Path, from which it diverges near the summit of Mt. Adams. (Round trip to the summit by either Israel Ridge or Lowe's Path adds about 25 min.) For about 0.5 mi. the Gulfside Trail and Israel Ridge Path coincide. They pass Peabody *Spring* (*unreliable*) just to the right in a small, grassy flat. A few yards beyond *more reliable water* is found at the base of a conspicuous boulder just to the left of the path.

At 1.5 mi. from the hut the Israel Ridge Path diverges right. Near this junction in wet weather there is a small pool called Storm Lake. The Gulfside turns a little left and approaches the edge of Jefferson Ravine, first passing Adams 5, a small peak 2 min. to the left of the trail. This part of the Gulfside was never graded. It is marked by cairns and keeps near the edge of the cliffs, from which there are fine views into the gulf. Descending southwest along the narrow ridge that divides Jefferson Ravine

THE NORTHERN PEAKS

from Castle Ravine, and always leading toward Mt. Jefferson, the trail enters Edmands Col at 2.2 mi. from the hut and 3.5 mi. from the summit of Mt. Washington.

Edmands Col

This col, between Mts. Adams and Jefferson, divides the Connecticut and Androscoggin watersheds. Its 4930-ft. altitude is almost the same as that of the Madison-Adams col at the Parapet, and within 50 ft. of that of the Clay-Jefferson col. Near the site of the former emergency shelter (*dismantled in 1982*) is a bronze tablet in memory of J. Rayner Edmands, who made most of the graded paths on the Northern Peaks. From Edmands Col the Randolph Path leads north into the Randolph valley. The Edmands Col Cutoff leads south about 0.5 mi. to the Six Husbands Trail. Branching from the Randolph Path about 0.1 mi. north of the col are the Cornice, leading west to the Castle Trail, and the Castle Ravine Trail. Thirty yd. south of the col is Gulfside *Spring* (*reliable water*). About 0.2 mi. north near the Castle Ravine Trail is Spaulding *Spring* (*reliable water*).

Gulfside Trail, Part I (map 6)

Distance from Madison Hut

to Edmands Col: 2.2 mi., 1½ hr.
to Mt. Jefferson Summit: *est.* 2.7 mi., 2 hr. 10 min.

Part II. Edmands Col-Clay/Jefferson Col

South of Edmands Col the Gulfside Trail ascends steeply southwest over rough rocks, with Jefferson Ravine on the left. It passes flat-topped Dingmaul Rock, from which there is a good view down the gulf, with Mt. Adams on the left. A few yards beyond, the Mt. Jefferson Loop branches right, and leads 0.2 mi. to the summit of Mt. Jefferson (5715 ft.), from which it continues about 0.3 mi. to rejoin the Gulfside at Monticello Lawn. To go over Jefferson by the loop, to Monticello Lawn, will add about 15 min. extra, excluding time spent at summit.

The path now turns southeast and rises less steeply. It crosses the Six Husbands Trail and soon reaches its greatest height on Mt. Jefferson, 5370 ft. Curving southwest and descending a little, it crosses Monticello Lawn, a comparatively smooth, grassy plateau (about 5350 ft.). Here, the Mt. Jefferson Loop rejoins the Gulfside in about 0.3 mi. (13 min.; ascending 20 min.) from the summit. A short distance southwest of the lawn the Cornice enters right from the Caps Ridge Trail.

The Gulfside continues to descend south and southwest. From one point there is a view of the Sphinx down the slope (left). Approaching the Clay-Jefferson col, the ridge and the path turn more south. The Sphinx Trail branches left (east) into the Great Gulf, through a grassy passage between ledges a few yards north of the col.

Part III. Clay/Jefferson Col-Mt. Washington

From this 4965-ft. col two paths lead toward Mt. Washington: the Mt. Clay Loop (a rough trail) to the left, which passes over the summits of Mt. Clay with impressive views into the Great Gulf, and the graded Gulfside Trail, which leads more to the right and avoids the summits. The trails unite beyond Mt. Clay. The Gulfside Trail is the easier and passes close to *water*, but misses the most impressive views.

The Gulfside Trail runs south and rises gradually, slabbing the west side of Mt. Clay. In about 0.3 mi. a loop leads a few steps down to the right to *water*. The path continues about 30 yd. farther to Greenough *Spring (more reliable)*, then rejoins the Gulfside farther up. The Gulfside continues its slabbing ascent. Just before it gains its highest point, one of the summits of Mt. Clay can be reached by a short climb to the left. Here, from the right, the Jewell Trail enters, ascending from the Marshfield station. The Gulfside swings southeast and descends slightly to the Clay-Washington col (5395 ft.), where the Mt. Clay Loop rejoins it from the left.

There is *no water* in this col. A little to the east is the edge of the Great Gulf, with fine views, especially of the east cliffs of

Mt. Clay. The path continues southeast, rising gradually on Mt. Washington. In about 0.1 mi. the Westside Trail branches right, crosses the cog railway, and leads to the Crawford Path and Lakes of the Clouds Hut. The Gulfside continues southeast between the cog railway and the edge of the Gulf. If you lose the path, follow the railway to the summit. At the extreme south corner of the gulf, the Great Gulf Trail from the left joins the Gulfside from the left, 5.4 mi. from the hut. The Gulfside turns sharp right, crosses the railway, and continuing west joins the Crawford Path just below (north) of the old corral. Just before this junction the Trinity Heights Connector, a link in the Appalachian Trail, leaves left for the summit of Mt. Washington (about 0.2 mi.).

Descending from the summit, the Gulfside Trail coincides with the Crawford Path for 0.3 mi. and turns right just below the old corral.

Gulfside Trail, Parts II and III (map 6)

Distances from Madison Hut

to Air Line Trail junction: 0.3 mi.
to Thunderstorm Junction: 0.9 mi.
to Israel Ridge Path junction: 1 mi.
to Edmands Col: 2.2 mi., 1½ hr.
to North end, Jefferson Loop: 2.4 mi.
to Six Husbands Trail junction: 2.6 mi.
to South end, Jefferson Loop: 3 mi.
to Cornice junction: 3.1 mi.
to North end, Clay Loop: 3.8 mi.
to Jewell Trail junction: 4.5 mi.
to South end, Clay Loop: 4.8 mi.
to Westside Trail junction: 5.0 mi.
to Great Gulf Trail junction: 5.4 mi.
to Mt. Washington summit (via Crawford Path):
 5.7 mi. (9.2 km.), 4 hr.
to Lakes of the Clouds Hut (via Westside Trail and Crawford Path): *est.* 6.8 mi., 4 hr. 40 min.

Distances from Mt. Washington Summit
to Great Gulf Trail junction (via Crawford Path) 0.3 mi.
to Jewell Trail junction: 1.2 mi.
to Sphinx Trail junction: 2.1 mi., 1 hr. 5 min.
to Six Husbands Trail junction: 3.1 mi.
to Edmands Col: 3.5 mi., 2 hr.
to Thunderstorm Junction: 4.8 mi., 2 hr. 50 min.
to Air Line Trail junction: 5.4 mi.
to Madison Hut: 5.7 mi. (9.2 km.), 3¼ hr.

Randolph Path (RMC)

This graded path extends southwest from the Dolly Copp Rd. over slopes of Mts. Madison and Adams, and joins the Gulfside Trail in Edmands Col between Mts. Adams and Jefferson. *Brooks* and *springs* supply *water* at short intervals. It was made by J. Rayner Edmands, the part above treeline in 1893 and following years, and the part below during 1897-99. Parts of it were reconstructed in 1978 as a memorial to Christopher Goetze, active RMC member and former editor of *Appalachia,* a journal published by the AMC.

The path begins at the parking space known as Randolph East, 0.2 mi. south of US Rte. 2 on the Dolly Copp Rd. and 0.3 mi. west of the Boston and Maine Railroad crossing. It coincides with the Howker Ridge Trail for approximately 80 yd. west, turns south, crosses the railroad, and 30 yd. beyond diverges right (west); the Howker Ridge Trail continues left (southeast). The Randolph Path keeps south of the power line for about 0.3 mi., where it enters the old location. It then turns southwest, crosses the Sylvan Way in about 0.5 mi., and in about another 0.8 mi. reaches Snyder Brook, where the Inlook Trail and Brookside diverge left. The Brookside and the Randolph Path cross the brook at the same place, then the Brookside diverges right and leads down to the Valley Way. A few yards beyond the brook it is crossed by the Valley Way, coming up from the Appalachia parking area. The Randolph Path soon crosses the Air Line Trail. At 2 mi. the Short Line, a short cut (1.3 mi.) from the Appalachia parking area, comes in on the right.

The Short Line coincides with the Randolph Path for 0.4 mi., then branches left for King Ravine. The Randolph Path descends slightly and crosses Cold Brook on Sanders Bridge where the Cliffway diverges right. At 3 mi. it crosses the King Ravine Trail at its junction with the Amphibrach. The Randolph Path crosses Spur Brook and in about 100 yd. the Spur Trail leads left and the Randolph Path climbs around the nose of the ridge. Soon two paths to the right lead to the RMC Log Cabin. At about 3.9 mi. from Dolly Copp Rd., Lowe's Path is crossed.

The grade on the Randolph Path moderates. Slabbing the steep west side of Nowell Ridge for about 0.8 mi., the path passes Franconia *Spring,* where there is a view of Mt. Lafayette. At about 4.9 mi. the Perch Path crosses, leading right (southwest) to The Perch and Israel Ridge Path and left (east) to the Gray Knob Trail. There is *water* on the Perch Path a few yards west of the Randolph Path.

Above this junction the Randolph Path rises due south through scrub. *Water* is usually found at a *spring* left. In about 0.5 mi. the scrub ends and Israel Ridge Path enters right (west), ascending from Bowman. Near this junction the Gray Knob Trail from Crag Camp and Gray Knob enters left. From this point the Randolph Path is nearly level to its end at Edmands Col, curving around the head of Castle Ravine. The path is above treeline and visible for a long distance ahead. For a few yards the Israel Ridge Path coincides, then branches left for Mt. Adams. Near the col, right, is Spaulding *Spring (reliable water).* The Castle Ravine Trail comes in from the right (northwest) and the Cornice leads west to Castle Trail. In about 0.1 mi. more the Randolph Path joins the Gulfside Trail in Edmands Col.

Randolph Path (map 6)
Distances from Appalachia parking area
to Randolph Path (via Air Line Trail and Short Line Trail or via Amphibrach Trail): *est.* 1.3 mi., 1¼ hr.
to Cliffway junction: *est.* 1.9 mi.

to King Ravine Trail crossing: *est.* 2.3 mi., 2 hr.
to Lowe's Path crossing: *est.* 3.2 mi.
to Perch Path junction: *est.* 4.2 mi., 3½ hr.
to Israel Ridge Path junction: *est.* 4.7 mi., 4 hr.
to Gulfside Trail junction, Edmands Col: *est.* 5.3 mi. (8.5 km.), 4 hr. 20 min.
to Mt. Jefferson summit (via Gulfside Trail and Jefferson Loop): *est.* 5.8 mi., 5 hr.
to Mt. Washington summit (via Gulfside Trail and Crawford Path): *est.* 9.2 mi., 7 hr. 5 min.
to Lakes of the Clouds Hut (via Gulfside Trail, Westside Trail, and Crawford Path): *est.* 10.5 mi., 7½ hr.

Distances from Randolph East parking area/Dolly Copp Rd.
add 0.7 mi. and ¼ hr. to above

The Cornice (RMC)

This trail, wholly above timberline, leads west from the Randolph Path in Edmands Col, 0.1 mi. north of the Gulfside Trail. After climbing slightly, it slabs around the north and west sides of Mt. Jefferson. It crosses the Castle Trail above the Upper Castle and enters the Caps Ridge Trail above the Upper Cap. It then turns left (east) up the Caps Ridge Trail about 50 ft., again diverges right (south), and climbs gradually to the Gulfside Trail on Monticello Lawn. Because the Cornice avoids the summit of Mt. Jefferson, it serves as an alternate connection — particularly in bad weather — between the Castle and Caps Ridge trails, and between those trails and Edmands Col on the east and Mt. Washington on the south. It is, however, a longer, rougher, and slower route than by the Gulfside Trail or by the Mt. Jefferson Loop: the rock-hopping can be hard on the knees. There is *no water* on the trail.

The Cornice (map 6)

Distances from Randolph Path junction, Edmands Col
to Castle Trail crossing: *est.* 0.5 mi., 40 min.
to Caps Ridge Trail junction: *est.* 1.5 mi., 1 hr. 50 min.

to Gulfside Trail junction: 2 mi. (3.2 km.), 2 hr. 25 min.

Edmands Col Cutoff (RMC)

This important link makes a quick descent possible from Edmands Col into the Great Gulf, a necessity in bad weather. The cutoff leads from the Gulfside Trail and Randolph Path at Edmands Col to Six Husbands Trail, slabbing the cone of Mt. Jefferson. Leaving the col, the cutoff shortly passes a fine *spring*, then rises slightly and begins a rough scramble of about 0.5 mi. over rocks and through scrub — follow cairns. The trail is mostly level, with only a few rises and falls over gullies and good views to the south and of the Great Gulf. The cutoff ends at the Six Husbands Trail about 0.5 below that trail's junction with Gulfside Trail.

Edmands Col Cutoff (map 6)
Distances from Gulfside Trail/Randolph Path junction
to spring: 50 yd.
to Six Husbands Trail: 0.5 mi.

The Link (RMC)

This path "links" the Appalachia parking area with the trails ascending Mts. Adams and Jefferson from the west. It connects with the Amphibrach, Cliffway, Lowe's, and Israel Ridge paths and Castle Ravine, Emerald, Castle, and Caps Ridge trails. The section between the Caps Ridge and Castle trails, although very rough, makes a circuit of the Caps and the Castles possible from Jefferson Notch Rd. It is graded as far as Cascade Brook.

The Link, with the Amphibrach, diverges right from the Air Line about 50 yd. south of its junction with the Valley Way and 100 yd. south of the Appalachia parking area. It runs west about 0.8 mi. to where the Beechwood Way diverges left, and just east of Cold Brook, Sylvan Way enters left. Cold Brook is crossed on the Memorial Bridge where there is a fine view of Cold Brook Fall, which is reached by Sylvan Way. West of the brook, after a few yards, the Amphibrach diverges left.

The Link then follows old logging roads southwest for about 1.5 mi. It enters the WMNF 1.2 mi. from the Appalachia parking area, and at 2 mi. the Cliffway leads east to viewpoints on Nowell Ridge. At about 2.1 mi. the Link turns left and runs south to Lowe's Path, which it crosses at about 2.8 mi. Continuing south about 0.4 mi. it crosses the north branch of the Mystic, and, turning a little to the right, crosses the main Mystic Stream at 3.3 mi. It soon curves left, rounds the western buttress of Nowell Ridge, and running southeast nearly level, enters Cascade Ravine on the mountainside high above the stream. It crosses a slide and keeps the same general direction at nearly the same altitude until it approaches and crosses the brook at 4.1 mi.

Before the Link reaches Cascade Brook, the Israel Ridge Path comes up right from Bowman (about 2.3 mi.) and unites with the Link at 4 mi. from the Appalachia parking area, coincides with it for 100 ft., then branches left for Randolph Path and Mt. Adams. The Cabin-Cascades Trail also intersects the Link just before the brook crossing. On the stream, a little below and a little above the Link, are the first and second cascades. The Link continues southeast for 100 ft., then crosses a slide, rounds the tip of Israel Ridge, and turns south and southeast into Castle Ravine, uniting at 5.1 mi. with the Castle Ravine Trail, with which it coincides for about 0.3 mi. The two trails pass Emerald Trail and cross Castle Brook. Then at 5.4 mi., the Link turns right and ascends west, slabbing the southwest wall of Castle Ravine. In about 0.6 mi. it crosses the Castle Trail below the first Castle at about 4050 ft. It then descends slightly, crosses three small brooks and continues southwest over sections of treacherous roots and hollows for 2.2 mi., slabbing a rough slope to the Caps Ridge Trail, which it enters 0.4 mi. above the Jefferson Notch Rd.

The Link (map 6)
Distances from the Appalachia parking area
   to Cold Brook Fall: *est.* 0.8 mi.
   to Cliffway junction: 2 mi.
   to Lowe's Path crossing: *est.* 2.8 mi., 1 hr. 40 min.

to Cascade Brook crossing: 4.1 mi., 2½ hr.
to Castle Ravine Trail junction: 5.1 mi., 3 hr. 5 min.
to Emerald Trail junction: 5.3 mi.
to Castle Trail crossing: 5.9 mi., 4¼ hr.
to Caps Ridge Trail: *est.* 8.1 mi. (13 km.), 5¾ hr.

PINE MOUNTAIN

Pine Mountain (2404 ft.), a northeastern spur of the Presidential Range, affords fine views up and down the Androscoggin, up the Moose, and up the Peabody rivers. There are also good views from the south cliff and from ledges along the crest, where the heavy virgin spruce growth was destroyed by fire during 1897-1903.

The 100 acres on the summit of Pine Mountain comprise Douglas Horton Center, a center for renewal and education operated by the New Hampshire Conference of the United Church of Christ (Congregational). The center consists of six buildings and an outdoor chapel on the more precipitous northeast peak. Although public camping is not permitted, day hikers are welcome to appreciate the views from Pine Mountain.

A trail around the south cliff — "Ledge Trail," maintained by the WMNF — gives beautiful views westward. The private road to the center gives easy access (on foot only) to the summit. The center road branches from Dolly Copp Rd. at 1650 ft., a little northwest of the highest point of that road, 2.4 mi. from US Rte. 2 and 1.9 mi. from NH Rte. 16, and opposite the foot of Pine Link. Hikers should watch for automobiles descending on this road. The road runs east across the col, and turns northeast and north to ascend along the west flank of the mountain, where the Ledge Trail branches right to climb around the south cliff and so to the summit. It enters the saddle between two of the summits, and runs south to the south summit. About 1.4 mi. from the highway a side trail leads left to a good *spring*. Opposite this path a shortcut leads right to the south summit.

Pine Mountain (map 6)
Distances to south summit
from Tractor Rd./Dolly Copp Rd. junction (via Tractor Rd.):
  1.8 mi., 1 hr.
from Tractor Rd./Dolly Copp Rd. junction (via Ledge Trail to
  south cliff): 1.6 mi., 1 hr. 5 min.

MOUNT MADISON

Farthest northeast of the high peaks of the Presidential Range, 5363-ft. Mt. Madison is remarkable for the great drop of over 4000 ft. to the river valleys east and northeast from its summit. The drop to the Androscoggin at Gorham — 4580 ft. in about 6.5 mi. — is probably the closest approach in New England, except at Katahdin, of a larger river to a high mountain. The views of nearby mountains south and southwest, and into the Great Gulf, are very fine. The distant view in these directions is cut off, though Chocorua is visible. In all other directions there is a distant view.

Mt. Madison (map 6)
Distances to summit
from AMC Pinkham Notch Camp (via Old Jackson Rd.,
  Osgood Cutoff, and Osgood Trail): *est.* 6.9 mi.,
  5 hr. 20 min.
from Glen House site, NH Rte. 16 (via Osgood Trail): 5 mi.,
  4 hr. 20 min.
from Glen House site, NH Rte. 16 (via Osgood Trail, Madison
  Gulf Cutoff, Madison Gulf Trail, and Osgood Trail):
  est. 5.6 mi., 5 hr.
from Dolly Copp Campground (via Daniel Webster-Scout
  Trail and Osgood Trail): *est.* 4 mi., 4 hr. 5 min.
from Appalachia parking area (via Sylvan Way and
  Howker Ridge Trail): 5 mi., 4 hr. 50 min.

from Appalachia parking area (via Valley Way and
  Watson Path): 3.4 mi., 3¾ hr.
from Appalachia parking area (via Valley Way,
  Madison Hut, and Osgood Trail): 3.9 mi.

Osgood Trail (AMC)

Made by B. F. Osgood in 1878, this is the oldest trail now in use to the summit of Mt. Madison. Above the Osgood Cutoff it is part of the Appalachian Trail.

Leave NH Rte. 16 (Pinkham Notch Highway) opposite the Glen House site, and follow the Mt. Washington Auto Rd. across the Peabody River to the edge of the woods, where a sign (right) shows the beginning of the trail. The trail gradually climbs the side of the ridge, then runs level for about 0.5 mi. After crossing a large brook it follows a former logging road, descends slightly, and crosses a dry channel of the West Branch. Crossing the West Branch on a bridge, it intersects the Great Gulf Trail 1.6 mi. from Rte. 16 (Glen House site) and about 2.3 mi. from Dolly Copp Campground.

At about 2.3 mi. the Madison Gulf Cutoff diverges left, affording a more sheltered and shorter (but very steep and difficult) route to Madison Hut. The Osgood Trail turns to the east, crosses a small brook, and soon begins a steeper ascent. A *spring* close to the trail on the right is the *last sure water*. Here the Osgood Cutoff comes in from the left. From this point to Madison Hut the Osgood Trail is part of the Applachian Trail. The steep ascent continues to treeline at 3.9 mi., where the trail emerges on the crest of Osgood Ridge. Ahead, on the crest of the ridge, ten or twelve small, rocky peaks curve to the left in a crescent toward the summit of Mt. Madison. Cairns mark the trail over these peaks. Keep on the crest of the ridge. Daniel Webster-Scout Trail enters right at Osgood Junction, ascending from Dolly Copp Campground. Here the Parapet Trail diverges left, slabbing the south side of the cone of Madison, to Madison Hut. As the Osgood Trail nears the last prominent hump below the summit and bears more west, it is joined on the right by the Howker Ridge Trail. It continues west over the summit and descends to Madison Hut.

In *reverse,* from Mt. Madison the trail runs east about 0.3 mi. over large fragments of rock to the crest of the southwest ridge of Mt. Madison, then swings a little north of east and ascends the ridge a little south of the crest, with the gulf on the right. A few yards from the summit it turns left, regains the crest of the ridge, and follows it to the summit, marked by a tall cairn.

Descending toward the Glen House site go east from the summit, keeping on the crest of the ridge. After about 0.3 mi. the crest (and trail) curve gradually to the southeast.

Osgood Trail (map 6)
Distances from Glen House site, NH Rte. 16
to Great Gulf Trail crossing: 1.6 mi., 50 min.
to Mt. Madison summit: 4.9 mi., 4 hr. 20 min.
to Madison Hut (via Parapet Trail): 5.4 mi. (8.6 km.), 4 hr. 40 min.
to Mt. Madison summit (via Parapet Trail and Madison Hut): 5.9 mi., 5 hr. 10 min.

Osgood Cutoff (AMC)

This link, about 0.5 mi. long, provides a convenient route from Pinkham Notch Camp to the summit of Mt. Madison. Part of the Appalachian Trail, it leads northeast from the junction of the Madison Gulf Trail and the Madison Gulf Cutoff to the *spring* on the Osgood Trail.

Osgood Cutoff (map 6)
Distance from AMC Pinkham Notch Camp
to Mt. Madison summit (via Old Jackson Rd., Madison Gulf Trail, Osgood Cutoff, and Osgood Trail): *est.* 6.9 mi. (11 km.), 5 hr. 20 min.

THE NORTHERN PEAKS

Daniel Webster-Scout Trail (WMNF)

This trail, cut in 1933 by the Boy Scouts, leads from Dolly Copp Campground to Osgood Junction on the Osgood Trail, about halfway between the timberline and the summit of Mt. Madison. It begins on the camp road about 0.8 mi. south of the point where the Dolly Copp Rd. joins the main camp road leading south, and in its course makes several zigzags not shown on the map, though the approximate location is shown. The trail is steep above timberline and, except for the last mile, it is abundantly supplied with *water*.

Daniel Webster-Scout Trail (map 6)

Distances from Dolly Copp Campground

to last sure water: 2.6 mi.

to Osgood Junction: 3.5 mi.

to Mt. Madison summit (via Osgood Trail): *est*. 4 mi., 4 hr. 5 min.

to Madison Hut (via Osgood Trail and Mt. Madison summit): *est*. 4.5 mi., 4 hr. 25 min.

The Parapet Trail (AMC)

This trail, marked with blue paint, leads from Osgood Junction, where the Osgood Trail joins the Daniel Webster-Scout Trail, west to Madison Hut, running nearly on a contour on the south side of the cone of Madison. It meets the Madison Gulf Trail where the latter leaves the scrub at the head of the gulf and continues beside the Parapet to join the Star Lake Trail to Madison Hut. Although above timberline and rough, in bad weather the Parapet Trail is sheltered from northwest winds and saves a climb of about 500 ft. over the summit of Mt. Madison. Use care in rainy weather.

Parapet Trail (map 6)

Distances from Osgood Junction

to Madison Gulf Trail junction: *est*. 0.6 mi., 20 min.

to Madison Hut: 1 mi., ½ hr.

Pine Link (AMC)

The Pine Link leads west from the Dolly Copp Rd. near its highest point directly opposite the tractor road to Pine Mountain and 2.4 mi. from US Rte. 2 and 1.9 mi. from NH Rte. 16 (Pinkham Notch Highway). Near it are a *spring* and small parking space. The trail generally follows the crest of a northeast spur of Howker Ridge. Below the outlook a fire in 1968 burned close to the south side of the trail opening fine views east and south. Above the outlook the trail unites with Howker Ridge Trail at the spring south of the second Howk. For about 0.3 mi. the two trails coincide, running southwest through a group of small Howks. At the foot of the highest Howk the trails diverge, Howker Ridge Trail leading left for Mt. Madison summit, and Pine Link, leading right, skirting the upper slopes of Bumpus Basin and high on Gordon Ridge crossing the Watson Path. Then running southwest, nearly level, with many fine views, it contours around the cone of Mt. Madison to Madison Hut.

Descending, start north from hut, soon turning northeast. Time to Dolly Copp Rd., about 2½ hr.

Pine Link (map 6)

Distances from Dolly Copp Rd.
to Howker Ridge Trail junction: *est.* 2.3 mi.,
   2 hr. 20 min.
to Watson Path crossing: *est.* 3.2 mi.
to Madison Hut: *est.* 3.8 mi., 3½ hr.

Town Line Brook Trail (RMC); Triple Falls

Three beautiful cascades on Town Line Brook just above its crossing of Dolly Copp Rd., 1.6 mi. southeast of the railroad, are known as Triple Falls: Proteus, Erebus, and Evans. The watershed is steep and the rainwater runs off very rapidly, so the falls should be visited during or immediately after a rain.

A good path, close beside the brook, leads from the road to the falls, about 0.1 mi.

Howker Ridge Trail (RMC)

Leading from the Dolly Copp Rd. to the Osgood Trail near the summit of Mt. Madison, this wild, rough trail gives good outlooks at different altitudes and passes three fine cascades.

The trail begins at the parking area known as Randolph East, 0.2 mi. south of US Rte. 2 on Dolly Copp Rd. and 0.3 mi. west of the railroad crossing. It runs with the Randolph Path approximately 80 yd. west, turns south, crosses the railroad, and 30 yd. beyond diverges left (southeast). It runs southeast to the former location of the trail, which it follows up the west bank of Bumpus Brook. The trail passes a cascade (Stairs Fall) that falls into the brook from the east, and at 0.7 mi. it passes Coosauk Fall where Sylvan Way enters from the right. The trail continues a little west of the brook, and the Kelton Trail diverges right. About 1 mi. from the highway the Howker Ridge Trail turns east and at 1900 ft. crosses the brook at the foot of Hitchcock Fall. Then it rises steeply southeast. Howker Ridge curves right, partly enclosing the deep bowl-shaped valley called Bumpus Basin. The trail follows the crest of the ridge, on which are several little peaks called the Howks. The first is a long, narrow ridge covered with woods. In the col south of the first Howk is a *spring (water unreliable)*. From the second Howk there is a fine view in all directions, especially into Bumpus Basin. South of the Howk the Pine Link enters left (there is a *spring* on the Pine Link about 50 ft. to the east). The two trails coincide for about 0.3 mi., ascend among several Howks in a group, and separate again at the foot of the highest Howk where Pine Link branches right. The Howker Ridge Trail climbs over the highest Howk (about 4200 ft), descends a little southwest, then ascends steeply to the crest of Osgood Ridge, where it enters the Osgood Trail a few hundred yards from the summit of Mt. Madison.

Howker Ridge Trail (map 6)
Distances from Randolph East parking area, Dolly Copp Rd.
  to Sylvan Way junction: 0.7 mi.
  to Hitchcock Fall: 1 mi., 50 min.
  to first Howk: 2.3 mi., 2 hr. 10 min.
  to second Howk: 3 mi., 2 hr. 50 min.
  to Mt. Madison summit (via Osgood Trail): 4.4 mi. (7 km.), 4½ hr.

Distances from Appalachia parking area
  add 0.5 mi. and ¼ hr. (via Maple Walk and Sylvan Way)

Kelton Trail (RMC)

This pleasure path branches right from the Howker Ridge Trail about 0.8 mi. from the Dolly Copp Rd. It climbs to Kelton Crag, then ascends, near the northwest arete of the "finger" of Gordon Ridge, to an upper crag at the edge of an old 1921 burn. From both crags there are restricted views, and there is usually *water* between them on the right. Ascending, with good views east, the trail reaches the Overlook at the edge of the unburned woods, and runs west to the Upper Inlook where the Inlook Trail enters (right) from Dome Rock. The Kelton Trail then runs south, nearly level through dense woods, crosses Gordon Rill (*reliable water*), another rill and Snyder Brook, and enters the Brookside 100 yd. below the foot of Salmacis Fall, 2 mi. from the road.

Kelton Trail (map 6)
Distances from Randolph East parking area, Dolly Copp Rd.
  to start of Kelton Trail: 0.7 mi.
  to Kelton Crag: 1 mi.
  to Inlook Trail junction: 1.6 mi., 1½ hr.
  to foot of Salmacis Fall: 2 mi. (3.2 km.), 2 hr.

Distances from Appalachia parking area
  add 0.5 mi. and ¼ hr. (via Sylvan Way)

Sylvan Way (RMC)

The Sylvan Way leads from the Memorial Bridge over Cold Brook to Howker Ridge Trail at Coosauk Fall. A few yards from the bridge it passes Cold Brook Fall. At 0.1 mi. Beechwood Way crosses. Sylvan Way crosses Air Line at 0.6 mi. and Valley Way at 0.7. Soon, at 0.8 mi., Fallsway crosses, and Maple Walk enters left. Sylvan Way then crosses Snyder Brook and immediately after, the Brookbank. Randolph Path crosses at 1.1 mi. from the Memorial Bridge, and, after a gradual ascent, the Sylvan Way ends at Howker Ridge Trail.

Sylvan Way (map 6)

Distances from Appalachia parking area

to start of Sylvan Way (via Link and Amphibrach Trails): 0.8 mi.

to Howker Ridge Trail junction, Coosauk Fall: 2.6 mi. (4.1 km.)

Fallsway (RMC)

The Fallsway leads from the east end of the Appalachia parking area, goes east for 0.1 mi., and then turns sharply right (south). It immediately crosses the railroad. Soon Brookbank diverges left and Fallsway enters the woods. At 0.4 mi. from the Appalachia parking area, the path passes Gordon Fall and Gordon Fall Loop diverges right. In a few yards Sylvan Way crosses and Maple Walk enters. Lower and Upper Salroc Falls are passed 0.8 mi. from the Appalachia parking area. Soon Fallsway enters Valley Way (below Tama Fall). In a few yards Fallsway leaves Valley Way and passes Tama Fall. Brookbank then enters, and Fallsway ends in a few yards at Valley Way, above Tama Fall.

Fallsway (map 6)

Distance from Appalachia parking area

to Valley Way junction above Tama Fall: 0.9 mi. (1.4 km.)

Brookbank (RMC)

Brookbank leads from Fallsway near the railroad, at the edge of the woods. It runs parallel to the railroad for about 0.1 mi., then crosses Snyder Brook, turns sharply right (south), and enters the woods. It runs up the east side of the brook passing Gordon Fall, Sylvan Way, Upper and Lower Salroc Falls, and

Tama Fall. Above Tama Fall it recrosses the brook and reenters Fallsway.

Brookbank (map 6)
Distances from Appalachia parking area
   to start of Brookbank (via Fallsway): 0.2 mi.
   to Tama Fall: 0.9 mi. (1.4 km)

Maple Walk (RMC) and Gordon Fall Loop (RMC)

The Maple Walk diverges left from Valley Way a few yards from the Appalachia parking area and runs to the junction of Fallsway and Sylvan Way. Gordon Fall Loop diverges right from Fallsway at Gordon Fall and joins Maple Walk about 0.1 mi. from the Appalachia parking area.

Maple Walk and Gordon Fall Loop (map 6)
Distances from Appalachia parking area
   to Gordon Fall (via Gordon fall Loop): 0.3 mi.
   to Sylvan Way junction: 0.3 mi.

Watson Path (RMC)

The Watson Path, completed by L.M. Watson in 1882, led from the Ravine House to the summit of Mt. Madison. The present path begins at the Scar Trail, leads across the Valley Way and to Bruin Rock, and then follows the original route to the summit.

Branching from the Scar Trail 0.3 mi. from Valley Way, it runs level about 0.2 mi. to the Valley Way, 2.2 mi. from the Appalachia parking area, then at an easy gradient to Bruin Rock, a large, flat-topped boulder on the west bank of Snyder Brook. Here the Brookside enters, coming up the west bank of the stream. The Watson Path crosses the brook at the foot of Duck Fall, but first the Lower Bruin branches to the right, and ascends to join the Valley Way. East of the stream, the Watson Path attacks the steep flank of Gordon Ridge and, slightly more than 3 mi. from the Appalachia parking area, emerges upon the grassy, stony back of the ridge. It crosses Pine Link and ascends to the

THE NORTHERN PEAKS

summit of Mt. Madison over rough and shelving stones.

Watson Path (map 6)

Distances from Appalachia parking area

to Valley Way crossing (via Valley Way and Scar Trail): 2.2 mi., 2 hr.

to Bruin Rock: *est.* 2.3 mi.

to Pine Link crossing: 3.3 mi.

to Mt. Madison summit: 3.5 mi. (5.6 km.), 4 hr.

Valley Way (WMNF)

The direct route from the Appalachia parking area to Madison Hut is preferred in bad weather. Formerly graded throughout, many portions of its upper section have washed, becoming rocky and rough.

The trail, in common with the Air Line, begins at the Appalachia parking area. After crossing the railroad, the Valley Way leads left and Air Line right across the power line location. In a few yards, the Maple Walk diverges left, and about 0.3 mi. from the railroad the trail crosses Sylvan Way. At 0.6 mi., within the WMNF, the Fallsway comes in on the left and soon leaves left for Tama Fall and the Brookbank. It reenters the Valley Way in a few yards and is a short but worthwhile loop.

The Valley Way leads nearer Snyder Brook and is soon joined from the right by Beechwood Way. About 30 yd. above this junction Brookside diverges left and in about 100 yd. the Valley Way crosses the Randolph Path and climbs the ridge at a comfortable grade.

At 1.8 mi. Scar Trail branches right and at 2.2 mi. the Watson Path crosses, leading to the summit of Mt. Madison. The Valley Way slabs the rather steep slopes of Durand Ridge considerably above the stream. At 2.5 mi. the Lower Bruin enters left, coming up from Bruin Rock and Duck Fall. At 2.9 mi. there is a *spring*. At 3 mi. the Upper Bruin, a graded path, branches right, leading in 0.2 mi. to the Air Line at the lower end of the Knife-edge.

The Valley Way steepens and approaches Snyder Brook. The

growth is mostly scrub, from which the path emerges close to the stream and near the hut.

Descending, the Valley Way enters the scrub just west of the outlet of Madison Spring.

Valley Way (map 6)

Distances from Appalachia parking area
to Tama Fall (via Fallsway): 0.6 mi.
to Randolph Path crossing: *est.* 0.9 mi., 50 min.
to Watson Path crossing: *est.* 2.1 mi., 2 hr.
to Upper Bruin junction: 3 min., 3 hr.
to Madison Hut: 3.5 mi. (5.6 km.), 3½ hr.
to Mt. Madison summit (via hut and Osgood Trail): 3.9 mi., 4 hr.

Inlook Trail (RMC)

This path was cut in 1932 from the junction of the Randolph Path and the Brookside east of Snyder Brook. It leads up to the Kelton Trail at the Upper Inlook (about 2700 ft.) near the crest of the finger of Gordon Ridge. There are good outlooks west, north, and east and several "inlooks" up the valley of Snyder Brook to John Quincy and Mt. Adams. The best outlook is at Dome Rock (about 2650 ft.), at the tip of the finger.

Inlook Trail (map 6)

Distances from Appalachia parking area
to start of Inlook Trail (via Valley Way and Brookside Trail): 1 mi.
to Dome Rock: 1.5 mi.
to Kelton Trail junction: 1.6 mi. (2.5 km.), 1 hr. 35 min.

The Brookside (RMC)

This trail goes up Snyder Brook and offers views of many cascades and pools. It branches left from the Valley Way about 30 yd. above the Beechwood Way and crosses Snyder Brook at the same point as the Randolph Path. East of the brook the Inlook Trail diverges left. In 0.3 mi. the Brookside recrosses the brook, and then becomes a moderate-to-steep trail to Salmacis Fall, just below which Kelton Trail enters on the left. The Brookside then follows the west side of Snyder Brook through virgin spruce and fir to Bruin Rock (3300 ft.), where it ends at the Watson Path. The brook between Salmacis and Bruin Rock is wild and beautiful, with cascades, mossy rocks, and fine forest.

The Brookside (map 6)

Distances from Appalachia parking area
   to start of the Brookside (via Valley Way): *est.* 1 mi.
   to Bruin Rock: *est.* 2.3 mi., 2¼ hr.

MOUNT ADAMS

Mt. Adams, at 5798 ft., is second in altitude of the New England summits. With its sharp, clean-cut profile, its four lesser summits, its large area above treeline, its great northern ridges (Durand sharp and narrow, Nowell massive and broad-spreading), its four glacial cirques, King Ravine and the three that it shares with its neighbors, and its inspiring views, Mt. Adams perhaps has more interesting features than any other New England mountain except Katahdin. The finest views are across the Great Gulf to Mts. Washington, Jefferson, and Clay.

Mount Adams (map 6)

Distances to Mt. Adams summit
   from AMC Pinkham Notch Camp (via Old Jackson Rd., Madison Gulf Trail, and Star Lake Trail): 6.7 mi., 5 hr. 35 min
   from Glen House site on NH Rte. 16 (via Osgood Trail, Madison Gulf Trail, and Star Lake Trail): *est.* 5.5 mi., 5 hr. 5 min.
   from Appalachia parking area (via Valley Way and Star Lake Trail): 4.3 mi., 4 hr. 25 min.
   from Appalachia parking area (via Air Line Trail): 4.1 mi., 4 hr. 20 min.

from Appalachia parking area (via Air Line Trail, Short Line Trail, King Ravine Trail, and Air Line Trail): 4.3 mi., 4¾ hr.

from Lowe's Store on US Rte. 2 (via Lowe's Path): 4.5 mi., 4 hr. 20 min.

from Madison Hut (via Star Lake Trail): 0.9 mi., 55 min.

Star Lake Trail (AMC)

This trail leads from Madison Hut to the summit of Mt. Adams, slabbing the southeast side of John Quincy Adams. It is often more sheltered from the wind than the Air Line Trail, and, in the lower part, is well supplied with *water*. It runs south from the hut, in common with the Parapet Trail, rising gently. In about 0.1 mi. the Parapet Trail branches to the left, passing east of Star Lake. The Star Lake Trail passes west of the lake and reaches the Adams-Madison col (about 4925 ft.) about 0.3 mi. from the hut. Here the Buttress Trail branches left and descends. The Star Lake Trail continues southwest on the steep southeast slope of John Quincy. There is usually *water* issuing from the rocks on the right. The trail continues to slab up the steep east slope of Mt. Adams to the summit.

Star Lake Trail (map 6)

Distance from Madison Hut

to Mt. Adams summit: *est.* 0.9 mi., 55 min.

Air Line (AMC)

This is the shortest route from the Appalachia parking area to Mt. Adams. It was completed in 1885 when Peek, Cook, Sargent, and Watson cut a path from the Ravine House in Randolph to a previously existing path on the crest of Durand Ridge.

The trail, in common with the Valley Way, begins at the Appalachia parking area. After crossing the railroad, the Air Line leads right and Valley Way left across the power line location. In a few yards the Link and the Amphibrach diverge right. The Air Line soon crosses Sylvan Way and, about 0.5 mi.

from the Appalachia parking area, crosses Beechwood Way and Beechwood Brook. A little beyond, the Short Line diverges right, and about 0.9 mi. from the Appalachia parking area, the Randolph Path is crossed. *Water* is found just short of 1.5 mi. in a *spring* 100 ft. east of the path (sign). From here the path becomes very steep for 0.5 mi. At 2.3 mi. is an old clearing known as Camp Placid Stream (*water unreliable*). The Scar Trail enters left, coming up from the Valley Way.

At 2.8 mi. the Upper Bruin comes up left from the Valley Way. Here the Air Line leaves the forest and ascends over the bare ledgy crest of Durand Ridge known as the Knife-edge. It passes over crags that drop off sharply into King Ravine on the right and the steep but not precipitous descent into Snyder Glen on the left. At 2.9 mi., just south of the little peak called Needle Rock, the Chemin des Dames comes up from King Ravine. At 3.1 mi. a branch leads left (southeast) 0.3 mi. to Madison Hut, which is visible from this junction in clear weather. *Water* is found on this branch not far from the main path.

The Air Line now departs a little from the edge of the ravine, going left of the jutting crags at the ravine's southeast corner. It rises steeply, and at 3.3 mi. passes the "Gateway" of King Ravine, through which the King Ravine Trail plunges between two crags into that gulf. There is a striking view of Mt. Madison. In a few steps the path enters the Gulfside Trail, turns right, and coincides with it for a few yards, attaining the high plateau at the head of the ravine. Then the Air Line leads to the left (southwest), passing west of Mt. John Quincy Adams, up a rough way over large, angular stones, to the summit of Mt. Adams.

Air Line Trail (map 6)
Distances from Appalachia parking area
- *to* Upper Bruin Trail junction: 2.8 mi., 3 hr.
- *to* King Ravine Trail junction at Gateway: 3.3 mi., 3 hr. 40 min.
- *to* Mt. Adams summit: 4.1 mi. (6.6 km.), 4 hr., 20 min.
- *to* Madison Hut (via branch path): *est.* 3.8 mi., 3 hr. 35 min.

Scar Trail (RMC)

This trail avoids the bad part of the Valley Way and the very steep and rough part of the Air Line on the way to Mt. Adams. It passes through virgin woods and has good outlooks at about 3200 ft. It leads from the Valley Way 1.8 mi. from the Appalachia parking area to the Air Line at an old clearing known as Camp Placid Stream (*water unreliable*) 2.3 mi. from Appalachia. It divides 0.2 mi. from Valley Way; a loop to the right goes over Durand Scar and another viewpoint. The main trail leads left to the beginning of Watson Path, then ascends to unite with the loop.

Scar Trail (map 6)
Distances from Appalachia parking area
- *to* start of Scar Trail (via Valley Way): 1.8 mi.
- *to* Durand Scar (via loop): 2.1 mi.
- *to* Watson Path junction: 2.2 mi.
- *to* Air Line Trail junction: 2.8 mi.
- *to* Mt. Adams summit (via Air Line Trail): *est.* 4.6 mi. (7.3 km.), 4 hr. 40 min.

Distances are the same via main trail or via loop to Durand Scar.

Short Line (RMC)

This graded path leading from the Air Line to the King Ravine Trail below Mossy Fall was made in 1899-1901 by J. Rayner Edmands. It offers easy access to the Randolph Path and to King Ravine from the Appalachia parking area.

The Short Line branches right from the Air Line 0.8 mi. from the Appalachia parking area. At 1.3 mi. from the parking area it unites with the Randolph Path, coincides with it for 0.4 mi., then branches left and leads south up the valley of Cold Brook toward King Ravine, keeping a short distance east of the stream. At 2.8 mi. from the Appalachia parking area, the path joins the King Ravine Trail just below Mossy Fall.

Short Line (map 6)
Distances from Appalachia parking area
to start of Short Line (via Air Line Trail): *est.* 0.8 mi.
to Randolph Path junction: 0.9 mi., 1¼ hr.
to King Ravine Trail junction: *est.* 2.8 mi., 2 hr. 10 min.

King Ravine Trail (RMC)

This branch from Lowe's Path through King Ravine was made by Charles E. Lowe in 1876.

It diverges left from Lowe's Path about 1.8 mi. from US Rte. 2 and rises over a low swell of Nowell Ridge. In 0.8 mi. it crosses Spur Brook below some cascades. In a few yards more it crosses the Randolph Path at its junction with the Amphibrach. Skirting the east spur of Nowell Ridge it enters the ravine and descends slightly. It crosses a western branch of Cold Brook, goes across the lower floor of the ravine, crosses the main stream, and in 0.2 mi. more is joined by the Short Line near the foot of Mossy Fall (*last sure water*). Just above this fall Cold Brook, already a good-sized stream, gushes from beneath the boulders that have fallen into the ravine.

So far the path has been fairly level, rising only 400 ft. in 1.5 mi.; but in the next 0.3 mi. it rises about 550 ft. and gains the upper floor of the ravine (3500 ft). The grandeur of the view of the ravine and to the north warrants a trip to the top of a bank of fallen rocks, even if you go no further. The Chemin des Dames branches left here. From this point to the foot of the headwall, about 0.4 mi., the path winds over and under boulders ranging up to the size of a small house. A short cut called the "Elevated" avoids some of the main boulder caves. The main trail, the "Subway," 550 ft. long, is more interesting and takes only a few minutes more.

The Great Gully Trail diverges right a little farther south. In a boulder-cave near the foot of the headwall, there is ice throughout the year. About 2.6 mi. from Lowe's Path the ascent of the headwall begins. It is very steep, rising about 1300 ft. in the 0.4

mi. to the "Gateway," where the trail issues from the ravine between two crags, and immediately joins the Air Line close to its junction with the Gulfside Trail. From the Gateway there is a most striking view of Mt. Madison. Madison Hut is in sight, and can be reached by the Gulfside Trail, left. The summit of Mt. Adams is about 0.5 mi. further, by the Air Line.

King Ravine Trail (map 6)
Distances from start of Lowe's Path, US Rte. 2
- *to* start of King Ravine Trail (via Lowe's Path): 1.8 mi., 1 hr. 20 min.
- *to* Amphibrach Trail crossing: 2.7 mi., 2 hr.
- *to* Short Line Trail junction: 3.4 mi., 2 hr. 35 min.
- *to* foot of King Ravine headwall: 4 mi., 3 hr. 40 min.
- *to* Air Line Trail junction at Gateway: 4.5 mi., 4½ hr.
- *to* Mt. Adams summit (via Air Line Trail): 5.1 mi. (8.2 km.), 5 hr. 10 min.

Distances from Appalachia parking area (via Amphibrach Trail or via Randolph Path and Short Line Trail) *subtract* about 0.8 mi. from distances above.

The Chemin des Dames (RMC)

This trail climbs the east wall of the King Ravine and joins the Air Line Trail above treeline. It is the shortest route out of the ravine. There is *no water*, and the trail is very steep.

Chemin des Dames (map 6)
Distance from King Ravine Trail junction
- *to* Air Line Trail junction: 0.3 mi. (0.5 km.), 40 min.

Great Gully Trail (RMC)

This very steep trail leads up the southwest corner of King Ravine and makes some use of the gully, crossing the brook above a high fall. Near the top of the headwall is a *spring (water unreliable)*. After emerging from the ravine the trail runs south to the junction of the Gulfside Trail and Lowe's Path, at Thunderstorm Junction.

THE NORTHERN PEAKS 89

Great Gully Trail (map 6)
Distance from King Ravine Trail junction
   to Gulfside Trail junction: *est.* 1 mi.

The Amphibrach (RMC)

This trail takes its name from its marking when it was first made, about 1883: three blazes — short, long, and short. It is a good approach to King Ravine or to any point reached via the Randolph Path or the Link, and also, via the Beechwood Way, to points reached by the Short Line, the Air Line, or the Valley Way. It ends at the Randolph Path and King Ravine Trail junction. For descent after dusk the Amphibrach has advantages over narrower footpaths, since this wider logging road is somewhat easier to follow.

The Amphibrach, in common with the Link, diverges right from the Air Line about 50 yd. south of its junction with the Valley Way and 100 yd. south of the Appalachia parking area. It runs west 0.8 mi. to where the Beechwood Way diverges left. Just east of Cold Brook the Sylvan Way enters left. Cold Brook is crossed on the Memorial Bridge. Shortly the Amphibrach turns left where the Link goes straight ahead. Just beyond, a side trail branches left 30 yd. to the foot of Cold Brook Fall. The Amphibrach now follows the course of Cold Brook, ascending west of the stream but generally not in sight of the water, and enters the WMNF. At 1.8 mi., near the confluence of Spur Brook and Cold Brook, the Monaway diverges right. The path crosses Spur Brook on the rocks, ascends the tongue of land between the two brooks, shortly diverges left (east), and climbs gradually, parallel to the badly eroded old trail. The Cliffway is crossed, and at 2.6 mi. the Amphibrach ends at "Pentadoi," the five-way intersection with the Randolph Path and King Ravine Trail.

Amphibrach Trail (map 6)
Distances from Appalachia parking area
   to Cold Brook Fall (via Air Line Trail): *est.* 0.8 mi., 20 min.
   to Monaway Trail junction: 1.8 mi.

to Randolph Path junction: 2.6 mi. (4.2 km.), 1½ hr.

Spur Trail (RMC)

This trail, cut in 1901 by Charles C. Torrey, leads up the east spur of the Nowell Ridge near the west edge of King Ravine, and at several points gives views into that gulf. The section known as the New Spur proved too steep for the amount of use it received and has been abandoned.

The Spur Trail diverges south from the Randolph Path west of Spur Brook about 100 yd. west of the King Ravine Trail. About 0.3 mi. above the Randolph Path, there is a short branch to Chandler Fall. About 0.3 mi. further up, the Hincks Trail to Gray Knob diverges right from the Spur Trail, and immediately above this point the Spur Trail crosses to the east side of the brook, the *last water* until Crag Camp. It ascends the spur that forms the west wall of King Ravine and goes over the Lower Crag, giving one of the best views of the ravine and an outlook east and north. A little farther on, a short branch leads to the Upper Crag, near which Crag Camp is situated. Here the Gray Knob Trail leads west to Gray Knob, 0.4 mi.

The trail continues up the spur, but not so near the edge of the ravine. It soon reaches the region of scrub and passes a trail that leads east to Knight's Castle, a crag at the edge of the ravine about 0.1 mi. from Spur Trail. Above this junction the trail leaves the scrub, ascends to the east of Adams 4, and merges with Lowe's Path just below the latter's crossing of the Gulfside Trail, or about 20 min. below the summit of Mt. Adams.

Spur Trail (map 6)
Distances from Appalachia parking area
to start of Spur Trail (via Randolph Path): 2.4 mi., 2 hr. 5 min.
to Crag Camp: 3.2 mi., 3 hr. 10 min.
to Mt. Adams summit: 4.6 mi. (7.4 km.), 4½ hr.

Hincks Trail (RMC) and Gray Knob Trail (RMC)

The Hincks Trail diverges right from the Spur Trail about 0.3 mi. above the Chandler Fall side trail and climbs steadily to Gray Knob. The Gray Knob Trail also leads from the Spur Trail, near Crag Camp, nearly on a contour to Gray Knob. The Gray Knob Trail then continues a few yards to cross Lowe's Path, and some distance beyond, the Perch Path diverges right. Ascending slightly, the Gray Knob Trail joins the Randolph Path near its junction with Israel Ridge Path. Gray Knob Trail is a route from Crag Camp and Gray Knob to Edmands Col without loss of elevation.

Hincks Trail (map 6)
Distance from Spur Trail junction
   to Gray Knob: *est.* 0.8 mi., ¾ hr.

Gray Knob Trail (map 6)
Distances from Spur Trail junction, Crag Camp
   to Gray Knob: *est.* 0.4 mi., 25 min.
   to Randolph Path junction: *est.* 1.4 mi., 1½ hr.

Perch Path (RMC)

This path runs right from the Gray Knob Trail, about 0.3 mi. south of Gray Knob. It descends slightly and, after crossing the Randolph Path, runs about level past the Perch and ends at the Israel Ridge Path.

Perch Path (map 6)
Distances from Gray Knob Trail junction
   to Randolph Path crossing: 0.4 mi.
   to the Perch: 0.5 mi.
   to Israel Ridge Path junction: 0.5 mi. (0.8 km.)
Distance from Gray Knob Camp
   to the Perch: 0.8 mi. (1 km.)

Beechwood Way (RMC)

This path starts from the Amphibrach 0.5 mi. from the Air Line. It follows a good logging road with moderate gradients. Just after it crosses Sylvan Way, there is *water* on the left. The path intersects the Air Line Trail and joins the Valley Way just below its junction with the Brookside Trail.

Beechwood Way (map 6)

Distance from Amphibrach Trail junction
to Valley Way junction: 1 mi., 40 min.

Cliffway (RMC)

This pleasure path leads from the Link 1.9 mi. from the Appalachia parking area, over some of the overgrown cliffs and ledges of the low swell of Nowell Ridge, then to Spur Brook Fall. It crosses the Amphibrach, then ends at the Randolph Path just west of Snyder Brook, 2.1 mi. from the Appalachia parking area. The only good view is from White Cliff. Gradients are easy, and much of the trail is level.

Cliffway (map 6)

Distances from Link Trail junction
to White Cliff: 0.7 mi.
to Spur Brook Fall: 1.6 mi.
to Randolph Path junction: 2 mi. (3.2 km.), 1 hr. 10 min.

Monaway, Ladderback Trail, Along the Brink (RMC)

The Monaway leads from the Cliffway near King Cliff to the Amphibrach at the confluence of Cold Brook and Spur Brook (Coldspur Ledges).

Ladderback Trail leads from Cliffway at White Cliff to Monaway 0.2 mi. above the Amphibrach.

A very short loop, Along the Brink, leads from Cliffway to Ladderback Trail via the mossy "brink" of White Cliff, affording good views of the Randolph valley.

THE NORTHERN PEAKS

Lowe's Path (AMC)

Cut in 1875-76 by Charles E. Lowe and Dr. William G. Nowell, from Lowe's house in Randolph to the summit of Mt. Adams, this is the oldest of the mountain trails that lead from the Randolph valley.

The trail begins on the south side of US Rte. 2 100 yd. west of Lowe's Store, where cars may be parked (a small fee is charged). It follows a broad wood road for 280 ft. and enters the woods right, crosses the railroad track and then the power line location. It ascends through woods at a moderate grade, at first toward the southwest then swinging more south, crosses several small brooks, bears left where it enters the old trail, and in 120 yd. crosses the Link.

In 0.2 mi. the King Ravine Trail branches left. The main path, about 2.3 mi. from US Rte. 2, passes close to the Log Cabin. Here two short spur paths lead left to the Randolph Path. Cabin-Cascade Trail to the Israel Ridge Path in Cascade Ravine (1 mi.) leaves on the right. *Water* is always found at the Log Cabin and midway between the cabin and treeline. About 0.3 mi. above the Log Cabin, Lowe's Path crosses the Randolph Path, and 0.5 mi. farther on the Gray Knob Trail crosses (leading left to Gray Knob). The mile ending at Gray Knob is steep.

The rest of the trail is above treeline and much exposed to wind. Views are very fine. The trail ascends steadily for 0.8 mi. to the summit known as Adams 4, the culminating peak of Nowell Ridge. It descends a little, keeping to the left of Sam Adams. The Spur Trail enters left. Lowe's Path then crosses the Gulfside Trail at Thunderstorm Junction (joined at the same point by the Great Gully Trail), turns a little more easterly, and ascends the summit of Mt. Adams. The Israel Ridge Path enters from the right about 0.2 mi. below the summit.

Lowe's Path (map 6)

Distances from US Rte. 2

to Link Trail crossing: 1.6 mi.

to King Ravine Trail junction: 1.8 mi., 1 hr. 20 min.

to Log Cabin: 2.3 mi., 2 hr.
to Randolph Path crossing: 2.5 mi.
to Gray Knob Trail crossing: 3 mi.
to Adams 4 summit: 3.9 mi.
to Mt. Adams summit: 4.5 mi. (7.2 km.), 4 hr. 20 min.

Israel Ridge Path (RMC)

This trail, which extends from near Bowman NH to Mt. Adams, was constructed as a graded path by J. Rayner Edmands beginning in 1892. Although hurricanes and slides have severely damaged the original trail, and there have been many relocations, the upper part is still one of the finest and most beautiful of the Randolph trails. (Some brook crossings may be difficult in high water.)

From Bowman follow the Castle Trail for 1.3 mi. Here, the Israel Ridge Path branches left and shortly crosses to the east bank of the Israel River. It follows the river for 1.6 mi., then diverges left where the Castle Ravine Trail proceeds straight ahead. The Israel Ridge Path bears southeast up the slope of Nowell Ridge. At 2.5 mi. it unites with the Link, follows it south on a level grade, and enters virgin growth. From this point to treeline, the forest has not been disturbed by lumbering, though slides have done much damage. In a very short distance the Israel Ridge Path branches left from the Link, and a short distance above, the Cabin-Cascades Trail from the Log Cabin enters left.

The first cascade is reached by following the Link a few yards right.

The Israel Ridge Path ascends on the north side of Cascade Brook to the head of the second cascade, where it passes to the south side. It runs southwest, then southeast, making a large zigzag up the steep slope of the ridge called Emerald Tongue or Israel Ridge, between Cascade and Castle brooks.

Soon the path turns sharply east, and Emerald Trail leads in 0.2 mi. to Emerald Bluff, a remarkable outlook, and continues down into Castle Ravine. The Israel Ridge Path zigzags up a rather steep slope where the Perch Path diverges left (east). The main path turns sharply south and ascends to treeline where it joins the Randolph Path 3.8 mi. from Bowman. It is a little north of this junction that the Gray Knob Trail from Gray Knob enters Randolph Path from the left. For a short distance the Randolph Path and Israel Ridge Path coincide. Then, the latter branches to the left and, curving east, ascends the southwest ridge of Mt. Adams, passes to the right of the viewpoint called the Eye and to the left of the summit known as Adams 5, to join the Gulfside Trail near Storm Lake. It coincides with the Gulfside for 0.5 mi., running northeast past Peabody *Spring* and south of Mt. Sam Adams, aiming for the Adams-Sam Adams col. Before reaching the col the Israel Ridge Path branches right from the Gulfside Trail, and in 0.1 mi. enters Lowe's Path, which leads in 0.2 mi. to the summit of Mt. Adams.

Israel Ridge Path (map 6)
Distances from US Rte. 2, Bowman NH
to start of Israel Ridge Path (via Castle Trail): *est.* 1.3 mi.

to Castle Ravine Trail junction: 1.6 mi.

to Link Trail junction: 2.4 mi., 1¾ hr.

to Perch Path junction: 3.5 mi., 3 hr.

to Randolph Path junction: 4 mi., 3 hr. 20 min.

to Gulfside Trail junction: 4.4 mi., 3 hr. 50 min.

to Mt. Adams summit: 5.2 mi. (8.4 km.), 4½ hr.

to Edmands Col (via Randolph Path): 4.4 mi., 3 hr. 40 min.

to Mt. Washington summit (via Randolph Path and Gulfside Trail): 8.4 mi., 6 hr. 25 min.

Castle Ravine Trail (RMC)

This trail leads through Castle Ravine, to the Randolph Path near Edmands Col.

From Bowman follow the Castle Trail and the Israel Ridge Path to a point 1.6 mi. from Bowman. Here the Israel Ridge Path turns left up a slope, while the Castle Ravine Trail leads straight ahead near the river. It crosses to the west bank (not easy in high water) and soon reaches a point abreast of the Forks of Israel, where Cascade and Castle brooks unite to form Israel River.

The trail crosses to the east bank, passes a fine cascade, and recrosses to the west bank. In general, it follows what is left of the logging road, but where that is too badly eroded, it goes through the woods. After entering Castle Ravine, the trail crosses to the east bank and follows a good logging road high above the brook. After about 0.6 mi. of steady ascent, the Link enters from the left. The two trails coincide for about 0.3 mi. when they cross to the southwest side of the brook in a tract of cool virgin forest beloved of *musca nigra*. Here the Link and the Castle Ravine Trail pass Emerald Trail, which diverges left for Israel Ridge. The Link then turns right while the Castle Ravine Trail continues up the ravine southwest of the brook. Close to the foot of the headwall it crosses again, and in a few yards. reaches the place where Castle Brook emerges from under the mossy boulders that have fallen from the headwall. At the foot of the headwall, the trail turns left and mounts the steep slope to Roof Rock, under which it passes *(last water)*. This is a good shelter from rain.

Rising steeply southeast, the trail soon winds up a patch of bare rocks, marked by small cairns and dashes of paint, re-entering the scrub at a large cairn. In a few hundred feet it emerges from the scrub at the foot of a steep slide of very loose rock (use caution when descending). It ascends, marked by paint, to the top of the headwall, over rocks and grass, marked by cairns, to Spaulding Spring. It joins the Randolph Path (sign) near Edmands Col.

Descending, leave the Randolph Path (left) at a sign about 0.1 mi. north of Edmands Col, go to Spaulding Spring, then follow cairns north.

Castle Ravine Trail (map 6)
Distances from US Rte. 2, Bowman NH

    to start of Castle Ravine Trail (via Castle Trail): *est.* 1.6 mi.

    to Forks of Israel: *est.* 1.9 mi.

to Link Trail junction: *est.* 3 mi., 2 hr. 20 min.
to Emerald Trail junction: *est.* 3.2 mi.
to Roof Rock, Castle Ravine: *est.* 3.6 mi.
to Randolph Path junction, Edmands Col: *est.* 4.3 mi. (6.8 km.), 4 hr. 10 min.

Cabin-Cascades Trail (RMC)

One of the very early AMC trails (1881), Cabin-Cascades leads from the Log Cabin on Lowe's Path to the Israel Ridge Path. It links the Log Cabin and the trails in the vicinity of Cascade Ravine, as well as the cascades themselves.

The trail begins at the Log Cabin, branching from Lowe's Path, and descends slightly to Israel Ridge Path just above its upper junction with the Link, near the first cascade of Cascade Brook and not far from the second cascade.

Cabin-Cascades Trail (map 6)

Distances from Log Cabin on Lowe's Path

to Israel Ridge Path junction: 1 mi.
to first cascade, Cascade Brook (via Link Trail): 1.1 mi.
to second cascade, Cascade Brook (via Israel Ridge Path): 1.1 mi. (1.7 km.)

Emerald Trail (RMC)

This trail provides a link in an attractive circuit from Bowman, up Israel Ridge, past Emerald Bluff, and down via Castle Ravine. It is steep and rough in spots, but the fine forest above Castle Ravine makes it worth the effort. The trail leaves the Israel Ridge Path high on the ridge about 0.3 mi. below the Perch, and runs level through high scrub for 0.1 mi., where a trail leads straight ahead 25 yd. to Emerald Bluff, an excellent outlook. The main trail bears left and shortly begins the steep and rough descent into Castle Ravine—follow blazes carefully. After 0.5 mi. the trail crosses several brooks, rises slightly, and enters the coinciding Castle Ravine and Link trails, about 0.2 mi. from their lower junction. Follow Castle Ravine Trail down to Israel Ridge Path and Bowman.

Emerald Trail (map 6)
Distances from Israel Ridge Path
   to Emerald Bluff: 0.2 mi.
   to Castle Ravine Trail/Link Trail junction: 0.7 mi.
Distance round trip from US Rte. 2, Bowman NH
   to Bowman NH (via Castle Trail, Israel Ridge Path, Emerald Trail, Castle Ravine Trail, and Castle Trail): *est.* 7.3 mi., 5 hr. 15 min.

MOUNT JEFFERSON

This 5715-ft. mountain has three summits a short distance apart, in line northwest and southeast, the highest in the middle. Perhaps the most striking view is down the Great Gulf with the Carter Range beyond, but there are others—of the Fabyan Plain and down the broad valley of the Israel. The Castellated Ridge, sharpest and most salient of the White Mountain ridges, extends northwest, forming the southwest wall of Castle Ravine. The view of the "Castles" from the village of Bowman is unforgettable. The Caps Ridge, similar in formation, but less striking, extends to the west. The two eastern ridges, Jefferson's "knees," truncated by the Great Gulf, have precipitous wooded slopes and gently sloping tops.

From the summit the Caps Ridge Trail leads west to Jefferson Notch, the Castle Path north then northwest down the Castellated Ridge, and the Mt. Jefferson Loop south to join the Gulfside Trail toward Mt. Clay. The Six Husbands Trail (see Section 5) and the Loop together run east from the summit, the Loop soon branching northeast to join the Gulfside toward Edmands Col, while the Six Husbands Trail continues east over one of the "knees" into the Great Gulf.

South of the peak of Mt. Jefferson is a smooth, grassy plateau called Monticello Lawn, traversed by the Gulfside Trail.

Jefferson Ravine, a glacial gulf tributary to the Great Gulf, has no trail.

THE NORTHERN PEAKS

Mt. Jefferson (map 6)

Distances to Mt. Jefferson summit

from Glen House site, NH Rte. 16 (via Osgood Trail, Great Gulf Trail, and Six Husbands Trail): *est.* 6.8 mi., 5 hr. 25 min.

from Appalachia parking area (via Randolph Path, Gulfside Trail, and Loop Trail): 6 mi., 5 hr.

from Appalachia parking area (via Link Trail, Castle Ravine Trail, Gulfside Trail, and Loop Trail): 6.8 mi., 5 hr. 35 min.

from US Rte. 2, Bowman NH (via Castle Trail, Israel Ridge Path, Randolph Path, Gulfside Trail, and Loop Trail): 4.9 mi., 4 hr. 20 min.

from US Rte. 2, Bowman NH (via Castle Trail): *est.* 4.8 mi., 4¾ hr.

from Jefferson Notch Rd. (via Caps Ridge Trail): *est.* 2.4 mi. (3.8 km.), 2 hr. 40 min.

Castle Trail (AMC)

Since it was made in 1883-84 by Cook, Sargent, Watson, Matthews, and Hunt, most of this trail has been relocated. It leaves US Rte. 2 at Bowman, 3 mi. west of the Appalachia parking area and 4.2 mi. east of the junction of US Rte. 2 and NH Rte. 115. Park on the Rte. 2 side of the track, cross the railroad, and follow the right driveway for 150 yd. to where the trail enters woods on the right. The trail circles left, crosses a power line, and at approximately 0.3 mi. crosses the Israel River at the site of an old footbridge.

At 1.3 mi. the Israel Ridge Path branches left (east). *(Last sure water* is a short distance along this trail.) The Castle Trail continues southeast, on the northeast flank of Mt. Bowman. At 2.3 mi. the trail passes a large boulder on the left and becomes much steeper for the next half mile. At 2.8 mi., near the saddle between Mt. Bowman and the Castle Ridge, about 3375 ft., it becomes less steep. The view into the ravine left and toward

Jefferson is quite spectacular. The trail dips slightly, then continues level along the ridge through thick growth. At 3.4 mi. it is crossed by the Link coming up from Castle Ravine and leading right to the Caps Ridge Trail. The ridge becomes very narrow and the trail is steep and rough. After passing over two ledges with an outlook from each, it reaches the first and most prominent Castle (4455 ft.) 3.6 mi. from Bowman. The view is very fine. The trail leads on over several lesser crags and ascends to where the Castellated Ridge joins the main mass of Mt. Jefferson. Above, the Cornice leads northeast to the Randolph Path near Edmands Col and south to the Caps Ridge and Gulfside trails. The Castle Trail continues to within a few yards of the summit of Mt. Jefferson, where it connects with the Mt. Jefferson Loop and the Six Husbands and Caps Ridge trails.

Castle Trail (map 6)

Distances from US Rte. 2, Bowman NH

to Israel Ridge Path junction: *est.* 1.3 mi.

to first Castle: *est.* 3.6 mi., 3½ hr.

to Mt. Jefferson summit: *est.* 4.8 mi. (7.6 km.), 4¾ hr.

to Mt. Washington summit (via Jefferson Loop and Gulfside trails): *est.* 8.1 mi., 7 hr.

Jefferson Notch Road: Jefferson Notch

This dirt road leads from the so-called Lower Rd. in Jefferson Highlands through the notch between Mt. Jefferson and the Dartmouth Range to the road to the Marshfield Base Station of the cog railway, officially called the Base Rd. The extension south from the Base Rd. to the Crawford House site is called the Mt. Clinton Rd.

Jefferson Notch Rd. is usually good for driving in summer and early fall. Use caution, since it is winding and narrow in places, and watch out for logging trucks. The beginning of the Caps Ridge Trail at Jefferson Notch (3000 ft.) is the highest point reached by the automobile roads surrounding the Presidential Range, so driving to Jefferson Notch permits the easiest ascent of

THE NORTHERN PEAKS

a high summit. Castellated Ridge can also be reached via the Link Trail.

Jefferson Notch Rd. (map 6)
Distances from Lower Rd. junction
- *to* Jefferson Notch: *est.* 5.5 mi., 2 hr. 40 min.
- *to* Base Rd. junction: *est.* 8.5 mi., 3 hr. 40 min.
- *to* Crawford House site (via Mt. Clinton Rd.): *est.* 12.5 mi.
- *to* Marshfield Station (via Boundary Line Trail): *est.* 8.3 mi., 3 hr. 40 min.

Boundary Line Trail (WMNF)

The trail begins on the north side of the Base Rd. about 0.5 mi. west of the Marshfield station of the cog railway. It soon crosses Franklin Brook, then the Ammonoosuc River. After heading east 100 yd., it turns north and runs north 1 mi. approximately along a surveyor's line, crossing Clay Brook, to Jefferson Notch Rd., about 1.5 mi. below the Caps Ridge Trail. (Signs may be missing.)

Caps Ridge Trail (AMC)

Because the Caps Ridge Trail starts at an elevation of 3000 ft., it makes possible an easy ascent of Mts. Jefferson, Clay, and Washington, and by the Sphinx Trail (see Section 3) gives access to the upper part of the Great Gulf. It can be reached from the Marshfield station by the Boundary Line Trail.

The Caps Ridge Trail leaves the Jefferson Notch Rd. at the north end of the height-of-land in Jefferson Notch. There is *no water* on the trail but water may be had at Jefferson Brook, which crosses the road 0.5 mi. south from the foot of the trail. About 0.4 mi. from the road the Link diverges left to the Castle Trail. Running east up the Ridge of the Caps, the trail passes an outcrop of granite that has several potholes, presumably formed by torrential streams, showing that the continental ice sheet covered the ridge at this point. About 1.5 mi. from the road the trail emerges from the woods at the lower Cap, a prominent ledge.

The trail follows the narrow crest of the ridge over minor ledges and the upper Cap (4830 ft.). Use care when ascending and descending the Caps: many of the ledges are steep and are slippery when wet.

About 0.1 mi. above the upper Cap the Cornice leads left to the Castle Trail and Edmands Col. By avoiding the summit of Mt. Jefferson the Cornice saves about 500 ft. of climbing, but it is very rough. Fifty feet above, the Cornice again branches right and leads southeast, rising gently, 0.5 mi. to the Gulfside Trail near Monticello Lawn. Hiking time to Mt. Washington, Mt. Clay, or the head of the Great Gulf is 25 min. less via this cutoff than via Jefferson summit. Above the Cornice, the Caps Ridge Trail continues east keeping a little south of the crest of the ridge, to the summit of Mt. Jefferson where it meets the Castle and Six Husbands trails and the Mt. Jefferson Loop.

Caps Ridge Trail (map 6)

Distances from Jefferson Notch Rd.

to lower Cap: 1.4 mi., 1½ hr.

to upper Cap: 1.8 mi., 1 hr. 50 min.

to Mt. Jefferson summit: 2.4 mi. (3.8 km.), 2 hr. 40 min.

to Gulfside Trail junction (via the Cornice): *est.* 2.2 mi.

to Sphinx Trail junction (via the Cornice and Gulfside Trail): *est.* 2.8 mi.

to Mt. Washington summit (via the Cornice and Gulfside Trail): *est.* 5.3 mi., 4 hr. 25 min.

MOUNT CLAY

Mt. Clay, usually counted as one of the Northern Peaks, is more properly a northern shoulder of Mt. Washington, corresponding to Boott Spur on the south and Nelson Crag on the northeast. Its 5532-ft. summit is only 135 ft. above the col that connects it with the main mass. Mt. Clay's most interesting feature is the eastern cliffs, which begin close to the summits and form the west wall of the Great Gulf. The Mt. Clay Loop off the

THE NORTHERN PEAKS

Gulfside Trail goes over all three summits. The south summit also can be reached by a short scramble from the Gulfside Trail.

Jewell Trail (WMNF)

This graded trail climbs the ridge that leads west from Mt. Clay. Named for a Sergeant Jewell, an observer for the Army Signal Corps on Mt. Washington, it leads from the Marshfield station (parking area privately owned and operated by the cog railway) to the Gulfside Trail north of the Clay-Washington col, and provides an easy ascent of Mt. Washington. In bad weather the Ammonoosuc Ravine Trail (see Section 6) is safer, since it leads past the Lakes of the Clouds Hut.

From the Marshfield station the trail immediately crosses the cog railway, then the Ammonoosuc, and zigzags to the crest of the low ridge between the Ammonoosuc and Clay Brook. It descends slightly to the latter, crosses at a fine cascade, switches back northeast up the south flank of the ridge, and winds around its west end. Avoiding the craggy crest, it slabs the north flank and comes out above treeline on the west slope of Mt. Clay. It zigzags up the slope of Mt. Clay and enters the Gulfside Trail 0.3 mi. northwest of the Clay-Washington col. For Mt. Washington, follow the Gulfside right. For Mt. Clay, scramble up the rocks above the junction.

Jewell Trail (map 6)
Distances from the Marshfield Station
to Clay Brook crossing: 0.5 mi.
to Gulfside Trail junction: 3 mi.
to Clay-Washington col (via Gulfside Trail): 3.2 mi.
to Mt. Washington summit (via Gulfside Trail): 4.6 mi. (7.4 km.), 3 hr. 55 min.

SECTION 5

The Great Gulf

This is the valley between Mt. Washington and the Northern Peaks. The views from the walls and from points on the floor of the Great Gulf are among the best in New England.

To preserve its unique scenic values, it was designated a Wilderness Area within the WMNF in 1959. Since 1980, *day-use permits* are no longer required for the Great Gulf Wilderness Area. Permits are, however, required for *overnight use,* with a limit of 60 campers in the Gulf on any night. Contact the USFS, Gorham, NH 03581 (603-466-2713); see also Section 2). There were formerly shelters in the Great Gulf, but careless campers left trash and damaged vegetation. Following wilderness policy, the USFS dismantled the shelters in 1976 and limited summer camping in the Gulf.

The Great Gulf, from 1100 to 1600 ft. deep, is a typical bowl-shaped gulf for 3.5 mi. from its head, and then becomes a more open valley that extends about 1.5 mi. farther east. It is drained by the West Branch of the Peabody River. Steep slopes and abundant water result in a great number of cascades. The Great Gulf and its tributary gulfs, Madison Gulf, Jefferson Ravine, and the Sphinx, were hollowed out by the action of glaciers, mainly before the last ice age.

The Great Gulf was observed by Darby Field in 1642. The name probably had its origin in 1823 in a casual statement of Ethan Allen Crawford, who, having lost his way in cloudy weather, came to "the edge of a great gulf." A few years later the name began to appear in the literature of the White Mountains. The region was visited in 1829 by Professor J. W. Robbins, but was little known until, in 1881, Benjamin F. Osgood blazed the first trail, from the Osgood Trail to the headwall.

Refer to map 6, the Mt. Washington Range, and the USGS Mt. Washington Quadrangle.

The Appalachian Trail follows the Osgood Trail, the Osgood Cutoff, and the Madison Gulf Trail.

GREAT GULF TRAIL (WMNF)

For use restrictions, see Section 2.

There are plans under consideration to relocate the start of this trail, together with the Osgood Trail, over new bridges to a point on NH Rte. 16 (Pinkham Notch Highway) 1.5 mi. north of the Glen House site.

The Pinkham B or Dolly Copp Rd. branches west from Rte. 16 4.4 mi. southwest of Gorham (Rte. 16 - Rte. 2 junction) and 3.5 mi. north of the Glen House site. It immediately crosses the Peabody River, runs west, passes the entrance to Dolly Copp Campground (left), and about 500 ft. beyond bears right, passes the entrance to the Barnes Field Camping area (right), and runs northwest to Randolph.

To reach the Great Gulf Trail bear left onto the entrance road, and shortly after bear left (south) on the main camp road. The Great Gulf Trail leaves the south side of the road just before reaching the site of the old bridge crossing.

For hikers with automobiles it is better to drive to the Glen House site and enter via the Osgood Trail. This saves 0.7 mi. of walking and may be drier in wet weather.

The Great Gulf Trail follows a logging road south, on the west bank of the Peabody River until it is joined by the West Branch, in about a mile. The trail then continues northwest of the West Branch. At about 2.3 mi. it crosses the Osgood Trail.

The trail soon approaches the West Branch and runs for about 0.3 mi. close to the north bank. Then, diverging from the stream, it ascends to the Bluff, where there is a good view of the Gulf and the mountains around it. The trail follows the edge of the Bluff, descends sharply left, crosses Parapet Brook on a bridge, then continues to the crest of the little ridge that separates Parapet Brook from the West Branch. At the top of this crest the Madison Gulf Trail enters right, and the two trails descend together for a short distance to cross the West Branch, on a suspension bridge. After ascending the steep bank, the Madison Gulf Trail branches left, while the Great Gulf Trail branches right, up the south bank of the river.

In 0.8 mi. the Great Gulf Trail crosses Chandler Brook, and on the far bank the Chandler Brook Trail diverges left and ascends to the Mt. Washington Auto Rd. The trail continues close to the river for more than 0.5 mi., passing in sight of the mouth of the stream that issues from Jefferson Ravine on the north, to join the Six Husbands (right) and Wamsutta (left) trails.

The Great Gulf Trail continues on the southeast bank, then in the bed of the stream, to the foot of a waterfall. Scrambling up to the left of this fall, it crosses a large branch brook and passes left of a beautiful cascade on the main stream. The trail soon crosses to the northwest bank, and in a short distance crosses the brook that descends from the Clay-Jefferson col. At this point the Sphinx Trail, leading to the Gulfside Trail, diverges right. The Great Gulf Trail soon crosses again to the southeast bank of the West Branch, passing waterfalls, including Weetamoo, the finest in the Gulf. There are remarkable views down the Gulf to Mts. Adams and Madison. The trail crosses an eastern tributary and, after a slight ascent, reaches Spaulding Lake, 4250 ft. elevation, 6.3 mi. from the Glen House site, and about 1.5 mi. by trail from the summit of Mt. Washington.

The Great Gulf Trail continues on the east side of the lake, and a little beyond begins to ascend the steep headwall. The trail runs south and southeast, rising 1600 ft. in about 0.5 mi., over fragments of stone, many of which are loose. The way may be poorly marked, because snow slides sweep away cairns, but paint blazes probably will be visible on the rocks. The trail curves a little left until within a few yards of the top of the headwall, then, bearing slightly right, emerges from the gulf and ends at the Gulfside Trail near the cog railway. It is 0.3 mi. to the summit of Mt. Washington by the Gulfside Trail and Crawford Path.

Descending from Mt. Washington, follow the Crawford Path west from the summit. Just below the old corral the Gulfside

Trail diverges right. Follow it north until it crosses the cog railway. A few yards beyond, where the Gulfside Trail turns sharp left, the Great Gulf Trail continues straight ahead north a few yards to the edge of the gulf, and plunges down.

Great Gulf Trail (map 6)
Distances from Glen House site, NH Rte. 16
to Great Gulf Trail junction (via Osgood Trail): 1.6 mi., 50 min.
to Madison Gulf Trail junction: 2.3 mi., 1 hr. 40 min.
to Six Husbands Trail/Wamsutta Trail junction: 4.4 mi., 3 hr.
to Sphinx Trail junction: 5.4 mi., 3 hr. 50 min.
to Spaulding Lake: 6.3 mi., 4½ hr.
to Gulfside Trail junction: 7.1 mi., 6 hr.
to Mt. Washington summit (via Gulfside Trail and Crawford Path): 7.5 mi. (12.1 km.), 6 hr. 20 min.

Distances from Dolly Copp Campground
add 0.7 mi. and ½ hr. to above

MADISON GULF TRAIL (AMC)

For use restrictions, see Section 2.

This trail begins at the Mt. Washington Auto Rd. a little more than 2 mi. from the Glen House site, opposite the Old Jackson Rd., and descends gently to the West Branch where it meets the Great Gulf Trail, then ascends along Parapet Brook to the Parapet, a point 0.3 mi. from Madison Hut. With the Osgood Trail, the Old Jackson Rd., or the Raymond Path, the Madison Gulf Trail affords routes to the hut from the Glen House site, from Pinkham Notch Camp, and from the Hermit Lake shelters respectively. It is well marked, well protected from storms, and has plenty of *water*. On the headwall of the Gulf it is very steep and possibly hazardous. In wet weather, stream crossings and steep slabs may be a problem. The last mile of the ascent to the Parapet is rough and very steep, going over several ledge outcrops, bouldery areas, and a chimney with loose rock. Hikers with full packs should allow extra time. From the Auto Rd. to

Osgood Cutoff it is part of the Appalachian Trail and so blazed in white; the rest is blazed in blue.

Leave the Auto Rd. after the 2-mile mark, at the end of a straight stretch, via the trail leading north to "Lowe's Bald Spot" opposite the Old Jackson Rd. junction. In a short distance, in a little pass west of Lowe's Bald Spot, the trail to this viewpoint branches right, reaching the summit in 5 min. The view is excellent.

The Madison Gulf Trail bears left and ascends about 75 ft. over a ledge with a limited view, descends rapidly for a short distance, then gently, crossing several water courses. The trail comes within sound of the West Branch of the Peabody River and continues along on contour until it meets the Great Gulf Trail on the south bank. The Madison Gulf Trail turns sharp right and, coinciding with the Great Gulf Trail, descends the steep bank to the West Branch.

Both trails cross a suspension bridge to the north bank, then coincide for a few yards farther up a slope east to the crest of the little ridge that divides Parapet Brook from the West Branch. At this point the Madison Gulf Trail diverges sharply left (northwest) and leads up the ridge. The Great Gulf Trail goes straight ahead northeast. Soon leaving the crest of the ridge, the Madison Gulf Trail crosses to the northeast side of Parapet Brook and is joined on the right by the Madison Gulf Cutoff from the Osgood Trail, affording a route from the Glen House site, about 2.9 mi. below, easier than that via the Bluff. At this junction the Osgood Cutoff continues ahead, leading in 0.5 mi. to the Osgood Trail for Mt. Madison and Madison Hut. The Madison Gulf Trail turns left, continues up the stream, soon crosses to the southwest side, and diverges from the brook, to which it later returns, crossing a small branch brook and turning sharply left just before it reaches the main stream. It soon crosses again to the northeast bank, follows that for a little way, then turns right, ascending steeply with good views.

The trail next turns left, slabbing the mountainside high above the brook, which it approaches again at the mouth of the branch stream from Osgood Ridge. It ascends rapidly between the two brooks, crosses to the west bank of the main stream, then recrosses, and, climbing more gradually, gains the lower floor of the gulf, crosses again, and soon reaches Sylvan Cascade, a fine fall.

The Madison Gulf Trail then ascends to the upper floor of the gulf, where it crosses four brooks. From the floor it rises gradually to Mossy Slide at the foot of the headwall, then ascends very rapidly by a stream.

The trail now turns left, continues near a brook partly hidden among the rocks, then ascends very steeply. Ultimately, it reaches the scrub, emerges on the rocks, and ends at the Parapet Trail. Turn left for the Parapet (400 ft.) and Madison Hut (0.3 mi.), and right for the Osgood Trail (0.6 mi.).

Madison Gulf Trail (map 6)

Distances from Mt. Washington Auto Rd.
  to Great Gulf Trail junction: *est*. 2.3 mi., 1¼ hr.
  to foot of Madison Gulf headwall: *est*. 4 mi., 3 hr.
  to the Parapet: *est*. 4.5 mi., 4 hr.
  to Madison Hut (via Osgood Cutoff and Osgood Trail): *est*. 5 mi. (8 km.), 4¼ hr.

Distances from Pinkham Notch Camp
  to Madison Hut (via Old Jackson Rd., Madison Gulf Trail, Osgood Cutoff, and Osgood Trail): *est*. 7 mi. (10 km.), 5¾ hr.
  to Mt. Madison summit (via Old Jackson Rd., Madison Gulf Trail, Osgood Cutoff, and Osgood Trail): *est*. 7½ mi., 6 hr.

Distance from Hermit Lake Shelters
  to Madison Hut (via Raymond Path, Madison Gulf Trail, Osgood Cutoff, and Osgood Trail): *est*. 7.8 mi., 5¾ hr.

CHANDLER BROOK TRAIL (AMC)

About 1 mi. in length, this trail diverges south from the Great Gulf Trail immediately after it crosses Chandler Brook. It follows the brook rather closely, crossing three times. Fine waterfalls can be seen from the trail. From the last crossing the course is southeast. Rising over a confused mass of stones, and keeping west of interesting rock formations, the trail enters the Mt. Washington Auto Rd. near a ledge of white quartz slightly less than 0.5 mi. above the 4-mile post, at the bend above the Halfway House. The trail is blazed in blue.

Descending, look for this white ledge, which is close to the Auto Rd. The trail is marked by cairns here and is visible from the road. For use restrictions, see Section 2.

WAMSUTTA TRAIL (AMC)

Weetamoo was a queen of the Pocasset Indians, and a beautiful waterfall in the Great Gulf bears her name. This trail was named for the first of her six husbands.

The Wamsutta Trail begins at the Great Gulf Trail opposite the start of the Six Husbands Trail, 4.4 mi. from the Glen House site on NH Rte. 16, and ends at the Mt. Washington Auto Rd. immediately above the 6-mile mark, opposite the north end of the Alpine Garden Trail. The Wamsutta Trail is blazed with yellow paint.

Leaving the Great Gulf Trail, the trail runs southwest to a small stream, then ascends gradually. Soon it climbs the very steep and rough northerly spur of Chandler Ridge. Passing a quartz ledge on the right, the trail continues steeply to a small, open knob on the crest of the spur, which offers a good view. It next goes through trees at a gradual ascent, passing a *spring* on the right. Continuing along the crest, the trail emerges at treeline and climbs to the winter shortcut of the Auto Rd. After turning right, it ends in a few yards at the Auto Rd.

Descending from the Auto Rd., be sure to turn left off the winter shortcut.

Wamsutta Trail (map 6)
Distance from Great Gulf Trail junction
  to Auto Rd.: 1.7 mi., 1 hr. 55 min.

SIX HUSBANDS TRAIL (AMC)

This name honors the six successive husbands of Weetamoo. The Six Husbands Trail begins at the Great Gulf Trail at the same point as the Wamsutta Trail, 4.4 mi. from the Glen House site on NH Rte. 16, descends northwest for a few yards, and crosses the West Branch. In times of high water go upstream to a better crossing. The trail bears right away from the West Branch, then ascends gently north until it comes close to the stream that flows from Jefferson Ravine, which it ascends on its southwest bank. At 0.6 mi. the Buttress Trail branches right and crosses the stream. The Six Husbands Trail continues a little farther beside the brook (*last sure water*), turns west and leads under two huge boulders. It ascends by ladders made of two-by-fours and passes near a cavern (10 yd. to left), where snow and ice may be found even in August. The trail soon comes to an overhanging ledge and leads along under its edge for a short distance, ascending again by ladders. It then leads to a crag affording a good view up the gulf, continues steep, and keeps close to the crest of the ridge until it comes out on the north "knee" of Jefferson (view). The ascent becomes easier. Across the bare stretches the trail is marked by cairns. The Edmands Col Cutoff branches right, leading in 0.5 mi. to Edmands Col. Beyond, the trail becomes steeper, begins to climb the cone of Mt. Jefferson, and leads past a snowbank that often lasts well into July. Marked by cairns, the trail crosses the Gulfside Trail and continues west to the summit of Mt. Jefferson, coinciding for the last 100 yd. with the Mt. Jefferson Loop. At the summit it meets the Castle and Caps Ridge trails. The trail is blazed in blue.

In *reverse:* enter the Great Gulf down this steep, difficult trail only in emergency (see also Section 2).

Six Husbands Trail (map 6)
Distances from Great Gulf Trail junction
 to Buttress Trail junction: *est*. 0.5 mi.
 to Gulfside Trail crossing: 1.9 mi., 2 hr. 5 min.

to Mt. Jefferson summit: 2.2 mi. (3.5 km.), 2 hr. 25 min.

BUTTRESS TRAIL (AMC)

This is the most direct route from the upper part of the Great Gulf to Madison Hut. The trail, blazed in blue, begins in the ravine between Mts. Adams and Jefferson, leaving the north side of the Six Husbands Trail at a point 0.6 mi. northwest of the Great Gulf Trail. It immediately crosses the brook (*last sure water*) flowing out of Jefferson Ravine, bears right (east) in 0.1 mi., and climbs diagonally across a steep slope of large, loose, angular fragments of rock. Some are easily dislodged, so care must be taken. The trail continues in the same direction, rising gradually along a steep, wooded slope. At the top of this slope, 0.6 mi. from start, the trail turns north across a gently sloping upland covered with trees. There is a *spring (reliable water)* on the left, at about 1 mi. As the trail nears treeline, it passes under a large boulder. At about 1.3 mi. the trail reaches the foot of the steep, rock-covered peak of Mt. Adams. Here, a little left of the trail, a small, ledgy summit provides a fine view.

The trail runs nearly level northwest and then north, passing through patches of scrub, across patches of rock fragments, and crossing two *brooks*. Then, rising slightly through scrub, it passes through a gap between the Parapet and John Quincy, and, just southwest of the lake, it enters Star Lake Trail, which leads in less than 0.3 mi. to Madison Hut.

Buttress Trail (map 6)
Distances from Six Husbands Trail junction
to Parapet: 1.9 mi.
to Madison Hut (via Star Lake Trail): 2.1 mi. (3.4 km.), 2 hr.

SPHINX TRAIL (AMC)

This trail derives its name from the profile of a rock formation seen from just below the meadow where *water* is found. The trail is important because it affords the best means of escape for anyone overtaken by storm on Mt. Clay or on the south part of Mt. Jefferson. It diverges east from the Gulfside Trail just north of the Clay-Jefferson col and descends to the Great Gulf Trail. Descending from the col, protection is quickly gained from the rigor of west and northwest winds.

The Sphinx Trail, blazed in blue, branches northwest from the Great Gulf Trail near the crossing of the brook that descends from between Mts. Clay and Jefferson, 5.4 mi. from the Glen House site on NH Rte. 16. It ascends through forest, first gradually, then very steeply. It follows the brook rather closely, using the bed for about 0.3 mi., and passes several small cascades. At 0.6 mi. the trail turns southwest, leaves the brook, and scrambles to a sloping shelf or plateau, partly covered with scrub, through which the trail is cut. A small meadow is crossed, where there is usually *water* under a rock north of the trail. After ascending slightly farther, the Sphinx Trail joins the Gulfside Trail on a level area a little north of the col.

Descending, go from the Clay-Jefferson col a short distance north along the Gulfside Trail. A grassy rock corridor leading east is the beginning of the Sphinx Trail, marked by a sign and cairns.

Sphinx Trail (map 6)
Distance from Great Gulf Trail junction
   to Gulfside Trail junction: *est.* 1 mi., 1¼ hr.

SECTION 6
The Southern Peaks

The southern part of the Presidential Range extends southwest from Mt. Washington and includes the following summits, from northeast to southwest: two peaks of Mt. Monroe (highest 5385 ft.); Mt. Franklin (5004 ft.); Mt. Eisenhower, formerly called Mt. Pleasant (4761 ft.); Mt. Pierce or Clinton* (4312 ft.); Mt. Jackson (4052 ft.); and Mt. Webster, formerly called Notch Mountain (3910 ft.). The Ammonoosuc River lies to the northwest, and the Dry River to the southeast. All of the southern peaks and trails in this section are within the Presidential Range Restricted Use Area or regulated Wilderness Area. See Section 2 for additional information.

On trail signs the word "Crawford's" is used to designate the locality near the Crawford railroad depot and the site of the former Crawford House (which burned down in 1977), where the Mt. Clinton Rd. meets US Rte. 302 (Crawford Notch Highway).

Refer to map 6, the Mt. Washington Range.

The Crawford Path (WMNF)

The first section, a footpath leading up Mt. Pierce (Mt. Clinton), was cut in 1819 by Abel Crawford and his son Ethan Allen Crawford. In 1840 Thomas J. Crawford, a younger son of Abel, converted the footpath into a bridle path, although it has not been used for horses for many decades. The trail still follows the original path, except for the section between Mt. Monroe and the Westside Trail. From Mt. Pierce to the summit of Mt. Washington, the Crawford Path is part of the Appalachian Trail, and so it is blazed in white.

Caution. The caution in Section 3 applies with particular force to this trail, because for at least 5 mi. it lies above treeline,

---

*Commonly referred to as Clinton, but legally Pierce, by a 1913 act of the New Hampshire legislature that named the mountain after the only US president from New Hampshire, Franklin Pierce. The name "Mt. Pierce" appears on the USGS maps, "Mt. Clinton" on most signs.

THE SOUTHERN PEAKS

exposed to the full force of all storms. Seven lives have been lost on the Crawford Path through failure to observe proper precautions. Always carry a compass and study the map before starting. If trouble arises on or above Mt. Monroe, use the Lakes of the Clouds Hut or go down the Ammonoosuc Ravine Trail. This is the most dangerous part of the path. If the path should be obscured in cloudy weather, go northwest if you are below Mt. Monroe, west if you are above, descending into the woods and following water. On the southeast nearly all the slopes are more precipitous, and the distance to a highway is much greater.

Because soils are thin and alpine plants are fragile above timberline, climbers are requested to stay on the path.

The path leaves US Rte. 302 (Crawford Notch Highway) opposite the Crawford House site just south of the junction with the Mt. Clinton Rd. (parking area). About 300 yd. from Rte. 302 a trail leads left to Crawford Cliff (20 min.). The main trail follows the south bank of Gibbs Brook. Gibbs Falls upper and lower are on short side paths left. After leaving the brook the trail ascends steeply for a short distance, then slabs the side of the valley. At 1.8 mi. above the Crawford House site the Mizpah Cutoff diverges east for Mizpah Spring Hut. *Water* is plentiful until the trail leaves the woods near the top of Mt. Pierce. The Webster Cliff Trail, which leads to the summit of Mt. Pierce about 150 yd. south, enters the Crawford Path on the right at treeline.

From Mt. Pierce to Mt. Washington, except for a few bits of scrub, the path is entirely exposed and gives magnificent views in all directions. Cairns and the marks of many feet on the rocks indicate the way. Though the path winds about, for the most part it remains on the top of the ridge, except where it passes Mt. Eisenhower and above the south end of the Mt. Monroe Loop. The general direction in ascending is northeast. There is usually *water* between Mts. Pierce and Eisenhower, nearer the latter. As the path approaches Mt. Eisenhower, the Mt. Eisenhower Loop diverges left, going over the summit of the mountain. The ascent is relatively easy, and the view is so fine that this loop is recommended in good weather. The Crawford Path continues right and slabs through scrub on the southeast side of the mountain: this is the better route in bad weather. In the col between Mts. Eisenhower and Franklin the path passes close to the stagnant Red Pond on the left, and just beyond, the Mt. Eisenhower Loop rejoins the Crawford Path left. A few steps beyond, the Edmands Path also enters left, and then the Mt. Eisenhower Trail from the Dry River enters right. There is a *spring* left just beyond this junction.

From this point to the shoulder called Mt. Franklin, there is a sharp ascent. A few yards to the right (south) of the path along the level ridge is the precipice that forms the side wall of Oakes Gulf. (Consideration is being given to relocating the trail to the northwest side of Mt. Monroe, to mitigate environmental problems on the southeast side. The area between the two ends of the Mt. Monroe Loop is one of great environmental importance and fragility. To protect this area, the most scrupulous care is required on the part of visitors.) South of Mt. Monroe the Mt. Monroe Loop diverges left, rejoining the Crawford Path near the Lakes of the Clouds Hut. Mt. Monroe has two summits, both easily ascended by this loop. There is *water* on the left, just as the Crawford Path reaches the level area at the foot of the higher peaks, and the path continues to Lakes of the Clouds Hut.

The Ammonoosuc Ravine Trail diverges left at the hut and a little farther on, the Dry River Trail diverges right. The Crawford Path crosses the outlet of the larger lake (*last water*) and passes between it and the second lake, where the Camel Trail to Boott Spur and the Tuckerman Crossover to Tuckerman Ravine diverge right. The path then ascends gradually, always some distance below (northwest) the crest of the ridge. The Davis Path, which here follows the original location of the Crawford Path, enters at the foot of the cone of Mt. Washington. A few yards beyond, the Westside Trail to the Northern Peaks diverges left. The Crawford Path turns straight north, switching back and

THE SOUTHERN PEAKS

forth as it climbs the steep cone through a trench in the rocks past the cross and cairn that mark where two hikers died on July 19, 1958. Above the flat where the Gulfside Trail enters left, the Crawford Path passes through the pen in which saddle horses from the Glen House used to be kept, and from there to the summit. It is marked by frequent cairns.

Descending, the path to the corral is on the north side of the railroad track. Beyond the buildings it leads generally northwest, then swings west. Avoid random side paths toward the south and the Gulfside Trail diverging north (right). Those bound for Bretton Woods will probably take the most direct route, Edmands Path, which joins the Crawford Path in the Eisenhower/Franklin col. For the Crawford House site, the Crawford Path is the most direct route. On arriving at Mt. Pierce (Mt. Clinton), many will be tempted to follow the Webster Cliff Trail over Mts. Jackson and Webster. Although this is a delightful route, it is much longer and harder than the direct route, and the difference is decidedly greater than a glance at the map would suggest.

Crawford Path (map 6)
Distances from Crawford House site, US 302 and Mt. Clinton Rd.

to Mizpah Cutoff junction: 1.8 mi., 1 hr. 20 min.
to Webster Cliff Trail junction: 2.9 mi., 2 hr.
to Mt. Eisenhower Loop junction: 4.4 mi., 2¾ hr.
to Edmands Path junction: 4.7 mi., 2 hr. 55 min.
to Mt. Franklin summit: 5.5 mi., 3¾ hr.
to Mt. Monroe Loop junction (south end): 6 mi., 4 hr. 5 min.
to Lakes of the Clouds Hut: 6.8 mi., 4½ hr.
to Westside Trail junction: 7.7 mi., 5 hr. 20 min.
to Mt. Washington summit: 8.2 mi. (13.2 km.), 6 hr.

Lakes of the Clouds Hut (AMC)

The original stone hut, greatly enlarged since, was built in 1915. It is located on a shelf near the foot of Mt. Monroe about 50 yd. west of the larger lake at an elevation of about 5050 ft. It is reached by the Crawford Path or the Ammonoosuc Ravine Trail, and has accommodations for ninety guests (see Section 9, *Appalachian Mountain Club*). The hut is open to the public from mid-June to mid-September, and closed at all other times. For current information contact Reservation Secretary, Pinkham Notch Camp, Box 298, Gorham, NH 03581 (603-466-2727).

Ammonoosuc Ravine Trail (WMNF)

This trail, which leaves from the Marshfield station of the cog railway, can be reached on foot from the Jefferson Notch Rd. via the Boundary Line Trail. There is a parking area below the Marshfield station (fee charged).

The Ammonoosuc Ravine Trail, together with the upper section of the Crawford Path, is the shortest route to the summit of Mt. Washington from the west. The views are spectacular. It is the best approach to the Lakes of the Clouds Hut in bad weather, since it lies below treeline to within 100 yd. of the hut.

Ascending by easy grades through open woods the trail follows the south bank of the Ammonoosuc River, and at 1.4 mi. crosses the river on a footbridge to a beautiful pool at the foot of some fine cascades. The trail crosses here to the east bank and begins the steep ascent. After a few hundred yards a side trail right leads about 100 ft. to a spectacular viewpoint at the foot of the gorge. Above this point the main brook falls about 600 ft. down a steep trough in the mountainside at an average angle of 45 degrees. Another brook a short distance to the north does the same, and these two spectacular waterslides meet at the foot of the gorge.

The main trail continues its steep ascent and in about 200 yd. comes within a few feet of the northern of these two brooks a little above their junction. The striking view of the gorge from the precipitous ledge separating the two brooks is worth the scramble out, but it is difficult to find unless the signs are in place. The trail then bears somewhat away from the brook, but soon returns, crosses it, and continues right to the main brook,

THE SOUTHERN PEAKS

which it also crosses at a striking viewpoint at the head of the highest fall. After crossing the brook twice more the trail emerges from the scrub and follows a line of cairns directly up some rock slabs, which may be slippery when wet, to the western end of the Lakes of the Clouds Hut.

Ammonoosuc Ravine Trail (map 6)
Distances from the Marshfield station of the cog railway:
to pool at foot of Ammonoosuc Ravine: 1.4 mi., 1 hr.
to side trail to view of falls: 1.6 mi., 1½ hr.
to Lakes of the Clouds Hut: 2.5 mi., 2¾ mi.

Edmands Path (WMNF)

The Edmands Path, leading from the Mt. Clinton Rd. to the Crawford Path in the Eisenhower-Franklin col, is the most comfortable route from the Bretton Woods region to the Southern Peaks and Mt. Washington, and the quickest way to civilization from points on the Crawford Path between Mts. Eisenhower and Monroe. It is a graded path throughout.

The path leaves the east side of the Mt. Clinton Rd. 2.4 mi. north of the Crawford House site and 1.4 mi. south of the junction of US Rte. 302 and the Base Rd. to the Marshfield station. It continues level for approximately 0.4 mi., crosses Abenaki Brook on a footbridge, and turns right on a logging road. After 0.5 mi. more the grade, which has been very gentle thus far, begins to steepen. At 2.3 mi., it crosses a brook at the foot of a small cascade, then quickly crosses two others. Cascade and brooks may be dry in dry weather. The trail then slabs the north face of Mt. Eisenhower at a slight grade, above treeline, to join the Crawford Path in the Eisenhower-Franklin col.

Edmands Path (map 6)
Distance from Mt. Clinton Rd.
to Crawford Path junction: 2.3 mi. (4.7 km.), 2½ hr.

SECTION 6

MOUNT WEBSTER AND MOUNT JACKSON

These peaks, the most southerly of the seven southern peaks in the Presidential Range, are ascended either via the Webster-Jackson Trail from the Crawford Depot, or via the Webster Cliff Trail, which leaves the east side of US Rte. 302 opposite the terminus of the Ethan Pond Trail and goes over the summits of Mts. Webster and Jackson to join the Crawford Path at Mt. Pierce (Mt. Clinton).

Webster-Jackson Trail (AMC)

The trail, blazed in blue, leaves the east side of US Rte. 302 0.1 mi. south of the Crawford Depot and 0.1 mi. north of the Gate of the Notch. The trail to Elephant Head, a ledge overlooking the Notch, leaves right at 0.1 mi. and reaches the ledge in 0.2 mi. The main trail bears a little left toward the brook and rises steadily on the south bank, then bears right (important turn) and up away from the brook at 0.2 mi. where a worn path continues straight ahead. The trail continues up the slope, crosses Little Mossy Brook at 0.3 mi., and continues in the same general direction, nearly level stretches alternating with sharp pitches. At 0.6 mi. from Rte. 302 a short trail (150 ft.) leads right to Bugle Cliff, a massive ledge overlooking Crawford Notch, where the view is well worth the slight extra effort required. The main trail then rises fairly steeply and soon crosses Flume Cascade Brook. About 0.5 mi. beyond the brook, within sound of Silver Cascade Brook, the trail divides, the left branch for Mt. Jackson and the right (straight ahead) for Mt. Webster. Since the two summits are connected by the Webster Cliff Trail, a circuit trip is possible.

Mount Webster

Continuing on the right branch, the trail immediately descends very steeply to the *brook (last sure water)*, which it crosses just below a beautiful cascade and pool. The trail continues straight ahead across the brook. Avoid a worn path leading downstream. The trail then climbs steadily south about 1 mi. to the Webster

THE SOUTHERN PEAKS

Cliff Trail, which it follows right about 200 yd. to the ledgy summit of Mt. Webster, where there is an excellent view of Crawford Notch and the mountains to the west and south.

Mount Jackson

Following the left branch of the fork of the Webster-Jackson Trail, the trail is fairly level until it comes within sight of the brook and begins to climb steadily. About 0.5 mi. above the fork, it crosses three branches of the brook in quick succession. Tisdale *Spring (last water, unreliable,* however there is frequently running water 10 to 20 ft. below the spring) is passed at the left (sign), a short distance below the base of the rocky cone, which the trail ascends rapidly. The summit is clear with the best view to be had of the southern peaks.

Webster-Jackson Trail (map 6)
Distances from US Rte. 302
- *to* Elephant Head: 0.1 mi.
- *to* Bugle Cliff: 0.6 mi.
- *to* Flume Cascade Brook: 0.9 mi.
- *to* Mt. Webster-Mt. Jackson fork: 1.4 mi., 1 hr.
- *to* Silver Cascade Brook: 1.4 mi.
- *to* Webster Cliff Trail junction: 2.3 mi.
- *to* Mt. Webster summit (via Webster Cliff Trail): 2.5 mi. (3.9 km.), 2¼ hr.
- *to* Mt. Jackson summit (via Webster Cliff Trail): 2.7 mi. (4.3 km.), 2½ hr.
- *to* US Rte. 302 (via Webster Cliff Trail): 5.3 mi.

Webster Cliff Trail (AMC)

This trail, a part of the Appalachian Trail, leaves the east side of US Rte. 302 (Crawford Notch Highway) opposite the terminus of the Ethan Pond Trail, and leads over Mts. Webster and Jackson to the Crawford Path at Mt. Pierce (Mt. Clinton). The entrance is about 1 mi. south of the Willey House Recreation Area at the Willey House site. It runs nearly east about 400 ft. to the Saco River, which it crosses by a bridge. The trail climbs to the terrace above and gradually ascends the south end of the ridge by a long diagonal through a hardwood forest. The trail grows steeper and rougher as it approaches the cliffs and swings more to the north. The trail bears right about 100 yd. below the slide, switches back and forth up the slope, climbs sunken steps and goes along left below an open ledge. Above the ledge, it turns left to a beautiful view down the Notch. After several level yards, the trail resumes the climb and soon emerges on the south end of the cliffs a little less than 1.8 mi. from the highway. It then turns north up the ridge for about 1 mi. at an easier grade, passing a 4-ft. cairn. Before reaching the summit of Mt. Webster, the trail alternates between woods and open cliff edges, where the finest views of Crawford Notch are obtained.

The trail then descends slightly toward Mt. Jackson, and in about 200 yd. the south leg of the Webster-Jackson trail to the Crawford Depot on Rte. 302 diverges left. The main trail runs generally north across three gullies to the end of the ridge connecting Mts. Jackson and Webster. It continues in the same direction with some further descent, then climbs sharply to the top of the ridge, runs over three small humps directly toward Mt. Jackson, and climbs a small gully to the cone. There is *no reliable water* on the trail. Tisdale *Spring (water unreliable)* is about 300 yd. below the summit of Mt. Jackson on the north leg of the Webster-Jackson trail to Rte. 302.

Toward Mt. Pierce, the trail leaves the summit of Mt. Jackson following a line of cairns running north and descends the ledges at the north end of the cone quite rapidly into the scrub. The Nauman Shelters formerly near this point have been removed. Water is not available here, and there is to be no camping in this area.

The trail soon emerges to wind through a large meadow with a good outlook on the right. North of the meadow the trail turns sharp left, drops into the woods, then continues up and down along the ridge toward Mt. Pierce. It descends gradually to Mizpah Spring Hut. Just before the hut, Mizpah Cutoff to the

Crawford Path diverges left (west), and the Mt. Clinton Trail to Oakes Gulf diverges right (southeast). Continuing past the west side of the hut, the trail ascends very rapidly for a few hundred yards, coming out at the lowest point of the meadow on the south summit of Mt. Pierce; it passes over the summit, turns somewhat right, and enters the woods. In about 0.3 mi. it emerges into the open on the main summit and follows cairns, cutting through the scrub to the large cairn at the peak. It then descends about 150 yd. in the same direction to the Crawford Path, which it joins at its highest point on the shoulder of Mt. Pierce, just after it leaves the woods.

Webster Cliff Trail (map 6)

Distances from US Rte. 302
- *to* south end of cliffs: *est.* 1.8 mi., 1½ hr.
- *to* Mt. Webster summit: *est.* 2.8 mi., 3 hr.
- *to* Mt. Jackson summit: *est.* 4 mi., 4 hr.
- *to* Mizpah Spring Hut: *est.* 5.8 mi., 5¼ hr.
- *to* Mt. Pierce summit: *est.* 6.5 mi. (10.5 km.), 5¾ hr.

Mizpah Cutoff (AMC)

This trail, which diverges right (east) from the Crawford Path 1.8 mi. above the Crawford House site, climbs the ridge at a moderate grade, passes through a fairly level area, and descends slightly to join the Webster Cliff Trail just before reaching Mizpah Spring Hut.

Mizpah Cutoff (map 6)

Distances from Crawford House site, US Rte. 302
- *to* west end of Mizpah Cutoff (via Crawford Path): 1.8 mi., 1 hr. 20 min.
- *to* Mizpah Spring Hut: 2.5 mi. (4 km.), 2 hr.

Mizpah Spring Hut (AMC)

The newest of the AMC huts was completed in 1965 and is located at about 3800 ft. elevation, on the site formerly occupied by the Mizpah Spring Shelter, at the junction of the Webster Cliff

Trail, the Mt. Clinton Trail, and the Mizpah Cutoff. The hut accommodates sixty guests, with sleeping quarters in eight rooms containing from four to ten bunks. This hut is open to the public from mid-June to mid-October. For current information contact Reservation Secretary, Pinkham Notch Camp, Box 298, Gorham, NH 03581 (603-466-2727). There are plans to move the campsite near the hut about 1 mi. west into the Elephant Brook watershed. The campsite has had a caretaker, and a fee is charged in summer.

OAKES GULF AND DRY RIVER

These areas are in the Presidential–Dry River Wilderness Area (see Section 2).

Dry River Trail (WMNF)

This trail leaves the east side of US Rte. 302, 0.3 mi. north of the entrance to Dry River Campground. From the highway the trail follows a clearly defined wood road, generally northeast, for 0.5 mi. to its junction with the bed of an old logging railroad. From here the trail follows the railroad bed for 0.4 mi. and stays on the north bank of the river to a point about 1.6 mi. from the highway, where it crosses to the east side on a suspension bridge. (The former Shelter #1 has been removed.) The trail continues on this side of the river, and at 3.0 mi. the Mt. Clinton Trail diverges left for Mizpah Spring Hut. In the next 1.5 mi. the Dry River Trail passes over some rough terrain, alternately climbing the hillside then descending to the valley floor. At approximately 4.5 mi. it turns sharply right, away from its former location, and climbs steeply for a short distance. The Isolation Trail diverges right a short distance beyond Isolation Brook, about 5 mi. from Rte. 302.

The Dry River Trail continues straight, and in about 0.1 mi. crosses another bridge, reaching a small island (formerly the location of Dry River Shelter #2, which was removed in March 1981). After the trail crosses a third bridge over the main river channel, the Mt. Eisenhower Trail diverges sharply left (downstream), and the Dry River Trail turns sharp right (northeast) and soon crosses the Dry River to the southeast bank (no bridge). This crossing may be impassable in times of high water. The trail follows a logging road away from the river and climbs steadily until it is above Dry River Falls. At 5.9 mi. a short side trail leaves left to a viewpoint a few yards away at the top of the falls and a pothole that should not be missed. Above the falls the trail crosses the river again and at 7.1 mi. passes Shelter #3. (It is planned to remove this shelter also by 1983.) The trail continues up through Oakes Gulf toward Mt. Monroe, then swings right up the headwall, passes a small alpine pool, and crosses over the top of the ridge passing south of the larger of the two Lakes of the Clouds to reach the Crawford Path, directly across from the Lakes of the Clouds Hut. The former route of the trail, which passes through an ecological area that is critical and very fragile, should be avoided.

Dry River Trail (map 6)
Distances from US Rte. 302
to Mt. Clinton Trail junction: 3 mi., 1¾ hr.
to Crawford Path junction: 10.8 mi. (17.3 km.), 7 hr. 25 min.

Mt. Clinton Trail (WMNF)

This trail diverges left from the Dry River Trail 3.0 mi. from US. Rte. 302, and immediately fords the Dry River. *Note*. This crossing may be impassable in high water. The trail soon begins a steady, generally northwest climb, following a brook, crossing it and several other small brooks many times. The second mile is less steep, but the last mile is mostly a steady climb that ends within about 100 yd. of Mizpah Spring Hut. The Dry River Cutoff enters from the right approximately 0.4 mi. below Mizpah Hut.

Mt. Clinton Trail (map 6)
Distances from Dry River Trail junction
   to Dry River Cutoff: 2.9 mi., 2½ hr.
   to Mizpah Spring Hut: 3.3 mi. (5.3 km.), 2 hr. 50 min.

Mt. Eisenhower Trail (WMNF)

The Mt. Eisenhower Trail diverges left from the Dry River Trail about 5.2 mi. from US Rte. 302, just beyond the third footbridge on the Dry River Trail. In a few steps, it leads right up a steep bank and joins an old logging road, which it follows for some distance. The Dry River Cutoff diverges left at 0.2 mi. The Mt. Eisenhower trail, generally leading north, keeps to the crest of the long ridge that runs south from a point midway between Franklin and Eisenhower. About 2 mi. from the Dry River Trail, the trail contours, and then descends somewhat before beginning the final ascent of the ridge crest by moderate grade, and continues for the most part along the ridge to treeline, joining the Crawford Path in the Eisenhower-Franklin col, 0.1 mi. north of the upper terminus of the Edmands Path.

Mt. Eisenhower Trail (map 6)
Distance from Dry River Trail junction
   to Crawford Path junction: 3 mi. (4.8 km.), 2 hr. 50 min.

Dry River Cutoff (AMC)

This trail diverges left from the Mt. Eisenhower Trail 0.2 mi. from its junction with the Dry River Trail. In approximately 150 yd. it descends steeply and crosses the northern fork of a branch of the Dry River, turns left, and in another 60 yd. crosses the southern fork to its south bank. The trail turns left, then bends right and follows the south bank of the stream in a generally northwest direction. At approximately 0.4 mi. the stream splits and the trail follows a narrow ridge between the two branches for 500 ft., where the stream recombines and the trail crosses to the north bank. It follows the stream, which is for the most part out of sight, at a moderate-to-steep grade until, at approximately 0.8

mi., the trail bends left to the stream. The trail parallels the stream for 40 yd., then crosses to the south bank, which it follows for another 40 yd. before bearing left away from the stream. It climbs at a moderate grade for another 0.3 mi. to the top of the minor ridge extending southeast from Mt. Pierce (Mt. Clinton). For the last 0.5 mi., to its junction with the Mt. Clinton Trail approximately 0.4 mi. below Mizpah Hut, the trail is practically level.

Dry River Cutoff (map 6)

Distance from Mt. Eisenhower Trail junction
  to Mt. Clinton Trail junction: 1.7 mi. (2.7 km.), 1 hr. 20 min.

SECTION 7

Montalban Ridge

The Montalban Ridge extends southward from Boott Spur and lies between the Rocky Branch and the Dry River. For convenience, it is subdivided into two parts in this section: the upper Montalban Ridge, which includes Mt. Isolation (4005 ft.), Mt. Davis (3840 ft.), Stairs Mountain (3460 ft.), and Mt. Resolution (3428 ft.); and the lower ridge — or southern Montalbans — which includes Mt. Parker (3015 ft.), Mt. Langdon (2423 ft.), Mt. Pickering (1945 ft.), and Mt. Stanton (1725 ft.). The Bemis Ridge extends southwesterly from Mt. Resolution to Mt. Crawford (3129 ft.), then south to Mt. Hope (2520 ft.) and Hart Ledge (2040 ft.).

The view from Mt. Davis is in the first rank of White Mountain views, and those from Mt. Crawford, Mt. Isolation, and Mt. Parker are scarcely inferior. The Giant Stairs are a wild and picturesque feature of this region. Notchland (formerly Bemis), not far from where the Davis Path begins, is the site of the historic Mt. Crawford House, usually referred to as the first White Mountain hotel.

NORTHERN MONTALBANS

The Davis Path, constructed by Nathaniel P. T. Davis in 1844, was the third bridle path leading up Mt. Washington. It was in use until 1853 or 1854, but soon after became impassable, and eventually went out of existence. It was reopened in 1910. Sections of it leading up Mt. Crawford and Stairs Mountain give some idea of the magnitude of the task Davis performed.

The Montalban Ridge north from Mt. Crawford and the upper Rocky Branch valley, both of which are covered in this section, are in the Presidential-Dry River Wilderness Area. Entry permits are no longer required.

Refer to map 6, the Mt. Washington Range.

DAVIS PATH (AMC)

This path leaves US Rte. 302 on the west side of the Saco River at the suspension footbridge (Bemis Bridge). There is a parking lot on the east side of the highway, about 100 yd. south of Bemis Bridge. Beyond the east end of the bridge, the trail passes through private land. Continue straight east across an overgrown field and a small brook and turn southeast on an embankment. Ignore other branching paths and blazes, which relate to new housing. At about 0.3 mi. the path turns east and enters the woods (WMNF and Wilderness Area) on a logging road. It then crosses a dry brook and, leaving the logging road at the foot of a steep hill 0.8 mi. from Rte. 302, soon enters the old, carefully graded bridle path and begins to ascend the steep ridge connecting Mt. Crawford with Mt. Hope. Attaining the crest, the Davis Path follows this ridge north, mounting over bare ledges with good outlooks. At 2.3 mi. from Rte. 302, at the foot of a large sloping ledge, a trail diverges left for 0.3 mi. to the peaked and higher summit of Mt. Crawford (3129 ft.), from which there is a view worth the extra walk.

From this junction the path turns northeast, descends slightly to the col between the peak and dome of Mt. Crawford, and resumes the ascent. It soon passes over the ledgy shoulder of Crawford Dome and dips to the Crawford-Resolution col. Leaving this col, the path runs north, rises slightly, and keeps close to the same level along the steep west side of Mt. Resolution. The Mt. Parker Trail, which diverges right (east) at 3.8 mi., leads in about 0.6 mi. to the open summit of Mt. Resolution. A trail that branches left at this junction descends a short distance to the AMC Resolution Shelter, an open camp with room for eight, situated on a small branch of Sleeper Brook. (USFS policies call for eventual removal of all shelters from Wilderness Areas, this one probably by 1983.) Ordinarily there is *water* just behind the shelter, but in dry seasons it may be necessary to go down the brook a short distance. In most seasons, this is the first *water* after starting up the grade of Crawford and the last before the site of the former Isolation Shelter.

At 4.1 mi. the path passes just west of the col between Mt. Resolution and Stairs Mountain. Here the Stairs Col Trail to the Rocky Branch diverges right. The path now veers northwest, passing west of the precipitous Giant Stairs, ascending gradually along a steep mountainside, then zigzagging boldly northeast toward the flat top of Stairs Mountain. Shortly before the path reaches the top of the slope, a branch trail leads right a few steps to the "Down-look," a good viewpoint. At the head of the ascent, 4.5 mi. from Rte. 302, a branch trail leads right (southeast) 0.2 mi. to the head of the Giant Stairs (about 3400 ft.) and an inspiring view.

The Davis Path continues down the north ridge of Stairs Mountain for about 1 mi., then runs east in a col for about 200 yd. Turning north again (watch for this turn), it passes over a small rise and descends into another col.

The path next begins to ascend Mt. Davis, whose successive summits are strung along north and south for 2.5 mi., keeping to the west slopes.

At 8.5 mi. a branch trail diverges right (east) to the summit of Mt. Davis (about 3840 ft.), where the view is considered the finest on the Montalban Ridge. This branch trail, marked by cairns, continues southeast to a *spring* (*water unreliable*) 150 or 200 yd. south and a little east of the summit. This side trip requires little more than 10 min. each way, and is well worthwhile in clear weather.

From its junction with this branch trail, the main path descends to the col between Mts. Davis and Isolation, then ascends the latter. At 9.6 mi. a branch trail diverges left, leading in a short distance to the summit (4005 ft.). The open summit provides impressive views in all directions.

At 10.6 mi. the path leads past the site of the former Isolation Shelter and the junction with the east branch of the Isolation

Trail, which leads to the Rocky Branch Valley. There is *water* down the Isolation Trail to the right (east).

Leaving the shelter site, the path climbs a southwest ridge and passes close to two minor summits. At about 0.5 mi. from the shelter site, the west half of the Isolation Trail descends left to the Dry River valley. At about 11.6 mi., just to the left of the path, there is a good view of the headwall of Oakes Gulf with its cascades. Turning northeast, the path reaches treeline (4700 ft.) at about 12 mi., and then passes a *spring (water unreliable)*. The path, marked by cairns, then leads across a broad, gently sloping lawn and passes close to a rocky summit at 12.5 mi. Here is a good view, and the Glen Boulder Trail joins on the right nearby.

At 12.9 mi. the path passes just west of the summit of Boott Spur (5500 ft.), and the Boott Spur Trail to AMC Pinkham Notch Camp diverges right (east). (The Boott Spur Link leaves the Boott Spur Trail in 0.8 mi. and descends to the Hermit Lake shelters. For overnight use, buy permit in advance at Pinkham Notch Camp; see Section 3.) Turning northwest the path leads along the almost level ridges of Boott Spur and crosses Bigelow Lawn. At 13.5 mi. the Lawn Cutoff diverges right to Tuckerman Junction, affording the shortest but not the easiest route to the summit of Mt. Washington. A short distance farther on, the Camel Trail diverges left (west) to the Lakes of the Clouds Hut.

At 13.9 mi. the Davis Path begins to follow the original location of the Crawford Path, crosses the Tuckerman Crossover, and in about 0.3 mi. is joined on the right by the Southside Trail. A little farther on the Davis Path enters the present Crawford Path, which affords an easy route to the summit of Mt. Washington.

Davis Path (map 6)

Distances from US Rte. 302

to Mt. Crawford summit branch trail junction: *est.* 2.3 mi.
to Crawford Dome: *est.* 2.6 mi.
to Resolution Shelter: 3.8 mi.
to Stairs Col Trail junction: 4.1 mi.

to Giant Stairs branch trail junction: *est*. 4.5 mi.
to Mt. Davis summit branch trail junction: *est*. 8.5 mi.
to Mt. Isolation summit: *est*. 10.4 mi.
to Isolation Trail, east branch junction: *est*. 10.6 mi.
to Glen Boulder Trail junction: *est*. 12.5 mi.
to Boott Spur Trail junction: *est*. 12.9 mi.
to Lawn Cutoff junction: *est*. 13.5 mi.
to Lakes of the Clouds Hut (via Camel Trail): *est*. 14.4 mi.
to Crawford Path junction: *est*. 14.4 mi.
to Mt. Washington summit (via Tuckerman Junction and Tuckerman Ravine Trail): *est*. 14.5 mi.
to Mt. Washington summit (via Crawford Path): *est*. 15 mi. (24.1 km.)

GIANT STAIRS AND STAIRS COL

The Giant Stairs are two great steplike ledges at the south extremity of the ridge of Stairs Mountain. They are quite regular in form and are visible from many points. The view from the top is striking, and the surrounding scenery is wild and unusual. There is no trail to a third and somewhat similar cliff, sometimes called the "Back Stair," east of the main summit. Stairs Col lies between the foot of the Stairs and Mt. Resolution. These points are reached via the Davis Path from US Rte. 302 in Crawford Notch, or via the Rocky Branch and Stairs Col trails from the Rocky Branch valley.

Stairs Col Trail (AMC)

This trail leaves the Rocky Branch Trail left opposite the Rocky Branch Shelter #1 area, and follows an old railroad siding 150 ft. It then turns sharp left, crosses a swampy area, and climbs several yards to a logging road where it enters the Dry River Wilderness Area.

From here nearly to Stairs Col, the trail follows a logging road along the ravine of a brook. The last part is rather steep. (Obtain *water* from the brook, or from one of its tributaries that cross the trail high in the ravine, because there is no permanent water in the col, on Stairs Mountain, or on the Davis Path below the col, except at Resolution Shelter; see Davis Path.) The trail crosses Stairs Col and continues down the west side a short distance until it meets the Davis Path.

Stairs Col Trail (map 6)
Distance from Rocky Branch Trail junction
  to Davis Path junction: 1.9 mi. (3.1 km.), 1 hr. 55 min.
Distances from Stairs Col Trail/Davis Path junction
  to Giant Stairs branch trail (via Davis Path): 0.6 mi., ½ hr.
  to Mt. Resolution summit (via Davis Path and Mt. Parker Trail): *est.* 0.7 mi., ½ hr.
  to Mt. Crawford summit (via Davis Path and branch trail): 2 mi., 1 hr.
  to US Rte. 302 (via Davis Path): 4.1 mi., 2 hr.

ROCKY BRANCH TRAIL (WMNF)

The middle portion of this trail is in the Presidential-Dry River Wilderness Area.

The valley of the Rocky Branch of the Saco River lies between the two longest subsidiary ridges of Mt. Washington — the Montalban Ridge to the west, and the Rocky Branch Ridge to the east.

From just east of the bridge where US Rte. 302 crosses the Rocky Branch, or 1 mi. west of the junction of Rte. 302 and NH Rte. 16, follow the Jericho Rd. — asphalt for about 1 mi., then a good unpaved road — about 4.4 mi. to the beginning of the trail.

The trail immediately crosses Otis Brook and in 0.7 mi. crosses to the west bank of the Rocky Branch. This crossing and the subsequent ones are difficult at high water.

The trail then bears right (northwest) and soon joins an old railroad bed, which it mostly follows from there on. At 1 mi. beyond the river crossing, the Stairs Col Trail diverges left, and a spur trail leads right about 200 ft. to WMNF Rocky Branch Shelter #1 area. (In addition to the shelter there are five 5-person and one 8-person tent platforms.)

The Rocky Branch Trail continues north along the old bed and crosses the main stream four times in the next 2 mi. At the first crossing it enters the Dry River Wilderness Area. Then, continuing generally north along the west bank, and at times on the old railroad bed, the trail reaches the Rocky Branch Shelter #2 in two more miles. (USFS Wilderness policies call for removal of this shelter, probably by 1983.) Just north of the shelter, where the trail crosses to the east bank, the Isolation Trail continues north along the river. The Rocky Branch Trail follows the east bank of the river for a short distance, then swings away right (east) to make an easy climb to a col on the Rocky Branch Ridge. At the height-of-land it leaves the Wilderness Area. From this col the trail follows an old logging road for more than a mile, close to a small brook for part of the distance, slabbing the side of an unnamed hump across the head of the valley of Miles Brook (*water*). Then, leaving the logging road right, it zigzags down the steep slope and, rejoining the logging road, descends at a moderate grade. At about 0.5 mi. from Rte. 16 a ski-touring trail enters from the left and shortly leaves right. The Rocky Branch Trail continues straight and terminates at a new parking lot on Rte. 16, about 400 yd. north of the Dana Place, 5 mi. north of Jackson.

Rocky Branch Trail (map 6)
Distances from Jericho Rd.

to Stairs Col Trail junction (Rocky Branch Shelter #1):
   1.8 mi., 55 min.

to Isolation Trail junction (Rocky Branch Shelter #2): 6 mi.,
   3 hr. 10 min.

to height-of-land (Wilderness Area Boundary): 6.5 mi.,
   3 hr. 40 min.

to NH Rte. 16: 10 mi. (16.1 km.), 5½ hr.

MONTALBAN RIDGE

Isolation Trail (WMNF)

This trail is part of the shortest route from a highway (NH Rte. 16) to Mt. Isolation. From the Rocky Branch Trail just north of Rocky Branch Shelter #2 (to be removed), the Isolation Trail diverges left and follows the river north, with several crossings, for 1 mi. The trail then strikes up a small brook to join the Davis Path at the former site of Isolation Shelter. Coinciding with the Davis Path, it climbs north for about 0.5 mi., then diverges left and descends southwest into Oakes Gulf. The trail finally reaches a branch of the Dry River and terminates at the Dry River Trail, 0.1 mi. south of the site of Dry River Shelter #2.

Isolation Trail (map 6)

Distances from Rocky Branch Trail junction

to Davis Path junction: 2.5 mi.

to Dry River Trail junction: *est.* 5.3 mi.

Distances from northeast end Rocky Branch Trail, NH Rte. 16

to Isolation Trail junction: 4.0 mi., 2¾ hr.

to Davis Path junction: 6.5 mi., 4½ hr.

to Mt. Isolation (via Davis Path): 7.5 mi. (11.6 km.), 5 hr.

THE SOUTHERN MONTALBANS

These mountains, with the upper Montalban Ridge, form the longest subsidiary ridge to Mt. Washington.

Mount Langdon Trail (WMNF)

From the four corners at the Bartlett Hotel in Bartlett follow River St. north about 0.5 mi., across the bridge over the Saco. The trail begins at the bend in the road (to the west) just beyond. In about 200 ft. it joins a new logging road and follows it north uphill toward Cave Mountain. The trail to Cave Mountain leaves left in about 0.3 mi. Continue on the main logging road to the WMNF boundary (red paint blazes) at 1 mi., where the logging activity ended and the trail becomes an old logging road. Just beyond the boundary the trail crosses a *brook (last sure water)*. About 0.3 mi. beyond brook the trail bears right, leaving the logging road, and then bears right uphill again, following another old logging road for a short distance.

The Mt. Langdon Trail ascends Oak Ridge through fine oak woods, heads north over the wooded summit, and descends sharply to the Oak Ridge-Parker col, where it bears right at a junction with the Mt. Parker Trail. The Mt. Langdon Trail leads in 0.5 mi. to the WMNF Mt. Langdon Shelter, capacity eight. A short distance down this trail from the junction is the beginning of a *brook (water unreliable)* on the left (north). In dry weather, *water* may be found in pools in brookbed both north and east from the shelter. The summit of Mt. Langdon is reached from the shelter via the Mt. Stanton Trail.

Mt. Langdon Trail (map 6)
Distances from River St., Bartlett NH
to Oak Ridge: *est.* 2.1 mi.
to Oak Ridge-Mt. Parker col: *est.* 2.5 mi.
to Mt. Langdon Shelter: *est.* 3 mi., 2 hr.
to Mt. Langdon (via Mt. Stanton Trail): 3.7 mi. (5.9 km.), 2 ¾ hr.

Mount Parker Trail (SSOC)

This trail begins in the Oak Ridge-Mt. Parker col, departing from the Mt. Langdon Trail about 2.5 mi. from Bartlett. (There is *no sure water* on the Parker-Resolution ridge before Resolution Shelter. The *last water* on the Mt. Langdon Trail is from the brook 1 mi. from Bartlett or from near the Mt. Langdon Shelter.)

The Mt. Parker Trail continues straight ahead north in the col from the junction, swinging right through some old blow-downs and then sharp left as it joins an old graded path at a switchback. It follows this, climbing easily with many switchbacks, to an open spot with good views to the southwest. It then slabs to the east of the ridge through beech and oak woods until it reaches the base of some cliffs, where a side path leads left up through a gully to a good viewpoint. Continuing, the trail descends right with a switchback before turning left and climbing steeply onto the main ridge. Heading generally northwest, the trail climbs easily to an outlook to the southwest, then turns right and levels off before the last short, steep climb to the open summit of Mt. Parker, where there are excellent views.

Continuing north, the trail descends to the long ridge between Mt. Parker and Mt. Resolution and passes over three "bumps," alternating between spruce woods and open ledges with good views. It then slabs the west and south sides of the remainder of the ridge until it reaches the southeast corner of Mt. Resolution, where it turns sharp right and zigzags steeply up to the col between the main summit ridge and the south summit (marked "3250" on the map). Here a short branch trail leads left over the open south summit, where there are fine views, and rejoins the main trail in about 100 yd. Beyond this junction the trail winds along the flat top of Mt. Resolution until it reaches a large cairn on an open ledge with excellent views. The true summit is about 200 yd. east-northeast off the trail. From the cairn the trail descends sharply into a gully where it crosses a *brook* (*water unreliable*), then heads northwest down past several ledges, and finally drops steeply to the Davis Path, opposite the branch trail to Resolution Shelter.

Mt. Parker Trail (map 6)
Distances from River St., Bartlett NH

to start of Mt. Parker Trail (via Mt. Langdon Trail): *est.* 1.3 mi., 1¼ hr.

to first "bump" Mt. Parker-Mt. Resolution ridge: *est.* 1.9 mi.

to third "bump" Mt. Parker-Mt. Resolution ridge: *est.* 2.1 mi.

to Mt. Resolution, south summit branch trail junction: *est.* 3 mi., 2¼ hr.

to cairn near Mt. Resolution summit: *est.* 3.5 mi., 2 hr. 40 min.

to Davis Path junction: 4.1 mi. (6.7 km.), 3 hr.

SECTION 7

Mount Stanton Trail (SSOC)

Leave the north side of US Rte. 302, 1.8 mi. west of Glen Station and a short distance east of the bridge over the Saco River, and follow an old CCC camp road west about 0.3 mi. past an old covered bridge to a new housing development. At the trail sign the yellow-blazed Mt. Stanton Trail leaves the road on the right (north). It enters the woods on an old logging road, which shortly merges with a new development road. In about 500 ft. it crosses another new road, then continues for about 400 ft. before turning right on a second crossroad. In about 200 ft. the trail enters the woods on the left (sign), and in about another 250 ft. crosses the WMNF boundary (red blazes). Shortly afterward it swings sharply left and climbs moderately to the base of White's Ledge. After a steep climb to the top of the ridge it swings left (west) and follows the crest, open to the south, to another short but very steep climb up the cone of Mt. Stanton to the south summit, where there are excellent views to the south.

The trail swings north over the true summit and descends to the top of a cliff with views to the north. Here the trail swings left and slabs down to the Stanton-Pickering col. Continuing west the trail ascends rapidly, with several switchbacks, to the cone of Mt. Pickering, bears north over the wooded summit, and reaches the top of a ledge with more fine views to the north. At this point the trail swings left, descends to the long ridge between Mt. Pickering and Mt. Langdon, and passes over four interesting humps known as "the Crippies." The last two have open summits with fine views in all directions.

From the last Crippie the trail descends somewhat along the north side of the ridge towards Mt. Langdon, then climbs steeply north along the east side of the mountain, finally swinging left uphill over open slabs, which afford fine views east over the Pickering-Stanton ridge. From the top of the slabs, the trail heads north through the woods to more open slabs with views to the north. The trail then swings sharply left, climbs to the wooded summit cone, which it passes on the right, and comes out on a gravel slope with views to the west. Here it turns right about 100 yd. across the top of the slope, bears northwest and descends rapidly for about 0.5 mi., and runs nearly level about 0.3 mi. to a *brook (first water)*. Mt. Langdon Shelter, where the Mt. Stanton Trail ends, is a short distance across the brook. In dry weather *water* can be obtained from a larger brook to the right (north) of the shelter. From the shelter to Bartlett is 3 mi. via the Mt. Langdon Trail; to the Davis Path at Resolution Shelter is 4.7 mi. via Mt. Langdon and Mt. Parker trails.

Mt. Stanton Trail (map 6)
Distances from Old CCC Camp Rd., off US Rte. 302
to Mt. Stanton south summit: 1.6 mi., 1 hr. 20 min.
to Mt. Pickering summit: 2.4 mi., 1 hr. 55 min.
to fourth Crippie: 3.6 mi., 2½ mi.
to Mt. Langdon summit: 4.8 mi., 3¼ hr.
to Mt. Langdon trail junction at Mt. Langdon Shelter: 5.5 mi. (8.8 km.), 3 hr. 50 min.

Cave Mountain

Remarkable for the shallow cave near its wooded summit, this 1397-ft. mountain is easily reached from Bartlett by River St., which runs north from the four corners at the Bartlett Hotel and crosses the Saco River. Follow the Mt. Langdon Trail for about 0.3 mi. to the left fork to Cave Mountain. In less than 0.5 mi. this branch trail leads up a steep gravel slope to the cave. A faint trail to the right of the cave leads, after a short scramble, to the top of the cliff in which the cave is located, where there is an excellent view of Bartlett.

Cave Mountain (map 6)
Distances from Mt. Langdon/branch trail junction
to cave: *est.* 0.5 mi.
to Cave Mountain summit: *est.* 0.3 mi.

Hart Ledge

This fine cliff, situated on a bend in the Saco River just above Bartlett, rises more than 1000 ft. above the meadows at its foot and affords commanding views to the east, west, and south. There is no trail. From Bartlett take the road leading north, cross the bridge to the north bank of the Saco, and turning west proceed about 2 mi. to the house at the second railroad crossing, directly across the ford from Sawyer's Rock. Follow the road north across the railroad tracks and turn left in about 300 ft. at the old Cobb maple sugar mill. In about 0.5 mi., where another road crosses diagonally from the left (and both roads are barricaded), continue straight ahead. In another 0.3 mi., just before a recent borrow pit, turn right (north) uphill. About 0.3 mi. farther, where the road turns sharply left, continue straight north, first on an old road, then through a logged area, into the ravine of a brook (not shown on maps). Follow the ravine up onto the ridge. This route permits an easy line of ascent west of the inaccessible line of crags. Give them plenty of leeway and approach the top from behind, turning right near the crest of the ridge. The distance from the house to the top of the ledge is about 2.3 mi.

SECTION 8

Presidential Range in Winter

According to Ticknor's *White Mountains,* published in 1887, the higher peaks of New Hampshire "seem to have received the name of White Mountains from the sailors off the coast, to whom they were a landmark and a mystery lifting their crowns of brilliant snow against the blue sky from October until June." Winter on the lower trails in the White Mountains may require only snowshoes and some warm clothing. But above timberline, conditions are often such that the equipment and experience needed to deal with them are of a different magnitude. Helpful information can be found in "Don't Die on the Mountain," by Dan H. Allen ($1, available from the AMC) and *Winter Hiking and Camping* by John A. Danielson (1982, Adirondack Mountain Club).

WINTER WEATHER

The conditions on the Presidential Range in winter are as severe as any in North America south of the mountains of Alaska and the Yukon Territory. On Mt. Washington summit in winter, winds *average* 44 mph, and daily high temperatures average 9° C. There are few calm days. The Mt. Washington Observatory, established in 1932, has often reported wind velocities in excess of 100 mph, and on April 12, 1934, a gust of 231 mph was timed. Temperatures are often below zero, record low for the present station being −46° F. The combination of high wind and low temperature has such a cooling effect that the worst conditions on Mt. Washington are approximately equal to the worst reported from Antarctica, despite the much greater cold in the latter region. Extremely severe storms also can come up suddenly and unexpectedly.

The winter of 1968-69 was the severest on record. New avalanches occurred on Lion Head and on Mt. Madison, in Madison Gulf, and in King and Ammonoosuc ravines. During the storm of February 24-26, 1969, the observatory recorded a snowfall of 97.8 inches. Within a 24-hour period during that storm, a total of 49.3 inches was recorded, a record for the mountain and for all weather observation stations in the United States. The previous 24-hour record (also nationwide) was February 10-11, 1969, when 40.6 inches was measured. The total snowfall from July 1, 1968, to June 30, 1969, was 566.4 inches, 222 inches more than the previous record.

PHYSICAL FITNESS, CLOTHING, AND EQUIPMENT

Severe weather and unfavorable snow conditions, for example deep powder below treeline or a breakable crust above, may put a climbing party to its ultimate test of physical fitness. People should not climb at this time of the year unless they have prepared by recent regular exercise, such as running, to face these adverse conditions. A safe size for a party is not less than three, or preferably four. Above treeline, they should stay close together at all times.

For a full day with a full pack, a hiker will need around 5500 calories. Candy, mintcake, and the like provide quick energy. Fats, like butter, provide prolonged energy.

A compass, map, and this *Guide*, well studied in advance, are more important than ever.

Clothing should be carefully chosen. Ordinarily, while climbing to timberline, relatively little should be worn, and the body should be suitably ventilated. Overdressing increases the possibility that clothing will become damp with perspiration. Once activity decreases or exposure increases, perspiration is the greatest cause of chill. Wool clothing is best for all winter hiking and climbing because of its insulating value, wet or dry. With two or three layers of wool clothing, winter hikers can better regulate body temperature when moving or resting. Wind parkas, alone or with wool depending on conditions, provide further versatility for body temperature maintenance. Cotton clothing, especially bluejeans, is not adequate, not safe, and not comfortable for winter hiking, skiing, or camping.

Parkas filled with down or with some synthetics provide excellent insulation for camping and some above-timberline hiking, but they are usually too hot and restrictive for hikers with packs. Down has the disadvantage of losing much of its insulating value if it becomes wet with snow, rain, or perspiration. High-loft fiberfills do not lose so much of their value when wet. In the White Mountains, where the weather can change very fast, hikers should always have rain gear and, if camping, a tent fly.

Hikers exposed to the wind, especially above timberline, are almost certain to want extra clothing, which must include a parka, warm mittens, and a face mask and goggles or a snorkel hood to avoid frostbite. Provisions for additional dry clothing should take into consideration the possibility that caps and mittens may be blown away.

Summer boots should not be used. Cold weather military boots — "Mickey Mouse" boots — are excellent as long as the felt inside them remains dry. For boots with removable liners, spare dry liners should be carried.

Crampons and snowshoes with creepers attached beneath the bindings are essential. During a trip, it may be necessary to switch from snowshoes to crampons and back several times, and these changes will be less agonizing if the equipment can be easily removed from or attached to the pack. It is vital to try on, try out, and adjust all equipment in a relatively warm place in advance. Camping equipment, such as stoves with pumps, also should be tried out in advance in winter conditions. If crampons might be needed on the upper half of a steep slope (as on Lion Head), it is better to put them on at the bottom.

Extra supplies, in addition to clothing and food, should include sun goggles and means to repair broken bindings and cope with possible emergencies. Strong nylon twine, rawhide, a knife, matches, and flashlights or, preferably, a headlamp, a first aid kit, and extra quick-energy food would be very useful at such times.

Finally, some people tend to overlook the possibility that they may get thirsty. Snow is not a good source of water because it requires energy to melt. It is advisable to carry a canteen of water, wrapped in a wool shirt or sock to keep it from freezing. Use a wide-mouthed water bottle. In the coldest weather, carry it next to the body. Dehydration is a more serious problem in winter than in summer in the mountains.

HYPOTHERMIA

Any winter emergency is likely to involve hypothermia or exposure. Hypothermia — the inability to stay warm because of injury, exhaustion, lack of sufficient food, and inadequate or wet clothing — is a very serious danger. The symptoms are uncontrolled shivering, impaired speech and movement, lowered body temperature, and drowsiness. The result is death, unless the victim (who usually does not understand the situation) is rewarmed. The victim should be given dry clothing and placed in a sleeping bag with someone else in it, then quick-energy food, and, when full consciousness is regained, something warm (not hot) to drink. Do not rewarm too quickly. Stay with the victim until help arrives. Many winter rescues in the White Mountains involve hypothermia victims.

Accordingly, a well-equipped party will carry at least one sleeping bag, a foam pad, and perhaps a tent shell, even on day trips.

INJURIES

Injuries are both more likely and more threatening in winter. An injured person unable to walk should be placed in a sleeping bag if possible. If outside help is needed for rescue, fill out an accident report form on back of a map. At least one person should stay with the victim while another goes for help, which is why parties should have at least three or four people.

REGISTERING

Winter hikers or climbers who leave from Pinkham Notch or from the Appalachia parking area should register at Pinkham Notch Camp, at Lowe's Store, or with John H. Boothman (WMNF Forest Warden) in Randolph. Note: On the summit of Mt. Washington, no buildings are open to the public in winter.

SNOWSHOEING

Each snowshoer should carry an ice axe or at least a ski pole. Since many trails are hard to find, it's a good idea to hike a trail in the summer or fall before doing it in winter. Take account of the short winter days: set a "turn around" time and stick to it, and carry lights. In general, don't split the group unless an emergency requires it, or unless each subgroup is strong enough on its own — which will not usually be the case, since the most common motive for splitting up is that some members are weaker.

Allow at least double the time needed to hike the same trail in summer. With full backpacks and fresh snow, a party may cover only 5 miles a day.

Air pockets can form under small fir or spruce trees that may be completely covered by snow, setting "spruce traps" for unwary hikers, especially those without snowshoes.

In summer or fall, it's nice to take circular hikes — going up one trail, crossing two or more summits, and descending another trail. In winter, you should be very sure you can find your trail for the descent. If you descend on the same trail you went up, you can usually follow your own tracks out unless, as occasionally happens, the wind has covered them with snow. But a different trail for the descent can cause problems if no one else has broken it out since the last snowfall, especially if the trail is steep and you try to follow it at the end of a relatively long hike on a short winter's day. (For example, don't plan to circle up the Old Bridle Path to Lafayette, Lincoln, and down the Falling Waters Trail.)

If in doubt, do consult this *Guide* and maps.

ABOVE TIMBERLINE

Winter hiking above the trees requires redoubled caution. On an average winter day in the White Mountains, the winds will be too strong. Ice axe and crampon experience under qualified instruction are mandatory, along with a good amount of below-timberline winter hiking.

WINTER CAMPING

Camping out in the winter in the White Mountains, with temperatures that can be $-20°$ F. or below, involves serious risk of frostbite and hypothermia, even for individuals who appear to be fully equipped. This is even truer at high elevations. Camping above timberline is extremely dangerous. It should be noted that the USFS has removed the Edmands Col emergency shelter, which had been improperly used for planned overnights.

As with rock climbing, it is doubtful that adequate skills for winter camping can be learned from a book, and this book does not presume to teach such skills.

WINTER TRAVEL

In the early 1960s, a trip to timberline in the winter often was a struggle in itself. But year-long use of trails in the 1970s and 1980s has been substantial. Frequently, a beaten path can be found heading toward most of the high peaks. A nice winter Saturday may find over a dozen people plodding up the Old Bridle Path to Lafayette. The danger is that it looks too easy, which leads to overestimating what is possible and underestimating the equipment required.

Obviously, many trails are infrequently used, and climbing just after a heavy snowfall can be like the "good" old days. If you have the option, avoid trails that ascend steeply or slab along a river valley. Steep slopes and the areas below them are subject to avalanches. Moderate grades, shortness, and shelter from the prevailing west winds are considerations in choosing a route. Among preferred snowshoe trails are: on Mt. Moosilauke, the Gorge Brook Trail; the Lonesome Lake and Fishin' Jimmy trails; the Liberty Spring Trail; on Mt. Lafayette, the Old Bridle Path; the Crawford Path up to Mt. Clinton; and the 19-Mile Brook and Carter Dome trails.

Sometimes trails are hard to follow even at the bottom. In a hardwood forest it is sometimes difficult in winter to tell where the trail does *not* go (this does not apply to the old logging railroads of the Pemigewasset "Wilderness"). Higher up, the snow may be so deep that the evidence of a cleared trail lies beneath the snow. Above timberline, trail signs and even the big cairns on the Gulfside Trail and the Crawford Path may be buried. In very deep snow, without a packed trail to follow, it would, for instance, be hard to locate and follow the Falling Waters Trail as it descends the broad ridge off Little Haystack.

Caution. In the Presidential Range, many ravines — the Great Gulf, Madison and Oakes gulfs, Raymond Cataract, the Gulf of Slides, and Castle, Huntington, Jefferson, King, and Tuckerman ravines — have open ice and snow slopes, with the accompanying danger of avalanche, that require a knowledge of technical climbing, which this chapter does not presume to give. Stay out until you have acquired the necessary skills. Ravines may be officially closed — even to qualified climbers — by the USFS during some periods of avalanche danger.

The most variable factor in winter hiking is the weather. Under no circumstances should you proceed or continue above treeline if conditions are deteriorating. To do so is to take a risk in which the odds are heavily against you. The cone of Mt. Washington in particular is no place to be in bad winter weather. During whiteout conditions, features of the terrain vanish, including such a seemingly obvious landmark as the Mt. Washington Auto Rd. Do not count on finding the cog railway either. Therefore, to circle the cone looking for either one makes little sense. In the face of bad weather, the only safe direction is down (with great caution and navigational care).

AMMONOOSUC RAVINE TRAIL

Because the road into the Marshfield station of the cog railway is not plowed, this trail is seldom used in the winter. However, a few notes for the descent are given here in case a climbing party is trapped by bad weather in the vicinity of the Lakes of the Clouds Hut.

The start from the hut is down a small ridge dividing two depressions and then into the right or more easterly of these. The direction is fixed exactly by a prominent slide showing as a broad band of snow on an opposite ridge of Mt. Washington; in a storm lay a compass course directly toward magnetic north. Once in the depression, follow the brookbed down to the first waterfall. Go around this, steeply, on the right (northeast) to the head of the big gorge. Here, on the right, a side trail leads right to the main trail. The main trail then descends on the right of the gorge to a pool at its foot, where it crosses to the left bank. Then the brook itself can probably be followed for some distance; in case of open water the trail lies for the most part on the left (south) bank and near at hand.

SKIING

For alpine skiing on Mt. Washington, see the end of Section 3. For cross-country skiing (ski touring), suitable trails are occasionally mentioned in this *Guide*, but a separate book is needed for adequate information.

SECTION 9

The Appalachian Mountain Club and Its Activities

The Appalachian Mountain Club (AMC) was organized in 1876 and was subsequently incorporated both in Massachusetts and in New Hampshire. It is the oldest, and largest, mountain club in the United States. It has made substantial contributions to various branches of geography, and has taken a leading part in efforts to preserve the beauty and economic value of the mountains and forests, and to promote backcountry research and education. It has built and maintains about 400 miles of foot trails and 20 shelters in New Hampshire and Maine.

The Club publishes a semiannual magazine, *Appalachia*, a monthly *Bulletin*, guidebooks, and other books.

AMC headquarters are in its own building, 5 Joy Street, Boston, Massachusetts. The information center and library are open to the public Monday through Friday, from 9:00 A.M. to 5:00 P.M. The information center is a resource for questions about trails and camping. It also sells guidebooks and books on outdoor recreation published by other publishers as well as by the AMC. Club-sponsored lectures, meetings, and social gatherings are held in Boston. The AMC also sponsors weekly outings and longer excursions, including some to foreign countries. Chapters in Maine, eastern New York, the Catskills, greater Philadelphia (Delaware Valley Chapter), New Hampshire, Connecticut, Rhode Island (Narragansett Chapter), Vermont, and Massachusetts (Worcester, Boston, Southeastern Massachusetts, and Berkshire chapters) also hold outings and meetings. There is opportunity to participate in trail clearing, skiing, canoeing, rock climbing, and other outdoor activities, in addition to hiking.

The Club now has more than 28,000 members. It invites all who love the woods and mountains and wish to contribute to their protection to join. Membership is open to the public upon completion of an application form and payment of an initial fee and annual dues. Information on membership, as well as the names and addresses of the secretaries of local chapters, may be obtained by writing to the Appalachian Mountain Club, 5 Joy St., Boston, MA 02108, or by telephoning (617-523-0636).

AMC Trails

Development, construction, and maintenance of backcountry trails and facilities have been a major focus of the AMC's public-service efforts since the Club's inception in 1876. Today, through twelve chapters, numerous camps, and its trails program, the AMC is responsible for maintenance and management of nearly 1000 miles of trails, including over 250 miles of the Appalachian Trail, many miles of ski trails, and more than twenty shelters and tent sites throughout the Northeast. The largest portion of these is in the White Mountain area of New Hampshire and Maine, where the AMC maintains over 100 hiking trails with an aggregate length of some 350 miles.

In general, trails are maintained to provide a clear pathway while protecting and minimizing damage to the environment. Some may offer rough and difficult passage. The Club reserves the right to discontinue any without notice, and expressly disclaims any legal responsibility for the condition of its trails at any time.

As a well-known and respected authority on hiking trails, the AMC works cooperatively with many federal, state, and local agencies, corporate and private landowners, and numerous other trail clubs and outdoor organizations.

AMC trails are maintained through the coordinated efforts of many members who volunteer their labor, and trails program staff and seasonal crew. Most of the difficult major construction projects are handled by the AMC trail crew, based in the White Mountains, which began operations in 1917 and is probably the oldest professional crew in the nation. Hikers can help maintain trails by donating their time for various projects and regularly scheduled volunteer trips with the AMC chapters and at AMC camps.

Funding for the AMC's trail and shelter maintenance comes primarily from membership dues, publication sales, fees from AMC facilities, and private and corporate donations. A Clubwide volunteer trails committee works closely with staff and other committees to develop program policy, budgets, and priorities.

For more information on any aspect of the Club's trail and shelter efforts, contact AMC Trails Program, Pinkham Notch Camp, Box 298, Gorham, NH 03581, or AMC Trails Program, 5 Joy St., Boston, MA 02108.

Comments on the AMC's trail work and information on problems you encounter when hiking or camping are always welcome.

AMC Hiker Shuttle

Shuttle service is available between Pinkham Notch Camp and major trailheads throughout the White Mountain National Forest. Connecting public transportation to Boston and points south via Concord Trailways is available through the ticket agency at Pinkham Notch Camp.

The shuttle operates daily from mid-June through Labor Day. Reservations are suggested. For additional information on fares and current schedule, write or call Reservations, AMC, Pinkham Notch Camp, PO Box 298, Gorham, NH 03581 (603-466-2727).

AMC Huts

There are eight AMC huts spaced a day's hike apart along the Appalachian Trail. They span the White Mountains from Lonesome Lake west to Carter Notch, and range in surroundings from lowland deciduous woods to alpine tundra. Each hut is operated by young men and women who pack in much of the food and supplies. Hearty meals prepared by the crew are served family-style at specific hours; bunks, blankets, and pillows are provided. All huts are open from mid-June through Labor Day. Many huts are open during the spring and fall on a caretaker basis. During caretaker season, the hut stove and utensils are available for use, but each guest must bring a sleeping bag and food. Zealand Falls and Carter Notch remain open on caretaker service through the winter.

All huts are open to the public; AMC members receive a discount on lodging. Reservations and deposits are necessary to guarantee space. For complete information, write or call Reservations, AMC Pinkham Notch Camp, Box 298, Gorham, NH 03581 (603-466-2727).

Pinkham Notch Camp

Pinkham Notch Camp is a unique mountain facility in the heart of the White Mountain National Forest. It is located along NH Rte. 16, twenty miles north of N. Conway, with public transportation via Concord Trailways available to the front door. The Joe Dodge Center, which accommodates over 100 guests in rooms with two, three, or four bunks, also offers a library that commands a spectacular view of the nearby Wildcat Ridge, and a living room where accounts of the day's activities can be shared by an open fireplace. The Center features a 65-seat conference room equipped with audio-visual facilities.

The Trading Post, a popular meeting place for hikers, has been a center of AMC recreational and educational activities since 1920. Weekend workshops, seminars, and lectures are conducted throughout the year. The building houses a dining room, and an information desk where basic equipment and guidebooks are available. The pack-up room downstairs is open 24 hours a day for hikers to stop in, relax, shower, and repack their gear.

Crawford Notch Hostel

Low-cost, self-service lodging is available in historic Crawford Notch. The main hostel holds 30 people in one large bunk-

154 SECTION 9

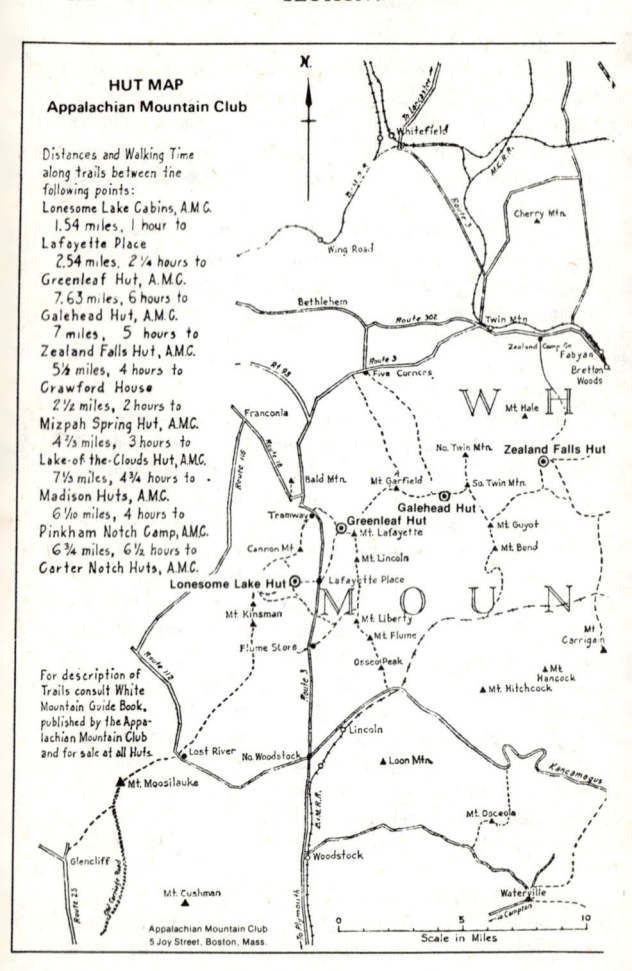

**HUT MAP
Appalachian Mountain Club**

Distances and Walking Time along trails between the following points:
Lonesome Lake Cabins, A.M.C.
1.54 miles, 1 hour to
Lafayette Place
2.54 miles, 2¼ hours to
Greenleaf Hut, A.M.C.
7.63 miles, 6 hours to
Galehead Hut, A.M.C.
7 miles, 5 hours to
Zealand Falls Hut, A.M.C.
5½ miles, 4 hours to
Crawford House
2½ miles, 2 hours to
Mizpah Spring Hut, A.M.C.
4⅔ miles, 3 hours to
Lake-of-the-Clouds Hut, A.M.C.
7⅓ miles, 4¾ hours to
Madison Hut, A.M.C.
6 1/10 miles, 4 hours to
Pinkham Notch Camp, A.M.C.
6¾ miles, 6½ hours to
Carter Notch Huts, A.M.C.

For description of Trails consult White Mountain Guide Book, published by the Appalachian Mountain Club and for sale at all Huts.

Appalachian Mountain Club
5 Joy Street, Boston, Mass.

THE APPALACHIAN MOUNTAIN CLUB 155

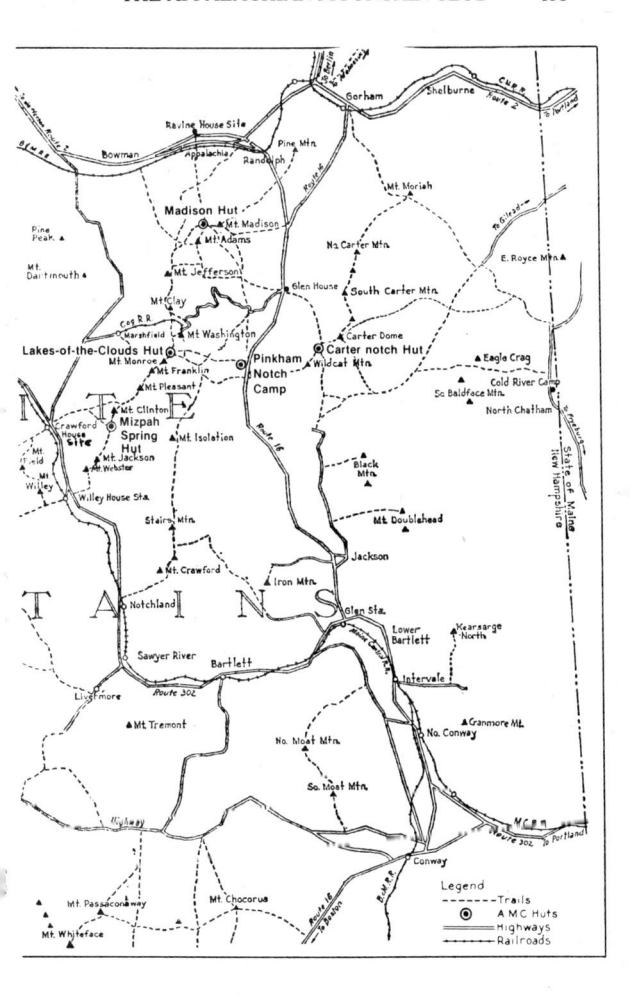

room. There are also a kitchen, bathrooms, and a common area. Three adjacent cabins accommodate 8 persons each.

The hostel is open to the public. AMC members receive a discount on lodging. Overnight lodging is available year-round. Guests must supply food and sleeping bags; stoves and cooking equipment are provided. The hostel is an excellent choice for families and small groups and offers a wide range of hiking and outdoor experiences.

Reservations are encouraged. Please write or call Reservations, AMC Pinkham Notch Camp, Box 298, Gorham NH 03581 (603-466-2727).

AMC Shelters and Tent Sites

The AMC is responsible for 15 of the more than fifty backcountry shelters and tent sites in the White Mountain area. These sites are maintained cooperatively with private landowners and state and federal land agencies. All are open on a first-come, first-served basis. Some sites have summer caretakers who collect an overnight fee to help defray expenses. Most sites have shelters, a few have only tent platforms, and some have both. The use of stoves is encouraged.

Hermit Lake Shelters in Tuckerman Ravine, also maintained by the AMC, have limited space available on a first-come, first-served basis. Tickets are available at Pinkham Notch Camp. An overnight use fee is charged. Some tenting is available near Hermit Lake, but only in the winter. Wood fires are not permitted, so bring stoves.

Shelter and tent site users must supply their own food, cooking equipment, sleeping bag, foam pad, and tent or tarp. Due to the popularity of the area, do not count on finding a vacant space in a shelter. Be prepared to use tent sites or to camp off-trail, which is feasible and legal in much of the area. Check with the AMC or USFS about regulations prior to your trip.

Please help keep the sites clean by carrying out all of your own trash as well as that left by others who are less thoughtful.

THE APPALACHIAN MOUNTAIN CLUB

AMC Reservations and Private Camps

The Club owns two reservations in New Hampshire for the benefit of the public. Madison Spring Reservation, with Madison Hut, is one acre.

The Cardigan Reservation, located in Alexandria, New Hampshire, contains almost 1000 acres of pasture and woodland on the north and east slopes of Mt. Cardigan. About sixty persons can be comfortably accommodated in the two lodges. It is open to the public on a seasonal basis. Reservations should be made with the Manager, Cardigan Lodge, RFD, Bristol, New Hampshire 03222 (603-744-8011).

The following camps, each under its own committee, afford comfortable summer vacations for AMC members, their guests, and friends of the Club. August Camp, where guests live in tents, changes its location from year to year. Cold River Camp is in N. Chatham, New Hampshire. Echo Lake Camp is on Mt. Desert Island, Maine. Ponkapoag Camp is in the Blue Hills Reservation near Boston, Massachusetts. Three-Mile Island Camp is on Lake Winnipesaukee, New Hampshire, and Wonalancet Cabin is in Wonalancet, New Hampshire. The Club also operates six campgrounds.

Glossary

For abbreviations see page 12.

blaze	a trail marking on a tree or rock, painted and/or cut
blazed	marked with paint on trees or rocks (blazes)
bluff	a high bank or hill with a cliff face overlooking a valley
boggy	muddy, swampy
boulder	large, detached, somewhat rounded rock
box canyon	rock formation with vertical walls and flat bottom
bushwhack	to hike through woods or brush without a trail
buttress	a rock mass projecting outward from a mountain or hill
cairn	pile of rocks to mark trail
cataract	waterfall
cirque	upper end of valley with half-bowl shape (scoured by glacier)
cliff	high, steep rock face
col	low point on a ridge between two mountains; saddle
crag	rugged, often overhanging rock eminence
grade	steepness of trail or road; ratio of vertical to horizontal distance
graded trail	well-constructed trail with smoothed footway
gulf	a cirque
gully	small, steep-sided valley
headwall	steep slope at the head of a valley, especially a cirque

GLOSSARY

height-of-land	saddle, col, or highest point reached by a trail or road
knob	a rounded, minor summit
lean-to	shelter
ledge	a large, smooth body of rock; or, but not usually in this book, a horizontal shelf across a cliff
ledgy	having exposed ledges, usually giving views
outcrops	large rocks projecting out of the soil
plateau	high, flat area
potable (water)	fit to drink
ravine	steep-sided valley
ridge	highest spine joining two or more mountains, or leading up to a mountain
runoff brook	a brook usually dry except shortly after rain, or snow melt
saddle	lowest, flattish part of ridge connecting two mountains; col
scrub	low spruce or fir trees near treeline
shelter	building, usually of wood, with roof and 3 or 4 sides, for camping
shoulder	point where rising ridge levels off or descends slightly before rising higher to a summit
a *slab* (n.)	a smooth, somewhat steeply sloping ledge
to *slab* (v.)	to walk across a slope
slide	steep slope where a landslide has carried away soil and vegetation
spur	a minor summit projecting from a larger one
spur trail	a side path off a main trail

GLOSSARY

strata — layers of rock

summit — highest point on a mountain; or, point higher than any other point in its neighborhood

switchback — zigzag in a trail to make a steep slope easier

tarn — a small pond, often at high elevation, or with no outlet

timberline — elevation that marks the upper limit of commercial timber

treeline — elevation above which trees do not grow

Index

Mountains are indexed alphabetically under the name of the individual peak.

Adams, Mt. (5798 ft.)	83
Adams, John Quincy, Mt. (5470 ft.)	56
Adams, Sam, Mt. (5885 ft.)	56
Adams 4	93
Adams 5	65,95
Air Line Trail	84
Along the Brink	92
Alpine Garden	49
Alpine Garden Trail	49
Ammonoosuc Ravine Trail	118
Amphibrach, The	89
Appalachia parking area, Randolph	57
Appalachian Trail	
Northern Peaks and Mt. Washington	52,57
Great Gulf area	104
Southern Peaks	114
Automobile Road, Mt. Washington	33
Skiing on	54
Back Stair	132
Barnes Field Camping Area	105
Base Road	100
Beechwood Way	92
Bigelow Lawn	51
Boott Spur (5500 ft.)	45
Boott Spur Link	47
Boott Spur Trail	45
Boundary Line Trail	101
Bourne Monument	34
Bowman, Mt. (3450 ft.)	56
Bretton Woods	117,119
Brookbank	79
Brookside, The	82
Bruin Rock	81,83
Bugle Cliff	120
Bumpus Basin	57,76,79
Burt Ravine	57
Buttress Trail	112
Cabin-Cascades Trail	97
Camel Trail	51
Camp Placid Stream	85,86
Caps Ridge (also called Ridge of the Caps)	56,100,101
Caps Ridge Trail	101
Carriage Road, Mt. Washington	33
Carter Notch Hut	47
Cascade Ravine	70
Castellated (or Castle) Ridge	98,99
Castle Ravine	95,98

161

INDEX

Castle Ravine Trail	95
Castle Trail	99
Cave Mountain	139
Chandler Brook Trail	109
Chandler Ridge	33
Chemin des Dames	88
Clay, Mt. (5532 ft.)	102
Mt. Clay Loop	102
Cliffway	92
Clinton, Mt. (4312 ft., also known as Mt. Pierce)	114
Mt. Clinton Road	114
Mt. Clinton Trail	125
Cloudwater Spring	41
Cog railway	31
Cold Brook Fall	79
Coosauk Fall	77
Cornice, The	68
Cow Pasture	34
Crag Camp	60
Cragway Spring	39
Crawford Cliff	115
Crawford Depot	114,120
Crawford Dome	129
Crawford House	114
Crawford, Mt. (3129 ft.)	128
Crawford Notch	120,121,122
Crawford Notch Highway (US Rte. 302)	114,115
Crawford Path	114
Crawford's	114
Crew-Cut Trail	36
Crippies, The	138
Crystal Cascade	35
Daniel Webster-Scout Trail	75
Davis, Mt. (3840 ft.)	128
Davis Path	129
Dingmaul Rock	65
Diretissima, The	36
Dolly Copp Campground	57,105
Dolly Copp Road (also called Pinkham B)	57,68,105
Dome Rock	78,82
Down-look	130
Douglas Horton Center	71
Dry River	124
Dry River Campground	124
Dry River Cutoff	126
Dry River Falls	125
Dry River Shelter #3	125
Dry River Trail	124
Duck Fall	81
Durand Ridge	81,83,85
Edmands Col	65
Edmands Col Cutoff	69
Edmands Path	119
Eisenhower, Mt. (4761 ft.)	114,115
Mt. Eisenhower Loop	115
Mt. Eisenhower Trail	126

INDEX

Elephant Head	120
"Elevated, The"	87
Emerald Bluff	94,97
Emerald Tongue (also called Israel Ridge)	94
Emerald Trail	97
Erebus Fall	76
Evans Fall	76
Eye, The	95
Fallsway, The	79
"Fan, The"	43,44
Forks of Israel	96
Franconia Spring	67
Franklin, Mt. (5004 ft.)	114
Gateway of King Ravine	85,88
George's Gorge Trail	36
Giant Stairs	128,130,132
Gibbs Falls	115
Glen Boulder	48
Glen Boulder Trail	47
Glen Ellis Falls	35
Glen House Bridle Path	50
Glen House site	33
Gordon Fall	79,80
Gordon Fall Loop	79
Gordon Ridge	78
Gray Knob Shelter	60
Gray Knob Trail	91
GREAT GULF	104-113
Great Gulf shelters	104
Great Gulf Trail	105
Great Gully Trail	88
Greenough Spring	66
Gulf of Slides	49
Gulf of Slides Ski Trail	55
Gulf Tank	32
Gulfside Spring	65
Gulfside Trail	60
Halfway House	34
Hanging Cliffs	40,46
Hart Ledge	139
Hermit Lake shelters	42
Hincks Trail	91
Hitchcock Fall	77
Hope, Mt. (2520 ft.)	128
Howker Ridge Trail	77
Howks, The	76,77
Huntington Ravine	43
Huntington Ravine Trail	43
Inlook Trail	82
Isolation, Mt. (4005 ft.)	128
Isolation Trail	135
Israel Ridge Path	94
Israel River	96

INDEX

Jackson, Mt. (4052 ft.)	114, 121
Jacob's Ladder	32
Jefferson, Mt. (5751 ft.)	98
Mt. Jefferson Loop	98
Jefferson Notch	100
Jefferson Notch Rd.	100
Jefferson Ravine	98
Jefferson's "knees"	56, 98
Jericho Road	133
Jewell Trail	103
John Quincy Adams, Mt. (5407 ft.)	56
John Sherburne Ski Trail	54
Kelton Trail	78
Kelton Crag	78
King Cliff	92
King Ravine	57, 87
Gateway of	85, 88
King Ravine Trail	87
"Knees" of Mt. Jefferson	56, 98
Knife-edge	85
Knight's Castle	90
Ladderback Trail	92
Lakes of the Clouds Hut	117
Langdon, Mt. (2423 ft.)	128
Mt. Langdon Shelter	136
Mt. Langdon Trail	135
Lawn Cutoff	51
Ledge, The (Mt. Washington)	34
Ledge Trail (Pine Mountain)	71
Liebeskind's Loop	36
Lila's Ledge	37
Link, The	69
Lion Head Trail	44
Lion Heads	45, 46
Log Cabin Shelter	59
Lower Crag	90
Lowe's Bald Spot	108
Lowe's Path	93
Madison Gulf	107
Madison Gulf Cutoff	73
Madison Gulf Trail	107
Madison Hut	58
Madison, Mt. (5363 ft.)	72
Madison Spring	58
Maple Walk	80
Marshfield Station, cog railway	31
Memorial Bridge	58
Mizpah Spring Hut	123
Monaway	92
Monroe, Mt. (5385 ft.)	114, 115, 116
Mt. Monroe Loop	116

INDEX

MONTALBAN RIDGE	128-140
Northern Montalbans	128
Southern Montalbans	135
Monticello Lawn	66,98
Mossy Fall	86
Mossy Slide	109
Mt. Clay Loop	102
Mt. Clinton Road	100
Mt. Clinton Trail	125
Mt. Eisenhower Trail	126
Mt. Eisenhower Loop	115
Mt. Jefferson Loop	98
Mt. Langdon Shelter	136
Mt. Langdon Trail	135
Mt. Monroe Loop	116
Mt. Parker Trail	136
Mt. Stanton Trail	138
Mt. Washington Automobile Road	33
Mt. Washington Railroad (cog railway)	31
Needle Rock	85
Nelson Crag Trail	39
NORTHERN PEAKS	56-103
Notch Mountain (now called Mt. Webster)	114
Notchland (formerly Bemis)	128
Nowell Ridge	70,83,87
Oak Ridge	136
Oakes Gulf	124,131
Observatory, Mt. Washington	32
Old Jackson Road	38
Skiing on	55
Osgood Cutoff	74
Osgood Junction	75
Osgood Trail	73
Parapet, The	59
Parapet Trail	75
Parker, Mt. (3015 ft.)	128
Mt. Parker Trail	136
Peabody Spring	95
Pentadoi	89
Pierce, Mt. (also called Mt. Clinton)	114
Perch, The	59
Perch Path	91
Pickering, Mt. (1945 ft.)	128
Pine Link	76
Pine Mountain (2404 ft.)	71
Pinkham B Road (also called Dolly Copp Rd.)	105
Pinkham Notch Camp	35
Pinnacle, The	44
Pleasant, Mt. (now called Mt. Eisenhower)	114
Proteus Falls	76

INDEX

Railroad, Mt. Washington (cog railway)	31
Randolph East parking area	57, 63
Randolph Path	62
Ravine Outlook	46
Raymond Cataract	49
Ravine of	44
Raymond Path	42
Skiing on	55
Resolution, Mt. (3428 ft.)	128
Resolution Shelter	129
Ridge of the Caps (also called Caps Ridge)	56, 100, 101
Rocky Branch shelters	134
Rocky Branch Trail	133
Roof Rock	96
Salmacis Fall	83
Salroc Falls	79
Sam Adams, Mt. (5885 ft.)	56
Sawyer's Rock	140
Scar Trail	86
Scout Trail (Daniel Webster Trail)	75
Short Line	86
Six Husbands Trail	111
Slide Peak	48
Snow Arch	40
Snyder Glen	85
SOUTHERN PEAKS	114-127
Southside Trail	50
Spaulding Lake	106
Spaulding Spring	65
Sphinx, The	112
Sphinx Ravine	104
Sphinx Trail	112
Spur Brook Fall	92
Spur Trail	90
Stairs Col	132
Stairs Col Trail	132
Stairs Fall	77
Stairs Mountain	128
Stanton, Mt. (1725 ft.)	128
Mt. Stanton Trail	138
Star Lake	59
Star Lake Trail	84
Storm Lake	64
"Subway, The"	87
Summit buildings	32
Summit House, Mt. Washington	33
Sylvan Cascade	109
Sylvan Way	78
Tama Fall	80
Thunderstorm Junction	64
Tip Top House	33
Tisdale Spring	121
Town Line Brook Trail	76

INDEX

Trinity Heights Connector	52
Triple Falls	76
Tuckerman Crossover	50
Tuckerman Junction	41
Tuckerman Ravine	39
Skiing in	53
Tuckerman Ravine Trail	39
Upper Crag	90
Valley Way	81
Wamsutta Trail	110
WASHINGTON, MT. (6288 ft.)	30-55
Automobile Road	33
Caution for climbers	31
Observatory	32
Cog railway	31
Skiing	35,52
Summit buildings	32
Watson Path	80
Webster Cliff Trail	121
Webster-Jackson Trail	120
Webster, Mt. (3910 f)	114,120
Weetamoo Fall	106,110
Westside Trail	52
"White Trail"	64
White Cliff	92
Willey House Recreation Area	121